Planning for Technology

Planning for Technology

A Guide for School Administrators, Technology Coordinators, and Curriculum Leaders

Bruce M. Whitehead

Devon F. N. Jensen

Floyd Boschee

CORWIN PRESS, INC.
A Sage Publications Company
Thousand Oaks, California

For information:

Corwin Press, Inc.
A Sage Publications Company
2455 Teller Road
Thousand Oaks, California 91320
www.corwinpress.com

Sage Publications Ltd.
6 Bonhill Street
London EC2A 4PU
United Kingdom

Sage Publications India Pvt. Ltd.
M-32 Market
Greater Kailash I
New Delhi 110 048 India

Printed in the United States of America

Library of Congress Cataloging-in-Publication Data

Whitehead, Bruce M.
Planning for technology: A guide for school administrators, technology coordinators, and curriculum leaders / Bruce M. Whitehead, Devon F. N. Jensen, Floyd Boschee.
      p. cm.
Includes bibliographical references and index.
ISBN 0-7619-4595-4 (cloth) — ISBN 0-7619-4596-2 (pbk.)
1. Educational technology—Planning. 2. Curriculum planning. 3. School management
2. and organization. I. Jensen, Devon. II. Boschee, Floyd. III. Title.
LB1028.3 .W48 2003
371.33—dc21

                                    2002007155

This book is printed on acid-free paper.

02 03 04 05 06 10 9 8 7 6 5 4 3 2 1

Acquisitions Editor:	Robb Clouse
Editorial Assistant:	Erin Clow
Copy Editor:	Hawley Roddick
Production Editor:	Diane S. Foster
Typesetter:	C&M Digitals (P) Ltd
Proofreader:	Scott Oney
Cover Designer:	Michael Dubowe
Production Artist:	Janet Foulger

Contents

Foreword xi
 Governor William J. Janklow

Preface xv
 Rationale xv
 Book Contents xvi
 Chapter Descriptions xvii
 Acknowledgments xviii

About the Authors xix

1. Changing Strategies in Technology 1
 Refocusing Efforts 1
  Changing Contexts 1
  School Technology Realities 3
  Student Achievement and Technology 9
  Classroom Technology 12
  Developing Local Community Awareness 13
  School Technology Goals 15
  State and National Levels of Awareness 16
 Strategies for Success 17
 Future Challenges 18
 Reflective Activities 19

2. Leadership and Planning 21
 Flexible Leaders 21
 Stakeholders' Role in Planning for Technology 24
  Factors to Be Considered 25
  Staff Development 27
  Financial Management 27
  Infrastructure 28
  Community Awareness and Support 28
  Evaluation and Assessment 29
  Technology Standards for Administrators 29
  Technology Leadership Tasks 32
   Superintendent: Technology Leadership Tasks 32
   Principal: Technology Leadership Tasks 33

District Program Director:
    Technology Leadership Tasks   35
    Formulating a Mission Statement   36
    Establishing and Maintaining Commitment   37
       School Administrators   37
       School Board Members   38
       Teachers   38
       Parents   39
Project Outline   40
    Project Calendar   40
    Developing a Schedule   40
Annual Plan   62
Reflective Activities   62

3. Technology and Staff Development   67
    Setting Priorities   67
       Staff Development Needs   67
    Cadres of Technology Specialists   71
       Management Planning Matrix   72
       Hardware, Software, and Services   72
       Regional Resource Centers   75
       Instructional Design and Computer Skills   75
    Strategies for Success   76
       Project-Based Approach   76
       Flexible Scheduling   77
       Rule of Traveling Pairs   77
       Early-Out Time for Students   77
       Presenter Stipends   77
       Extended Contracts   78
       Adult Education   78
       Substitute Rotation   78
       Free Consulting Services   78
       Staff Development Cooperatives   78
       Staff Development Consortiums   78
       College and University Preservice Programs   79
       School, University, and College Partnerships   79
       Community Resources   79
    Technology for Learning Audit   79
    Future Challenges   80
    Reflective Activities   80

4. Teaching and Learning With Technology   83
    The Power of Teachers   83
    Providing Connectivity   85
       Educational Technology Standards   86
    How Technology Facilitates Learning   89
    How Technology Facilitates Teaching   91

Benefits to Educators 91
Classroom Computer Networks 91
Classroom Curriculum Connections 92
Technology Scope and Sequence 93
Content Software and Tool Software Selection 93
Classroom and Cooperative Learning 94
Classroom Technology Strategies 94
Learning-Styles Applications 95
Student Writing 95
Cross-Age Tutoring via Technology 96
Distance Learning 96
Community Links 97
Keyboarding Skills in the Classroom 97
Keyboarding Software Checklist 97
School to Work 98
Student Assessment and Technology 98
Technology Applications 99
Impacting Disadvantaged Youth 99
Meeting State and National Standards 99
Strategies for Success 100
Future Challenges 101
Reflective Activities 101

5. **Selling Your Technology Plan** 103
Public Relations 103
Barriers to Quality School
and Community Relations 103
Administrative Role in Public Relations 105
Promoting Public Relations and Technology 106
The Public Relations Process 107
Public Relations Plan 107
Mission Statement 107
Internal and External Analysis 108
Objectives and Strategies 108
Action Plans 108
Research 108
Communication Strategies 110
Communication Strategies for Internal Groups 112
Classroom Teachers 112
Improving Communication Through
Instructional Leadership 112
Improving Staff Morale 113
Noncertified Staff Members 114
Using Noncertified Staff 114
Board Members 115
Board Member Communication 115
Students 115

Student Communication 115

Communication Strategies for External Groups 116

    Parents and the School 116

    Increasing Communication With Parents 117

    Business and Community Leaders 118

    Communication with Business
      and Community Leaders 118

School-Community Relations 119

    Teacher-Directed Community Relations 119

    Administrator-Directed Community Relations 119

Where Should We Go From Here? 120

Strategies for Success 121

Reflective Activities 122

6. Financial Management 123

Creative Financing 123

    Federal Allocations 124

    State Financial Support 124

Successful Grant Writing for Technology 125

    Grant Proposal 125

    Special Grant-Writing Strategies 126

    Grant Configuration 126

    Writing the Grant 127

Funding Resources 127

Success in Financing Technology 143

    Setting Priorities 143

    Purchasing Policy 143

    School Technology Purchasers 145

    E-Rate 145

    Funding Staff Development 145

    Fund-Raising Campaign 145

    Finding Local Funds for Technology 146

Strategies for Success 147

    Effective Finance Strategies 147

Future Challenges 149

Reflective Activities 149

7. Infrastructure 151

Coordinating the Effort 151

Network Classroom Technology Centers 152

    Technology Learning Stations 153

    Teacher Work Stations 153

National Telecommunications Infrastructure 154

    State Telecommunications Infrastructure 154

    State Telecommunications Networks 155

State Regulations and Guidelines 156

    Equity Issues 156

    Technology Plans 156

Evaluation 156
Staff Development 156
Maintenance and Service 157
Infrastructure 157
Regional Centers and Technology Hubs 157
Distance Learning Programs 157
Procurement 158
Research and Evaluation 158
Financial Advice on Technology Implementation 159
Technology Cooperatives 159
District Technology Configurations 159
Wide Area Networks 159
Local Area Networks 160
Local Intranet 160
Laptop Computing 160
Interactive Television 161
Wireless-Keypad Response Systems 161
Automated Networked Libraries 162
Compatibility of Hardware 162
Upgrading 162
Management, Service, and Maintenance 162
Technical Director 162
Teacher Technology Coordinators 163
Student Technology Assistants 163
Work-Tracking System 165
Strategies for Success 165
Three Main Parts 168
Networking Costs 169
Infrastructure Costs 170
Future Challenges 172
Reflective Activities 172

8. **Program Evaluation** 173
The Final Piece in the Puzzle 173
Challenges to Program Evaluation 173
Focusing on Student Performance 175
Data Collection 175
Leadership 176
Technology Plan Assessment 177
Staff Development and Evaluation 177
Assessing Teaching and Learning 178
Integration of Curriculum 178
Classroom Technology Environment 178
Student Outcomes 179
Equity Issues 179
Measuring Connectivity 179
Accreditation Standards 180
Student Performance Assessment 180

Integrated Learning System Assessments   180
Program Guidelines   180
Evaluation Checklist   181
Strategies for Success   182
Future Challenges   182
Reflective Activities   183

Resource A: Individual Teacher and Administrator Technology Profiles   185

Resource B: Cupertino Union School District: Technology Scope and Sequence   205

Resource C: ISTE National Educational Technology Standards (NETS) and Performance Indicators: Educational Technology Foundations for All Teachers   211

Resource D: ISTE National Educational Technology Standards (NETS) and Performance Indicators: Technology Foundation Standards for All Students   215

Resource E: Glossary   217

Notes   221

Name Index   229

Subject Index   231

Foreword

Inventions can provide momentary enjoyment, as did the Hula-Hoop, or create massive cultural and personal changes, as did the alphabet and movable type.

Today, at the beginning of the 21st century, the people of the world are experiencing the first stages of humankind's third major, massive change in the way we communicate with each other and with future generations yet unborn.

In the same manner that the alphabet and movable type changed everything about work and living in the decades after they were invented, the invention of the computer is changing and will continue to change our lives and our children's lives dramatically.

THE EMERGING INFORMATION AGE

Until the invention of the first alphabet around 4000 BC, people acquired information primarily by listening. Information was organized through human memory, and the sharing of information was limited to speaking and gesturing.

With the alphabet came the ability to actually store and save information through writing and the ability to share information with others through reading.

With the invention of moveable type in 1440 AD, all of that was accelerated. Huge volumes of knowledge, new ideas and imaginations could be printed in mass quantities and shared with millions of people individually, one by one, book by book.

In the 20th century, the inventions of mass media, such as the phonograph, the motion picture, the radio, and the television, enabled information to be shared with millions of people simultaneously and immediately.

Now, technology's offspring—computers, word processors, electronic spreadsheets, databases, the Internet, networks, and myriad of other devices and connections—have encapsulated all of the past communications methods and given people even more new ways to acquire information, organize information, store information, and share information.

Acquiring information is no longer limited to just listening to another human being. Organizing and storing information is now much, much more than passing stories down from generation to generation. Sharing information isn't limited to how many people a person can personally visit in a lifetime.

The new technologies enable a person with a computer and a phone line or cable in the remotest part of South Dakota to connect to the equivalent of a million libraries worldwide. The use of an Internet browser and search engine allows people to acquire within seconds the exact information that they need.

Then those same tools allow those people to organize and analyze huge quantities of acquired information to use in solving problems and creating new opportunities. Those same tools also enable people to share information with one other person or with many millions of people worldwide.

THE BASICS PLUS TECHNOLOGY

To survive and prosper in the 21st century, people need to be technology smart.

Of course, students need to learn basic knowledge and acquire basic skills so that they have the basic tools—reading, writing, and 'rithmetic—to be excellent lifelong learners. That's the first, most-important purpose of schooling. But now, in the 21st century, there is a new, fourth basic—technology. So the challenge is not the basics or technology, it's the basics *plus* technology.

When students learn the basics plus technology, nobody will be able to stop them from learning whatever they need to know to be successful and happy in their lives in the 21st century. The right use of technology can also help students learn the basics and also reemphasize and reinforce the basics over and over again.

But, more important, computer and other technology skills can enable a student to process the huge amounts of data available in the modern world and change that data into productive, useful information that solves problems and benefits people.

WHAT MAKES IT ALL HAPPEN

Obviously, the school should be the catalyst for, and a very important teacher of, the basics plus technology. But how can that happen? What makes it happen?

Schools can buy computers, servers, routers, liquid crystal display (LCD) projectors, and many other technological devices. They can connect them to networks and the Internet. They can build videoconferencing classrooms. They can buy and distribute the latest software to their teachers and students. But all of those items are only ingredients.

Someone must put them all together and integrate those tools into the learning experience so that learning is enhanced and achievement is accelerated. The end results will be students who will graduate from school with all the basics plus technology that they need to make their dreams come true.

Only individual teachers, administrators, and parents can make that happen. It can't be bought in a box or achieved by hooking wires together.

That's why this book is so important. It shows educational leaders what they can do to make it happen.

This book shows the reader how to overcome the financial, organizational, and implementation roadblocks that often kill the best projects and innovations. This book is a roadmap for technology integration success.

William J. Janklow
Governor, South Dakota

Preface

Milestones in science and technology have marked the march of human progress. Gutenberg's creation of moveable type in the 15th century laid the foundation for universal literacy. Watts's invention of the steam engine in the 18th century launched the Industrial Revolution. The inventiveness of Bell and Marconi in the 19th and 20th centuries—creating the telephone and radio—helped bring a global village into being.

Secretary of Education Richard W. Riley provided some realistic facts.[1] He indicated that the United States and the world are now in the midst of an economic and social revolution every bit as sweeping as any that has gone before: computers and information technologies are transforming nearly every aspect of American life. They are changing the way Americans work and play, increasing productivity, and creating entirely new ways of doing things. Every major U.S. industry has begun to rely heavily on computers and telecommunications to do its work.

America's schools, however, have been an exception to this information revolution. Computers and information technologies are not a part of the way most American students learn. Today's students spend an average of only a few minutes a day using computers for learning. Only four states have five or fewer students per Internet-connected computer, and the nation's average is 11.3 students per instructional computer. As a parent at the Southwest Regional Forum said, "If classes aren't offered on how to use computers and technology to build skills, it is a disgrace. Think of the future and all the skills our children will need."[2]

RATIONALE

The reason for writing this book has come from both practical experience and a recognized technology gap evident in current research conducted in this field. For years, school administrators and teachers have struggled with appropriate and relevant ways to integrate technology into the curriculum. Far too often, however, schools have depended on classroom computer labs as their sole outlet for helping students and teachers with the integration process. The weakness with this approach is that teachers are bound by set times and schedules for computer use. The result is that computers are both physically and pedagogically distant from the curriculum. Current research and practical experience are directing administrators toward establishing a system of five to six networked computers in each classroom. It is in this environment that teachers can truly link technology with the curriculum in both structured and spontaneous ways improving results in student achievement. This is a very new approach to integrating technology with the curriculum and is the path that most schools need to consider if they are going to establish effective and efficient means for computer use in their schools. Since it is such a new approach, most administrators are both technologically and administratively ill equipped to deal with many of the issues related to this transition. This book provides essential information and activities that will help school administrators, technology coordinators, and curriculum developers as they seriously consider establishing a school plan that supports in-class technology usage for students and teachers.

BOOK CONTENTS

The essence of this book is to provide a practical framework in which administrators can address the issues pertinent to this shift in technology focus. The content of the book is intermixed with personal experiences, current research, and practical activities in which school administrators can explore and consider how to best adapt their context with the direction suggested in the book.

Bruce Whitehead has actually gone through the transition of implementing technology classroom designs of five to six networked computers in each classroom and thus provides invaluable insights and advice for other administrators. Since he is a practicing school administrator himself, he is able to address issues that other administrators can relate to.

The book is also dependent on current research that provides essential quantitative and qualitative findings that address the need for this technology initiative. Some of the research referenced in the book includes a recent empirical technology study[3] in which the authors concluded that despite the rapid infusion of computers into American schools, inequities persist in access to educational technology and how it is used to enhance learning. Layton[4] found that students of the 21st century are different and, subsequently, require different learning models. Since educators are trying to apply outdated models of technology use to current realities, Layton highlights why they are having a hard time realizing the full potential that technology can offer to learning environments of today. Also included is essential research conducted by Mid-Continent Research for Education and Learning (see Chapter 3 and Resource A) regarding teacher and administrator technology profiles, as well as foundational work by the Technology Standards for School Administrators Collaborative, which proposes national technology standards for administrators and teachers (see Chapter 2).

CHAPTER DESCRIPTIONS

Chapter 1 provides the context and rationale for the technology shift suggested in this book. The justification for the new technology design is supported by case studies, qualitative and quantitative research, and statistical data that direct the reader to see how properly implemented technology can improve student achievement. The chapter also directs the reader to the basic elements and processes of bringing computers into the classroom.

Chapter 2 outlines how crucial administrative planning and leadership are to making this technology initiative a practical reality. Readers are provided with essential information that helps them to ponder their own personal educational contexts and how the proposed technology changes can best fit their needs. The administrative responsibilities and structures essential to getting the technology plan off the ground are outlined through a hands-on worksheet provided in the chapter.

Chapter 3 establishes a case for developing a strong-technology professional-development plan with all its supportive administrative features. Most research indicated that teachers do not receive the essential training necessary for effective implementation of computers into the curriculum. Schools spend vast amounts of money on bringing computers into the school and then provide little professional development for teachers. Most recommendations indicate that 30% of a technology budget should be for professional development.

Chapter 4 provides a practical framework for bringing computers into the classroom and issues that teachers, through administrative support, need to address in trying to develop a closer link between computers and the curriculum. Computers and student achievement have been one of the biggest issues related to technology in schools. Unfortunately, most researchers, practitioners, and academics are undecided on the impact that computers have on student achievement. Current research related to the implementation of classroom computer-learning centers is showing that it can impact achievement. One of the key elements of this chapter is the discussion on the five principles of educational technology that provides a framework for bringing computers into classrooms.

Chapter 5 contains key processes, structures, reflective activities, and research necessary for administrators as they consider developing their own technology public relations plan. School administrators have been placed in an increasingly complex educational position. One of their expanding responsibilities is that of public relations. Current efforts on establishing this technology initiative indicate that a properly developed public relations plan can greatly enhance the successful implementation of computers in the classroom.

Chapter 6 helps administrators become aware of the financial options available to them. Due to the fact that most school administrators are held tightly accountable for their school's financial status, implementing a costly technology initiative could appear impossible at first. Therefore, one of the key elements of this chapter is an activity for writing a successful grant proposal.

Chapter 7 addresses the key factors that school administrators must explore as they implement classroom-networked learning centers throughout their schools. It is evident that any changes in technology can be a very complex physical and administrative endeavor. The challenges range from selecting appropriate hardware to having an effective school technology director. The chapter also addresses the technology initiative from its internal challenges to state issues. Upon completion of working through this chapter, public school administrators will have a good handle on how they can address the technological infrastructure issues pertinent to their school situation.

Chapter 8 provides a structural model for developing an effective evaluation and assessment plan. Without this element of the plan, many people will revert to familiar frameworks to the detriment of the technology initiative. The overall effort of this chapter is to help school administrators realize that through detailed planning, they can increase the links between technology, the curriculum, and student learning.

Each chapter also concludes with a series of Reflective Activities. The purpose of these activities is to allow readers to apply reflective strategies as they attempt to employ the book's technology framework to their local contexts and realities.

ACKNOWLEDGMENTS

The contributions of the following reviewers are gratefully acknowledged.

Senator Max Baucus, Montana
   Chair, Senate Finance Committee
Dr. George Dennison
   President, University of Montana
Dr. Vince Ferrandino
   Executive Director, National Association of Elementary School Principals
Gary Graves
   Senior Research and Evaluation Associate, Technology in Education Center, Northwest Regional Educational Laboratory
Dr. Marlene Jacobsen
   Acting Dean, Statewide Educational Services, The University of South Dakota
Nancy Keenan
   Senior Vice President of State Relations, Hawthorn Group, Washington, DC, Former State Superintendent of Schools in Montana

About the Authors

Bruce M. Whitehead, Principal at Hellgate Intermediate School, Missoula, Montana, and Adjunct Professor at the University of Montana, is recognized at both state and national levels for his work in education. As an author, coauthor, and illustrator, he has produced work that includes numerous monographs and articles in national journals as well as four books. He is known for his work in developing a model for implementing technology in schools via classroom technology centers and received the Milken National Educator Award. In addition, he received the National Distinguished Principal's Award, Montana's Citation of Merit Award for History, Montana's Administrator in Reading Award, University of Montana Distinguished Alumni Award, and the National John F. Kennedy Center Award for Arts in Education. Dr. Whitehead is a past president of the Montana Association of Elementary and Middle School Principals and of the Montana State Reading Council.

Devon F. N. Jensen is Assistant Professor in the Division of Educational Administration, School of Education, at The University of South Dakota. He recently completed his graduate studies at the University of Alberta in Edmonton, Canada. He brings with him both practical and academic experience in the field of educational policy studies. While in Canada, he worked for seven years as an administrator and teacher in a private English language school for secondary students, university visa students, and adults. Over the past few years, he has had the privilege of presenting research studies at several national conferences in both Canada and the United States. His current research focus is on the pedagogical issues of online educational delivery.

Floyd Boschee is Professor in the Division of Educational Administration, School of Education, The University of South Dakota, where he teaches and conducts research in educational leadership, supervision, and curriculum. He also serves as a member of the board of education for the Vermillion School District No. 13-1 in Vermillion, South Dakota. In 18 years of public school service, he has served as a teacher, coach, athletic director, and assistant superintendent for curriculum and instruction. He has also served as chairman of departments of education, published extensively in national journals, and authored or coauthored six books.

Dedicated to our families: Charlotte, Rye, and Paige; Sandra, Lena, Kyle, Samantha, and Emily; Marlys Ann, Barbara, Brenda, Bonni, and Beth; and to James O. Atkinson (1951-1999), an elementary school principal in Charlo, Montana, who devoted his life to the improvement of education through technology and who had a profound effect on many children, teachers, and administrators. His work in educational curricula is well known, and his ideas for educational reform have been imprinted on many schools in Montana. Jim continued to stand tall in his fight with leukemia to the very end. He was the best of the best!

1

Changing Strategies in Technology

REFOCUSING EFFORTS

After several decades of having computers in public education, it is amazing that questions still abound regarding their usefulness and purpose in the classrooms of the nation. It is also interesting that governments, public businesses, and private enterprise are not asking these questions regarding the implementation of technology into their sectors. Schools have access to the same hardware that the external community does, and they also have access to a plethora of software programs designed specifically to meet educational needs. Unlike the external community, most school districts have the ability to access a variety of means of financial support for implementing technology into the classrooms. So why has business succeeded, and in what areas has education failed?

Changing Contexts

Layton noted that administrative leaders have misdirected planning efforts by envisioning technological direction around where educators are and how to move forward. Instead, he suggested that we envision where we want to be and then work backward in designing the appropriate frameworks to get us there.[1] The important realization in this process is that students of the 21st century are different and do require different learning styles. Since we are trying to apply outdated models of technology use to current realities, it highlights why we are having a hard time realizing the full potential that technology can offer to learning environments of today.

Layton focused on the following key factors that describe the unique qualities of today's schoolchildren.

Time. Children in our schools today perceive working, learning, and playing as interconnected. With the content of their daily lives so influenced by technology and entertainment, the lines among these three groups actually intersect, and they no longer feel comfortable in a reality that attempts to compartmentalize time into specific activity blocks. Twenty-first-century schools must implement curricula where working, learning, and playing converge on an academic praxis. As such, learning can occur at any time and in any place.

Relationships. Children of the 21st century are beginning to reestablish a strong connection to community, and linkages with other human beings form the fabric of their existence. The difference is that their communities are vastly different than those of their parents. They now learn and play in a community that is highly diverse—diverse in age, religion, culture, language, and location. Within these communities, collaboration is the primary expression of life experience, and this is important because it is representative of the working realities that are developing and being created in our society today.

Technology. The children in our schools today live in a reality of change and especially changing technologies. Students are prepared and are constantly waiting for the next level of advancement that will provide them with new learning and pleasure experiences.

Learning Style. Students today learn more effectively in groups. It doesn't negate that they will spend time working alone, but individual learning is reinforced through membership in a social group—even if that group is thousands of miles away. Their perception is that knowledge is for sharing and not for possessing. As such, students want to solve real problems in which they can make some contribution to their school, community, city, and so on. They also recognize that knowledge is fleeting and changing, and so they desire to develop analysis skills that will help them succeed in a liquid reality.

Flexibility. Students can no longer depend on a stable and unchanging reality; therefore they desire a curriculum that is open to a diverse range of options and educational choices. Learning opportunities are expanding beyond the classroom, and so the curriculum must take this into account. Learning can occur through an interaction of public schools, home schooling, distance learning, private lessons, travel, community groups, and Internet groups.

The dilemma is that in implementing technology into the schools of America, we have not connected technology to the changing learning contexts that students find themselves in. Under the existing structures, various entities concerned with technology and education have spent significant dollars in establishing school computer labs where students can learn to be computer literate and can learn the value of technology. The problem with this approach is that computer labs counter the notions of time, relationships, flexibility, and learning style that students rely on. As the President's Panel on Educational Technology stated, "One of the enduring difficulties about technology and education is that a lot of people think about the technology first and the education later, if at all."[2] It is in response to this changing student context that educational administrators should consider adding technology classroom designs to their existing school infrastructures.

Moving technology into our nation's classrooms has the capability of significantly reshaping education in America. Today's schools are exploding with new technological innovations and a host of educational changes. Satellite dishes are popping up on school roofs all over the nation, and fiber-optic cables are being dropped through classroom ceilings, and three educational buzzwords are *video conferencing, virtual reality,* and *wireless technology.* Interested and knowledgeable teachers and administrators are becoming media specialists, and students are stepping into a learning environment that was unimaginable only a decade or two ago.

School Technology Realities

A careful look around the country reveals that some schools are making giant steps in their use of computer technology, while a vast majority of schools and teachers remain tied to past educational strategies. For instance, "While 84% of teachers have at least one computer in their classrooms, only 36% have between two and five computers and a scant 10% have more than five class computers."[3] As illustrated in Table 1.1,[4] most schools locate the majority of their computers not within the individual classrooms but in specialized computer labs that are shared among all classes. This makes student computer use by individuals and small groups impractical within most classrooms. Knowledgeable school superintendents and principals are beginning to express concern over this state of affairs. These administrators feel a strong need to refocus district and state efforts to continue to challenge school technology infrastructures so that they more appropriately address students' academic and social needs. With their help, a movement is now under way to bring the benefits of electronic information gathering and other technological advances to classrooms across America. According to the regional data shown in Table 1.1, Wyoming leads the nation with the lowest number of students (three) per instructional computer, and Alaska leads with the lowest number of students (seven) per instructional unit in the classrooms.

The current movement toward putting the latest technology into classrooms is causing educators to reassess school programs and policies and to examine the impact computers and other data-processing equipment are having on teaching and learning. As a result, many school

Table 1.1   Regional Data on Students Per Instructional Computer

Northeast Region	Connecticut	Maine	Massachusetts	New Hamp.	New Jersey	New York	Pennsylvania	Rhode Island
Statewide	5.4	4.6	5.2	6.1	4.6	5.3	4.6	6.5
Classrooms	11.4	10.3	12.8	13.2	11.8	11.7	11.5	14.3
	Vermont							
Statewide	4.9							
Classrooms	8.6							
Midwest Region	Illinois	Indiana	Iowa	Kansas	Michigan	Minnesota	Missouri	Nebraska
Statewide	4.9	3.7	3.8	3.3	5.1	4.2	4.5	3.7
Classrooms	13.2	8.8	9.6	8.1	14.3	12.8	10.9	9.6
	N. Dakota	Ohio	S. Dakota	Wisconsin				
Statewide	3.6	4.4	3.2	3.7				
Classrooms	8.8	8.9	8.2	12.1				
South Region	Alabama	Arkansas	Delaware	Florida	Georgia	Kentucky	Louisiana	Maryland
Statewide	5	5.1	4.4	4.2	4.7	4.2	6.8	5.6
Classrooms	12.4	13.3	7.2	8.4	9.8	10	15	17.6
	Mississippi	N. Carolina	Oklahoma	S. Carolina	Tennessee	Texas	Virginia	W. Virginia
Statewide	6.4	5.2	4.6	5	5.4	4.3	4.7	3.9
Classrooms	14.2	13	11.3	10.8	10.5	10.9	10.7	8.7
West Region	Alaska	Arizona	California	Colorado	Hawaii	Idaho	Montana	Nevada
Statewide	3.7	4.8	7.2	4.6	5.8	3.8	3.1	6.1
Classrooms	7	11.4	14.5	11.4	10.1	8.6	8.7	14.1
	New Mexico	Oregon	Utah	Washington	Wyoming			
Statewide	4.9	5.2	5.5	4.7	3			
Classrooms	11	12.3	15.2	11.3	8.1			

administrators are finding that computers and associated software programs, often purchased at great expense, are not having the impact that was once envisioned (see Box 1.1).

When school administrators and teachers begin to carefully analyze the academic and social needs of their students, they quickly see the value of putting technology into the hands of teachers and students. Researchers and educators are now discovering that a bank of four to six computers in a classroom is one of the most pedagogically sound ways to create connections between the curriculum and technology.

Box 1.1. Reasons for Lack of Technological Progress

➢ Limited numbers of up-to-date computers and programs available for use in classrooms (see Table 1.2)[5]
➢ Limited computer networks and a critical shortage of school-based expertise to service network problems quickly and effectively
➢ Improper coordination (linkage, integration) of computer software to school needs
➢ Lack of compatibility between various ages and brands of computers
➢ Scarcity of quality staff development programs and lack of time for teachers to help each other (see Table 1.3)[6]
➢ Overemphasis on computer labs to the exclusion of classroom learning centers
➢ Past failure of universities and colleges to train computer-smart graduates (see Table 1.4)[7]

Table 1.2   Regional Data on Computer Hardware in Public Schools

Northeast Region	Connecticut	Maine	Massachusetts	N. Hampshire	New Jersey	New York
286, 386, or Apple IIS	15	12	19	21	13	19
486 or non-Power Macs	23	40	30	30	24	25
586, Pentium II, or Power Macs	62	48	51	49	63	56
	Pennsylvania	Rhode Island	Vermont			
286, 386, or Apple IIS	18	19	12			
486 or non-Power Macs	25	34	33			
586, Pentium II, or Power Macs	56	47	55			
Midwest Region	Illinois	Indiana	Iowa	Kansas	Michigan	Minnesota
286, 386, or Apple IIS	18	19	19	20	16	17
486 or non-Power Macs	24	29	32	31	25	32
586, Pentium II, or Power Macs	58	53	49	49	58	51
	Missouri	Nebraska	N. Dakota	Ohio	S. Dakota	Wisconsin
286, 386, or Apple IIS	17	21	21	12	20	15
486 or non-Power Macs	27	31	28	17	28	27
586, Pentium II, or Power Macs	56	48	50	71	52	58
South Region	Alabama	Arkansas	Delaware	Florida	Georgia	Kentucky
286, 386, or Apple IIS	25	27	8	19	21	23
486 or non-Power Macs	20	23	15	34	29	33
586, Pentium II, or Power Macs	55	50	77	47	50	44
	Louisiana	Maryland	Mississippi	N. Carolina	Oklahoma	S. Carolina
286, 386, or Apple IIS	28	22	25	25	21	20
486 or non-Power Macs	23	25	24	30	27	21
586, Pentium II, or Power Macs	48	53	51	45	52	59
	Tennessee	Texas	Virginia	W. Virginia		
286, 386, or Apple IIS	21	14	18	28		
486 or non-Power Macs	32	29	26	21		
586, Pentium II, or Power Macs	47	57	56	51		
West Region	Alaska	Arizona	California	Colorado	Hawaii	Idaho
286, 386, or Apple IIS	16	18	20	17	15	20
486 or non-Power Macs	39	31	31	35	38	19
586, Pentium II, or Power Macs	46	52	49	48	47	60
	Montana	Nevada	New Mexico	Oregon	Utah	Washington
286, 386, or Apple IIS	23	15	20	15	18	20
486 or non-Power Macs	28	31	26	34	25	39
586, Pentium II, or Power Macs	49	54	54	51	55	43
	Wyoming					
286, 386, or Apple IIS	22					
486 or non-Power Macs	34					
586, Pentium II, or Power Macs	44					

The success of state-of-the-art classroom technology centers is causing school administrators, board members, trustees, and teachers to shift their ideas about how technology best works in schools. Within this alternative structure, school administrators are compelled to ask several penetrating questions.

Does the new technology enhance academic achievement?

Can technology be integrated into our existing classroom arrangement and educational programs without significant disruption?

Will the new technological approach have the impact we expect?

Is changing our technological program worth the financial expenditures required to upgrade or replace existing facilities, equipment, and programs?

Are there new technological advances on the horizon that will render our intended equipment purchases obsolete in the not-too-distant future?

Where can we go as a school (or school district) to get the best advice about serving our technological needs to upgrade or stay current?

Table 1.3   Regional Data on Initial Teacher Tech Training and Requirements for State Licensure

Northeast Region

	Connecticut	Maine	Massachusetts	New Hampshire	New Jersey	New York
Teachers who are tech. novices	32%	15%	28%	26%	29%	34%
Must pass a technology test						
Must receive tech. training	✔					✔
	Pennsylvania	Rhode Island	Vermont			
Teachers who are tech. novices	24%	26%	28%			
Must pass a technology test						
Must receive tech. training	✔	✔				

Midwest Region

	Illinois	Indiana	Iowa	Kansas	Michigan	Minnesota
Teachers who are tech. novices	31%	13%	13%	18%	31%	18%
Must pass a technology test					✔	
Must receive tech. training			✔		✔	
	Missouri	Nebraska	N. Dakota	Ohio	S. Dakota	Wisconsin
Teachers who are tech. novices	28%	21%	34%	34%	25%	23%
Must pass a technology test						
Must receive tech. training	✔		✔			✔

South Region

	Alabama	Arkansas	Delaware	Florida	Georgia	Kentucky
Teachers who are tech. novices	34%	37%	43%	32%	25%	20%
Must pass a technology test						
Must receive tech. training			✔	✔	✔	✔
	Louisiana	Maryland	Mississippi	N. Carolina	Oklahoma	S. Carolina
Teachers who are tech. novices	35%	24%	37%	22%	36%	30%
Must pass a technology test				✔		
Must receive tech. training		✔	✔	✔		
	Tennessee	Texas	Virginia	W. Virginia		
Teachers who are tech. novices	28%	28%	21%	25%		
Must pass a technology test						
Must receive tech. training	✔	✔	✔	✔		

West Region

	Alaska	Arizona	California	Colorado	Hawaii	Idaho
Teachers who are tech. novices	19%	35%	31%	20%	31%	18%
Must pass a technology test						✔
Must receive tech. training	✔		✔	✔		✔
	Montana	Nevada	New Mexico	Oregon	Utah	Washington
Teachers who are tech. novices	27%	32%	36%	21%	36%	20%
Must pass a technology test						
Must receive tech. training			✔			
	Wyoming					
Teachers who are tech. novices	39%					
Must pass a technology test						
Must receive tech. training						

At present, only limited research is available that shows a correlation between increases in student achievement and the use of technology in schools. As a result, some people question technological changes in education when it is not clear to them that such resources are directly tied to student achievement. However, a few of the better-known examples of the successful application of technology to K-12 education may help to convey an intuitive feeling for the potential of educational technology.[8]

- **Blackstone Junior High School (California).** This school has 10 "smart classrooms," including one in which students can use computer-aided design (CAD) software to describe products that are then fabricated using a computer-controlled, flexible manufacturing system. Higher test scores and improvements in comprehension, motivation, and attitude have been reported for the predominantly Hispanic student body.

- **Carrollton City School District (Georgia).** Computer technology is used in this school district as part of a novel program that has succeeded in reducing the dropout rate from 19% to 5% and the failure rate in ninth-grade algebra from 38% to 3%.

- **Carter Lawrence School (Tennessee).** Students in selected classrooms within this Nashville middle school used technology in various

Table 1.4   Regional Data on State Tech Professional Development Incentives and Requirements

Northeast Region

	Connecticut	Maine	Massachusetts	New Hampshire	New Jersey	New York
Tech. training for recertification	✔					
Tech. development required						
Professional/financial incentives	✔		✔		✔	

	Pennsylvania	Rhode Island	Vermont			
Tech. training for recertification						
Tech. development required						
Professional/financial incentives			✔			

Midwest Region

	Illinois	Indiana	Iowa	Kansas	Michigan	Minnesota
Tech. training for recertification						
Tech. development required						
Professional/financial incentives		✔			✔	

	Missouri	Nebraska	N. Dakota	Ohio	S. Dakota	Wisconsin
Tech. training for recertification						
Tech. development required						
Professional/financial incentives				✔	✔	

South Region

	Alabama	Arkansas	Delaware	Florida	Georgia	Kentucky
Tech. training for recertification					✔	
Tech. development required		✔		✔		
Professional/financial incentives			✔	✔		✔

	Louisiana	Maryland	Mississippi	N. Carolina	Oklahoma	S. Carolina
Tech. training for recertification						
Tech. development required				✔		
Professional/financial incentives	✔		✔			

	Tennessee	Texas	Virginia	W. Virginia		
Tech. training for recertification			✔			
Tech. development required	✔			✔		
Professional/financial incentives				✔		

West Region

	Alaska	Arizona	California	Colorado	Hawaii	Idaho
Tech. training for recertification						
Tech. development required						
Professional/financial incentives					✔	

	Montana	Nevada	New Mexico	Oregon	Utah	Washington
Tech. training for recertification						
Tech. development required						
Professional/financial incentives					✔	

	Wyoming					
Tech. training for recertification						
Tech. development required						
Professional/financial incentives						

ways as part of a program called Schools for Thought (SFT), which is based largely on constructive principles. Sixth-grade SFT participants scored higher on a number of components of Tennessee's mandated standardized achievement test than students in matched-comparison classrooms, and demonstrated substantially stronger critical-thinking skills in complex performance assessments involving high-level reading and writing tasks. Absenteeism and student withdrawal rates were also dramatically lower among SFT students.

- **Christopher Columbus Middle School (New Jersey).** Perhaps the most widely publicized example of the successful application of educational technology, this inner-city school in Union City implemented a reform program that (along with other important changes) provided all seventh-grade students and teachers with access to computers and the Internet both at school and at home. The performance of its 91% Hispanic student population, the majority economically disadvantaged, improved from significantly below to somewhat above the statewide average in reading, language arts, and math.

- **Clearview Elementary School (California).** A restructuring program involving the use of advanced technology resulted in an increase in standardized achievement test scores from the lowest 10% to the highest 20%.

- **East Bakersfield High School (California).** A school-to-work program at this school made extensive use of technology to provide its 60% Hispanic student body (including many students having very limited English proficiency) with the skills required for any of five different career tracks, resulting in increased graduation and job placement rates.

- **Northbrook Middle School (Texas).** Interdisciplinary teams use computing and networking resources to teach critical-thinking and problem-solving skills to this student population, which consists primarily of the children of migrant workers, 76% of whom are economically disadvantaged. Highly significant increases in test scores have been reported.

- **Ralph Bunche School (New York).** Information technology has been used for collaborative work and project-oriented learning by 120 randomly selected students in this elementary school, which serves primarily low-income black and Hispanic residents of Central Harlem. These students outperformed a control group by 10 percentage points in mathematics on New York City standardized exams. Progress has also been reported on problem-solving skills.

- **Taylor Elementary School (Indiana).** Self-paced individualized learning is the central focus of this suburban school, whose students are drawn largely from lower-middle-class white families. Technology is used to support project work conducted by teams that include students of different ages. Internet access and sophisticated information retrieval tools are used to support self-directed inquiries. While the program is relatively young, some improvement has been reported in test scores along with a significant increase in student interest and enthusiasm for learning.

Hellgate Elementary School in Missoula, Montana, provides another excellent example. This school is using an electronic testing system called Measures of Academic Progress (MAP) that has been developed by the Northwest Evaluation Association (NWEA) of Portland, Oregon. It is being used effectively in over 370 school districts nationally. At Hellgate Elementary, teachers are using several labs made up of Pentium computers to test over 800 students in Grades 3 to 8. These electronic tests, however, can be adapted to be used with classroom-networked computers as well. The electronic tests are especially useful in placing new students in appropriate educational programs. The tests are adapted to measure each student's performance level. If a student answers a question correctly, the next survey question will be more challenging. If a student answers a survey question incorrectly, the student will receive a less difficult item. This process continues back and forth until all items are focused at the student's achievement level. Electronic tests are criterion-based and thus can be tailored to local, state, and national goals and benchmarks. They can also be designed to provide additional information for teachers and local school officials. Tests are drawn from a database of 15,000 items and are interpolated to correspond with national norm-referenced tests. The MAP test couples the advantages of achievement level tests with the power of technology. While most tests provide scores that compare and rank students and schools, the MAP electronic test provides growth information that is vital in classrooms faced with helping students meet rigorous standards.

In addition to the success by individual schools, the KPMG Economic Consulting Service conducted a comprehensive study in Ohio and found that at least 97% of surveyed superintendents and principals in Ohio agreed that computers improved learning achievements within their districts.[9] In support of this finding, other studies show that computers, if used appropriately, can have the following positive effects on children.

- Interesting and engaging educational software and nonprofit Web sites offers children opportunities to explore the world and to create original works of art and literature.
- Communicating through the Internet can enable children to keep in touch with friends and family and to form online communities with others who share their interests.
- Children's use of home computers is linked to slightly better academic performance.
- Through training in media literacy and computer fluency, children can learn to recognize and seek out higher-quality software and Web sites, and learn to use computers in more active ways to create, design, and invent.[10]

The reality is that new developments in technology, changing societal and career needs, and new learning strategies are challenging schools to accommodate a symbiotic relationship among technology, curriculum, and the learning environment. In support of this reality, "Rigorous, systematic, well-controlled research is required to identify the specific factors responsible for successful outcomes and to ascertain their range of applicability and the extent to which they can be generalized."[11]

Student Achievement and Technology

Placing wide area computer networks and other forms of advanced technology in schools has been taking place for a number of years now. This implementation process has been expensive for school districts and, at times, a source of controversy and frustration for school boards, upper- and mid-level administrators, and teachers. This is mainly due to the fact that technology has not yielded the intended curricular and student learner achievements thought possible. On the other hand, a growing body of evidence is now substantiating the notion that, when implemented appropriately, technology does have a relevant impact on student achievement.

Box 1.2. Academic Benefits of Technology

➢ Improve problem-solving skills significantly
➢ Enhance the quality and quantity of writing processes and content
➢ Facilitate independent work, teamwork, and collaborative inquiry
➢ Increase performance in basic skills learning, especially in math and reading
➢ Widen the scope of instructional opportunities
➢ Increase mastery of vocational and workplace skills
➢ Promote higher student retention rates
➢ Encourage higher-order thinking skills (organizing, analyzing, and communicating complex information)
➢ Serve students with special needs effectively and efficiently[12]

Several positive beneficial outcomes that accrue when a symbiotic relationship is established among technology, curriculum, and the learning environment have been cited (see Box 1.2).

According to the available research reports and articles on the effectiveness of technology in the student-learning environment, a variety of conclusions and opinions are offered. On one end of the continuum, supporters allude to research studies showing the positive impact of technology on student learning. On the other end of the spectrum, critics present arguments that there is little, if any, evidence from the research to support the claim that the use of technology in classrooms is worthy of the resources it requires. The supporters of technology point out that, in addition to student achievement, creating a technology culture that is more indicative of student needs has made a significant impact in at least 10 areas.

1. Increased student writing. Simply measuring the amount that students are using computers to write reveals one positive impact of technology. Students are writing more compositions and doing so more often. Many teachers now find that students are producing three times the amount of written documents than they did before word processors were made available to them. Teachers who carefully watch students find that it often appears to be easier for their pupils to use a keyboard than a pen or pencil to write. The direct result is that students are writing more often and with seemingly greater ease. This trend is likely to become even more pronounced with the advent of voice recognition programs and other technological applications soon to be available for school use.

2. Higher quality student writing. Analysis of student writing by numerous researchers has shown that word processing helps students become more effective writers. This is not surprising to anyone who uses word processing to any degree because today's user-friendly computers and powerful programs allow students to check grammar and spelling and revise all or part of their work as often as they wish.

3. **Enhanced cooperative learning.** Schools whose teachers are using five wide area networked computers and a printer in classrooms are finding that this format enhances and supports cooperative learning strategies. By using classroom computer centers as learning stations, many teachers are finding it easier to have students engage in collaborative efforts. When collaborative learning is linked with technology, it is known to have a strong positive influence on student achievement.

4. **Enhanced integration of curriculum.** Teachers whose classrooms have access to the Internet and electronic scanning devices are finding that using computers can make it easier to integrate social studies, literature, math, and science into a more coordinated series of learning experiences for students. A practical example of this type of learning opportunity occurs when students use the Internet and scanner to create content-integrated presentations using material from several disciplines. In addition, maps, graphs, tables, and illustrations from a variety of subject areas can be incorporated into student projects and visual presentations by means of computers.

5. **Greater application of learning style strategies.** A significant correlation exists between the use of technology and the ability to accommodate different student learning styles in the classroom. Dunn pointed out in her research that multimedia computer technology is structured to enhance the visual, auditory, and kinesthetic components of student learning.[13]

6. **Increased applications of cross-age tutoring.** Students having access to high-speed, wide area networked systems are now able to use computers at any site in the school district. As a result, teachers are finding that older students can work with younger students on cooperative or tutorial projects across the network.

7. **Increased teacher communication.** An analysis of message logs across school districts indicates an interesting trend. Teachers having access to e-mail and Internet services at their schools are communicating more with their administrators as well as with other teachers at the same grade level. Today's new wave of technological advances is allowing teachers to more easily exchange information with other educators on local, state, national, and international levels. A very positive consequence of this increased use of electronic communication is the improvement of communication between school staff members at all levels.

8. **Greater parent communication.** Voice mail as well as e-mail capabilities have provided a promising new link between home and school. Many teachers can now have parents contact the school via computer and receive updated reports on homework assignments and upcoming school activities. Looking at a school's message logs also demonstrates the impact

and effectiveness of computers in helping to bridge the information and understanding gaps that can occur between school and home.

9. **Enhanced community relations.** Bringing the school and community together provides another compelling reason for implementing technology into schools. In many school districts, community residents and local business members are regularly invited to take part in on-campus training programs using classroom facilities and computer labs. As a result, adult education classes using technical instructors and school computer facilities are on the rise. In addition, students and teachers across the country are helping civic groups and small businesses develop Web pages, formulate listservs, and use e-mail.

10. **Enhanced global learners.** Never before have educators and students been able to develop a better understanding of other cultures and people than is possible today. Many schools are now using computers to access information from all parts of the globe. New advances in voice translation and voice recognition will improve this capability even more in the future. As one considers this phenomenon, it becomes increasingly evident that technology in schools is paving the way for students, teachers, and citizens to enter a new community of global learners.

Classroom Technology

New understandings of systemic leadership and management frameworks are melding with technological advancements to revitalize concepts and designs for the computer-aided classroom of the future. These new designs redirect educational technology away from use as a mere tool to something that addresses the academic needs of a new generation of learners. The concentration of this theory makes the implementation and regular use of technology student centered. The philosophy is to build an awareness of how technology can advance education, enhance student opportunities for exploration, and provide a transition between present and future forms of learning.

This educational vision creates a suitable climate for the use of technological advances in both computer labs and classrooms. For those schools having access to computer labs, advances in technology are providing opportunities for teachers and students to use high-speed and high-memory machines to access the Internet as well as assist with curricula programs. For the first time in our educational history, teachers and students will have the hardware, courseware, and service support to truly enhance curriculum and instruction in a lab setting. Some educators, however, are deciding to make technology even more accessible by using clusters of computers in their classrooms. Such opportunity is due to recent advances in technology that allow administrators to place a minimum of five high-quality, networked computers and a printer in every classroom. Developing a cluster of classroom computers promotes collaboration and cooperative-learning activities among students and creates an environment for school improvement.

Additionally, computer networks now link classrooms with centralized file servers and provide powerful information-gathering tools for students and teachers. Many teachers are now finding that they are learning to use technology effectively in their classrooms because they have open access to the appropriate equipment and software programs. Ruth Wishengrad, educational editor and former teacher, offered three reasons for making computers part of a student's regular classroom education:

1. Computers can make learning all subjects easier and are especially valuable in developing students' language and problem-solving skills.

2. Students can use computers to reach hundreds of telecommunication networks, and these sources provide a huge amount of information students cannot get from textbooks and more traditional learning tools.

3. Computer literacy (understanding computer technology) is necessary for many high-paying and interesting careers in a computer dependent economy.[14]

Innovative teachers now access and use information from a wide array of multimedia formats. Technologically integrated classrooms provide opportunities for using automated libraries, interactive video, voice recognition, hypertext presentations, Internet access, CD-ROMs, cellular phones, and satellite feeds to improve learning opportunities for students. As a result, teachers in technologically advanced schools are discovering that the classroom of tomorrow is here today.

Most educators now realize the contribution that technology is making in schools. Barbara Mean, educational researcher at SRI International in Menlo Park, California, noted that more states are becoming aware that technology is an important part of the school restructuring movement. She listed several ways in which technology can bolster reform (see Box 1.3).

We are said to be living in the Information Age, and some theorists have suggested that we are now entering the Learning Age.[16] The reality is that many people are also living and working in an age of increasing interconnectedness. There seems to be little doubt that new advances in technology are capable of providing America's classrooms and citizens with a new and long-awaited window to the world. Since students thrive on creating and being a part of a community, technology design is beginning to make a difference in teaching and learning as it is in society as a whole.

Developing Local Community Awareness

Michael Lowe, a school principal in Lawrence, Kansas, declared that the overarching theme to be developed throughout new-millennium schools involves the nature and significance of community.[17] Increased community awareness about the uses of educational technology is directly

---

Box 1.3. Support for Technology

➢ Internet and desktop presentation tools support student exploration.

➢ Computers provide a powerful tool for use with constructivist teaching methods.

➢ Technological awareness gives teachers an added sense of professionalism.

➢ Electronic communications reduce isolation and lead to the development of professional communities.

➢ Specialized computer programs help educators measure academic achievement and assess student performance.

➢ Networks and databases streamline information collection and help teachers target additional resources and appropriate teaching methods.

➢ Technology simplifies.[15]

---

impacting the role of technology in the classroom. In many districts, parents and community members are now communicating with teachers in their classrooms via e-mail, school hotlines, and interactive Web pages. Additionally, some progressive schools are providing students and parents with portable laptop computers that can be used for homework or class projects.

Public involvement is growing in many schools as advances in educational technology occur, and as a result, community members are beginning to revise their views about education. A positive example of community-directed responsiveness is the Foshay Learning Center,[18] a school in Los Angeles that now uses eight satellite-learning centers in low-income apartment complexes across the city to provide educational programs to students. Without leaving home, students can now get help with their homework, learn about technology, and participate in enrichment activities.

Increasingly, business leaders are recognizing the connection between students' technological skills and their ability to be successful in the world of work. This consciousness has led to the formation of school-to-work programs funded by state money and local taxpayers. In addition, school and business partnerships are on the rise. Students and teachers routinely help businesspeople by doing such things as creating Web pages for them. In return, local businesses often donate equipment to schools in an effort to capitalize on a new market for educational products. An important by-product of these various forms of contact between schools and citizens is that community members are often more willing to support tax levies for education when they understand where their tax dollars are going. The resulting interaction between schools and community members is being seen more and more as a positive outcome for both groups.

School Technology Goals

A key standard for school jurisdictions to consider is the provision of four clear and practical technological goals that will expand the boundaries of traditional schooling and help children reach new levels of learning development. First, school administrators should coordinate school-based services and resources in order to heighten access to interactive technology for students in their schools. Statewide telecommunication infrastructures are usually most capable of providing the necessary level of linkage and delivery for schools.

Second, guidelines for equipment use and programs designed to enhance communication and technological awareness within communities need to be developed. A study in Ohio found that 77% of the school superintendents indicated they had a strategic plan in place, but only 28% had shared that vision or its accomplishments with their stakeholders; and 53% of the parents surveyed indicated that they had never received information about technology goals at their schools.[19] Improved public awareness of what technology is available often leads to a greater understanding of how technology can benefit students and citizens. Community appreciation also leads to the creation of shared vision and mission statements, joint technology committees, appropriate financing programs, infrastructure development, staff development, maintenance and service arrangements, favorable program evaluation, and finally, successful public relations programs. Education leaders must expand traditional school boundaries to involve the community in planning, financing, implementing, and evaluating technology.

Third, school leaders would be wise to share school success stories with their communities. Data obtained from student assessments can add substantial credibility to the positive things happening in schools when effectively presented to the public. This information can be easily retrieved and presented with the aid of computers.

Fourth, data from student assessments can provide school administrators and teachers with a valuable mechanism for checking exam results to ensure that student performance meets or exceeds local, state, and national standards. If required, a statewide data retrieval system for student performance could assist school leaders in determining aggregate achievement levels for all schools. As well, an accompanying item analysis of standardized test questions would provide administrators and teachers with a means of making a sound appraisal of strengths and weaknesses in the school or district curriculum.

It is through the development of clear public information programs that state legislators and citizens will best understand how technology is impacting student achievement. As community support increases, school leaders are better able to provide the administrative support necessary to accommodate the needs of teachers and students. Community support also breaks down the "classroom walls" by making the positive activities in schools more visible and educators more accessible to parents. Computers and other technology provide a practical avenue to connect teachers and students with learning opportunities that await them as they begin to make contact with the rest of the world. There is little doubt that leading-edge technology holds the promise of many positive elements for American education. A few of these positive outcomes would be the fostering of exploratory learning, the empowering of teachers, and the equipping of school leaders with advanced resources needed to manage schools. In reality, the task of illuminating the role of technology in our nation's classrooms is a complex and important one. It is only through an effective public information campaign that policymakers, practitioners, and citizens can be equipped with the facts needed to make wise decisions about the new electronic advancements available to their schools.

State and National Levels of Awareness

State and national organizations are now working to develop a shared vision that will establish a workable frame of reference for school technology programs. It is crucial that education leaders at state and national levels develop a coordinated plan directed at helping schools use technology. It is unfortunate that, at present, state and federal agencies often confound this process by duplicating each other's efforts. While numerous government agencies are capable of providing financial and technical support to schools, they are often unable to offer this aid efficiently. As a result, many schools are trying to work with a mishmash of networks, database providers, hardware and courseware applications, and all the difficulties associated with such a technological conglomeration. In practice, this uncoordinated array of appliances and applications creates confusion for educators. Fortunately, a concerted effort is under way to eradicate this problem. In an effort to improve the situation, savvy school leaders are spearheading a movement to develop new frameworks for including influential noneducators into the brainstorming and implementation process before bringing new technologies into their districts.

The creation of national and state standards for the use of computers and other electronic resources is a major factor in the development of an overall plan to deal with the complexity of today's hi-tech educational landscape. The National Council for Accreditation of Teacher Education (NCATE), for example, requires schools of education to meet verifiable technology standards for program accreditation. This accreditation body recognizes the importance of advanced technology in schools and supports this stance by stating that technology needs to move from the periphery to the center of teacher education.

Many local and state educational leaders are considering a proposal to collaborate closely with the U.S. Department of Education on matters related to computers in schools. The results of these coordinated efforts would be specifically directed at better understanding Internet use, the integration of curriculum via technology, software and courseware development, and course content for technology classes. This national organization will comprise a consortium of capable people from the ranks of higher education, business, research institutes, and governmental agencies. An opportunity will exist to share research information and data from many sources to develop a national technology initiative. The outcome of subsequent proposals made by the national and state technology task forces will be to place a greater emphasis on technology in classrooms by fostering close cooperation between teachers, administrators, parents, experts from higher education, and business. Individual states are also moving forward with initiatives designed to capitalize on the benefits of technology for schools and students. Some perceptive state lawmakers are advancing legislation to provide teachers with computer skills to allow for a wider use of technology in classrooms, while legislators in other states are establishing statewide standards to regulate the use of personal computers in schools and classrooms.

STRATEGIES FOR SUCCESS

To be successful in our increasingly technological world, all learners and educators must be skilled in the use of computers. Also, to bring about change and establish equity, factors such as proper training programs, technical support, and time for learning must be provided simultaneously for educators (see Box 1.4).

In our rapidly changing world, the economic vitality of communities and individuals will depend more and more on the ability to access information, build knowledge, solve problems, and share success. Because technology will increasingly play a key role in this process, students must

---

Box 1.4. Successful Technology Goals

➤ Community involvement in planning and implementing the use of computers and other technology in schools should be a high priority for school leaders.

➤ Developing quality technological leadership and planning for effective computer use within the jurisdiction must receive considerable attention.

➤ Finances for computers and other forms of school technology should come from the general budget of the district.

➤ Emphasis should be placed on incorporating computer learning centers into classrooms.

➤ Curriculum should use technology, but not be driven by it.

➤ Staff development involving technology should be made highly practical by having teachers instruct teachers.

➤ Planning and implementation phases for the inclusion of new technology should include assessment and evaluation standards.

➤ A well-planned public relations program should be used to share the benchmarks of a successful program with the community.

develop the necessary skills to use computers capably while they are in school. This means that today's students must be prepared now for the technological world that will be a very real part of their lives in the future.

FUTURE CHALLENGES

One might say that technology is here to stay. The 88 million children of baby-boomer adults find using digital technologies no more intimidating than using a VCR or an overhead projector. These children are often referred to as the net generation because they are media literate and watch much less television than their parents did at the same age. That two thirds of the children today use a personal computer either at home or at school implies that they want to be active participants, not just viewers or listeners. In fact, TV to many in the current generation is somewhat old-fashioned. A survey by Teenage Research Unlimited, in which more than 80% of the teenagers polled said it is "in" to be online, puts being online on a par with dating and partying.[20] To meet the challenge for the future, the following questions beg answers:

1. How do we engage youth in our schools to be active participants in all our classrooms with online activities?

2. If only 20% of the 2.5 million teachers who work in our public schools feel comfortable using technology in their classrooms, what must a school district do to make 100% feel comfortable with technology?

As Perry and Areglado stated, "Technology-support curricular transformation demands visionary leadership and effective management from school [administrators]."[21] Today, with the heightened national interest in improved student performance, high-stakes testing, and school accountability, the school administrator's role must change. Traditionally, principals have been seen as managers responsible for implementing district policies. Until the arrival of the Information Age, which includes computers, the attitude of school administrators was, "If it ain't broke, don't fix it." At present, because investments in equipment have not always been accompanied by changes in teaching, school administrators must take on the role of leadership. Teachers need help to overcome obstacles and integrate technology into their instructional practice. The overriding question is, "What must school administrators do?" Also—according to Henry Jay Becker, professor of education at the University of California, Irvine—disparities between rich and poor must be addressed if computer technology is to help create a more egalitarian society.[22]

As educators give further thought to the impact of technology in our present world, and as they consider the nature of the world our children will inherit from us, it becomes readily apparent that we must carefully meld computers and other technologies into the current structure of individual classrooms. The potential for creating schools and school districts of high quality is only possible through the timely and adroit application of existing knowledge. In order to benefit from this knowledge, it is important that a comprehensive blueprint be adopted and followed. It is recommended that educators and community leaders carefully consider and adhere to suggestions from the chapters that follow as they explore ways to integrate technology into the curriculum to enhance student learning.

REFLECTIVE ACTIVITIES

1. List and analyze the outcomes expected from computers and other forms of technology in our schools.

2. Explain how your school district computer purchases and software programs are meeting students' needs. If they are not meeting students' needs, list the shortcomings (e.g., equipment inadequacies, lack of qualified personnel, or facility limitations).

3. Identify other forms of technology available that could improve learning opportunities for students in your school district.

4. Reflect on the type of students you see in your school district today. Compare and contrast their relationship with learning and technology.

5. Determine whether computer labs or classroom-based learning centers should be the main configuration for the use of technology in our schools. List the advantages and disadvantages of each as well as for a combination of both.

6. Analyze the positive and negative aspects of computer use in your school district.

7. Decide how much access community members should have to the school's technologies.

8. Provide a rationale for why school-community communication via e-mail and other technologies should or should not be promoted.

9. Identify what organizations exist in your school district and state for the coordinated implementation of computer hardware and software.

10. Describe your state and national standards for computer programs and purchases.

2

Leadership and Planning

FLEXIBLE LEADERS

Capable leadership and careful planning are critical factors that are consistently interwoven within the fabric of successful school technology initiatives. In fact, leadership and planning are common threads invariably found in the design of any successful program in K-12 schools. Currently, school administrators face one of the most challenging and exciting times in the educational history of this nation. The changes that schools are being asked to accommodate can be both academically threatening and liberating for teachers and administrators. At this critical juncture, the quality of educational leadership is clearly one of the essential elements required for the organization and realization of successful technology initiatives in schools. Conversely, inadequate leadership will merely maintain the status quo. At its worst, mediocre direction from administrators will likely nullify the positive contributions that technology can make to education, frustrate teachers and their students, and cost taxpayers a good deal in ill-directed expenditures.

John Morefield, principal of Hawthorne School in Seattle, Washington, succinctly places the importance of accomplished leadership in proper perspective by noting, "We all know intuitively, and the research on effective schools shows empirically, that quality schools require quality principals."[1] The men and women who provide leadership to schools make a significant contribution to the teaching and learning that happen behind classroom walls. As a result, their leadership is not insignificant, although it may be misunderstood at times.

One of the taxing features of contemporary leadership is its ambiguity. School leaders usually have no predetermined set of rules or formulas to follow in their quest to provide the most appropriate equipment and programs for teachers and students. Often, they have only general guidelines, vague suggestions, and past successes to rely on, and these are not tools that support proficient decision-making! Be that as it may, acceleration in the discovery of new learning technologies, coupled with the ever-more-pervasive use of computers in education, are providing perceptive leaders with many opportunities to positively guide their schools through this changing learning environment. Those school administrators who supply the foresight required to create and sustain cutting-edge technology programs will be worthy of the encouragement and recognition extended by their communities and peers. It is also very possible that they will be the forerunners of a new type of administrator who will usher in a renewed vision of school and education.

In order to exercise the level of leadership required to develop and maintain programs of exceptional quality, superintendents and principals must reach clear answers to four basic questions:

What equipment (hardware and software) is required to make the improvements necessary to construct student-centered learning environments in schools?

Why commit a great deal of time and money to this initiative for technological change—are these motives focused on improving student learning?

Who is the best person to lead the technological initiative under consideration?

Who will be best suited to assess and maintain the quality of technology programs after the initial stages of implementation are completed?

Quality leadership involves the unique human ability of being able to anticipate change and adapt administrative roles and responsibilities to meet the needs of their schoolteachers and students. It is the art of knowing how and when to be flexible within a structured administrative framework. Administration now requires a person to possess a good deal of technological knowledge and flexibility. This flexibility is helpful because it allows the practitioner to shift from a purely administrative focus to a more teacher-learner oriented approach.

The ability of the school administrator to shift leadership styles can provide a supportive climate for broad-based discussions between administrators and teachers. Such discussions can also build a platform for shared decision making when opportunities are appropriate. Involving teachers in technology deliberations may well take a good deal of courage on the part of the administrator, but there can be real benefits for the overall feasibility and attainment of school or district objectives. Also, student needs can often be more easily gauged.

It makes sense to broaden leadership responsibilities whenever the job is too large to be effectively done by one person. Instead of one administrator trying to provide adequate leadership for a comprehensive technology project, it is more responsible to spread the leadership to perceptive individuals from a group of professional educators. The corollary to this line of thinking is that if we trust teachers to work with students and make decisions about their academic welfare, school administrators should be willing to involve teachers in discussions that are technology related.

School administrators who have comprehensive ways of thinking about their jobs also realize the importance of parents as stakeholders in technology reforms. Public engagement is no longer a theoretical phrase to be used exclusively in discussions between academics. The development of changed environments that are broad based and supportive requires initiative and foresight on the part of administrators. A good deal of this foresight involves the willingness and moxie to cultivate and capitalize on the potential knowledge, energy, and support of parents and community members. Current research shows that many site and district level administrators are aware of the importance of parents and interested community members to the educational constituency. For example, Jeffery Kimpton, former director of public engagement for the Annenberg Institute for School Reform, and Jonathan Considine, a former researcher in public engagement at the Annenberg Institute, described public engagement in the following manner.

> Frustrated by the rising tide of the community's concern over public education, school leaders are developing a tool for building solid new relationships among educators, parents, citizens, business and civic leaders, and elected officials. The tool can take many forms—parent involvement or advocacy, school-business partnerships, community visioning and public dialogue, a broad-based bond referendum or a community-wide program for putting academic standards into use. Collectively, this work is called public engagement.[2]

Researchers are finding many examples of school leaders who are willing to involve parents and community members in the school technology process. Researchers at the Annenberg Institute for School Reform at Brown University canvassed the country, documenting the practice of public engagement in schools that were large and small, urban and rural, and rich and poor. The researchers found many examples of school leaders who were willing to engage parents and community members in the search for solutions to thorny educational issues. However, they were quick to add a warning. They sensed that

> the number of those [school leaders] willing to forge new collaborations for positive school change is insufficient. For every leader who is interested, many more are looking for a quick-fix workshop and 10 "how to's" to take back to the school board and their central office colleagues. Still others think public engagement is a temporal, short-term process. . . . It is the age-old "we vs. they" dichotomy. . . . We just don't find enough school leaders taking the concept of public engagement very seriously . . . [and] this lackadaisical attitude will produce few winners and a lot of losers.[3]

Understanding how to support educational change, evaluating instructional strategies, and initiating new programs are perhaps the most critical abilities required by those wishing to become outstanding educational leaders. It is also important that these leaders are able to translate their knowledge and abilities into community support for needed programs and reforms. When consideration of the great extent to which properly functioning schools can positively influence student lives, there should be little doubt that communities should be major supporters and encouragers of their children's schooling. That this support and encouragement is often unavailable is troubling. Public disengagement from schools is not a reality that is likely to be reversed without the intentional outreach of accomplished educational leaders. Kimpton and Considine stated:

> Public engagement represents the only way in which schools will garner the necessary local support to negotiate the treacherous waters of school change, creating the energy for the vision that . . . so many . . . Americans are seeking.[4]

The high-quality, broad-based leadership behavior discussed in the above paragraphs is the same type of leadership required to properly connect technology to the learning styles of students in the 21st century. As well, it is this type of leadership that will effectively accommodate the demands for curricular and technological change that are unmistakably evident on the educational horizon.

STAKEHOLDERS' ROLE IN PLANNING FOR TECHNOLOGY

Most school administrators know that computers and advanced-information technologies are touching the lives of students at school and at home. These administrators also realize that in the future, many students will attend schools whose curricula will increasingly rely on computers and advanced information-gathering programs. According to Thomas Shannon, Executive Editor of Technology Leadership Network,[5] planning that takes direct aim at the educationally productive use of school computers is one of the most important tasks a school district can undertake. He described planning as a two-tailed enterprise designed to establish detailed strategies and blueprints as well as to accomplish objectives. This type of planning carefully considers the overall effort that will be required to implement new technologies into schools and is particularly critical because it is through this process that the significant investments of time, effort, and funding will be guided wisely.

Comprehensive planning for the introduction of technology into classrooms is a lot of hard work for administrators. In addition to the back-room deliberations that precede and underpin any major project, administrators must provide considerable leadership in a number of other areas. Such project components as state guidelines, outside funding sources, plant facilities, community expectations, student needs, and teacher preferences must be considered. In addition, the importance of involving the right people in the enterprise cannot be overstated. Discerning leaders will encourage school staffs and supportive community members to work closely with their school and district to establish the parameters and implement the newest technology in the educational environment of the classroom.

It is important for planners to be considerate of all people affected by the refocusing of technology efforts and to provide opportunities for their viewpoints to be heard. With this in mind, planners should incorporate able people having various types of expertise into an advisory committee. If possible, such a committee should include a financial expert, a person knowledgeable about project implementation, another with knowledge of staff development strategies, a technology specialist, and a person to handle public relations.

One unique characteristic of education in America is that the whole community shares a group responsibility for schools. As a natural consequence of this responsibility, community members should be included on committees where their expertise or judgment can really help with the technology initiative. As Rebecca Jones writes, "To be effective, studies show community involvement must be well designed and focused—and that requires a school's wise direction."[6]

Factors to Be Considered

A number of important factors must be addressed in any major technology plan. Information included in the three paragraph headings that follow provides a brief overview of each element in a successful technology outline. In most cases, these paragraph headings also provide concise categories for administrator and committee actions to focus on. Readers are referred to specific chapters for additional discussion and information.

Student Needs. In any technology initiative, the needs of students must be placed above any other factor being considered. The present drive toward computer-aided education often derives support from viewpoints that fail to take into account the importance of student needs. As a result, many well-meaning administrators and committee members make decisions about technology that really don't acknowledge the needs of the people who will use it. Educationally questionable reasons for making major decisions about technology include international competitiveness, skilled labor force, and getting good jobs. As important as these reasons are, no other motivation can be allowed to supplant students' needs as the central focus for schools and their technology programs. For more in-depth information on students' needs, refer to Chapter 4.

Teaching and Learning. Teaching and learning are two complex but complementary entities. Therefore, they must be considered simultaneously when deciding how the technology will be brought into the classroom. For a more complete discussion of teaching and learning with technology, refer to Chapter 4. Several points to remember when considering the effects of technology on teaching and learning are as follows:

- Consider carefully how the technology program will affect teaching and learning. Make sure to have a purpose that reflects teaching and learning when bringing technologies into the school and its classrooms.

- Evaluate hardware purchases and coordinate them to student needs. Consider features like user-friendliness, dependability, and speed.

- Evaluate projected software purchases to determine which programs will best complement, support, and expand classroom teaching and learning.

- Evaluate planned software purchases for comprehensiveness and user-friendliness. Comprehensiveness is important because a program must be able to do a number of jobs in the classroom. User-friendliness is important because ease of use flattens the learning curve and helps ensure that the program will be used.

- Determine the simplest approach that will effectively bring computers into the teaching and learning environment. Simplicity aids understanding and allows stakeholders to support the process more readily.

- Establish dialogues with teachers to evaluate classroom space and decide on computer locations within each classroom.

- Determine the amount of use teachers will make of the new technology.

Leadership and Planning. Quality leadership must prevail at all stages of the project. Planning opens the project to view so participants understand the structure of the project and what is required of each committee and person. Planning will address the who, what, when, where, why, and how aspects of the project. The traits listed below provide a brief overview of several important factors to consider when a technology project is being planned and led:

- Keep students' and teachers' needs at the forefront during the various stages of the technology planning process.

- Consider how students and staff members will be affected by the technology changes and develop appropriate support structures like training, changes in classroom layout, and inclusion into curricula.

- Review school programs to determine how course subjects may be adjusted to make use of technologies in the classroom.

- Locate research that both supports and counters the major assumptions on which the technology project is based. Make sure everyone knows both sides of the issue.

• Consider the possibility of having to modify school practices or upgrade regulations.

• Look at the likelihood of having to adjust the school's philosophy and mission statements to align with the technology initiative you are creating.

• If necessary, create or borrow surveys to probe stakeholder viewpoints.

• Envision what the completed project will look like and what it will do for teaching and learning. This mental picture can help provide focus for the entire enterprise.

Staff Development

One of the most important aspects of this initiative is staff development. It is critical that consideration be given to teacher learning well in advance of the arrival of computers into the classroom. For a detailed description of staff development and its importance to technology implementation, refer to Chapter 3. The list that follows is a brief synopsis of beneficial staff development suggestions.

• Formulate detailed plans for staff development and implementation. Plans for staff development should be developed well in advance of the actual implementation of technology in the classrooms.

• Decide who will lead staff development programs and evaluate each stage of implementation.

• Develop a working schedule for the staff development program.

• Determine appropriate staff development activities for special services and support staff.

• Identify who will lead and evaluate staff development for auxiliary staff members.

• Identify in-house technical consultants who will help teachers deal quickly with problems that might arise.

Financial Management

Most determinations about finance are generally dealt with at middle- and upper-management positions. While many of these deliberations are held in small groups, their impact will be critical to the success of the larger groups and committees that will guide the technology project. For more information about financial management, see Chapter 6. Several points are listed below to provide a general overview of the financial management process.

• Determine what financial resources are available for in-house projects and equipment.

• Itemize equipment resources owned by the school or district. The goal is to look to reduce unnecessary duplication in new purchases.

• Compute financial resources available 3 years in advance.

• Consider canvassing civic organizations for financial or equipment support.

• Determine if the proposed equipment will be purchased locally or from a national distribution company. Decide who will be responsible for handling the recommended purchases.

• Review all costs to make sure the technology project is affordable in all of its phases.

Infrastructure

When speaking of infrastructure, one is generally referring to the basic facilities and the mechanical and electrical installations found in a school. These facilities and installations form the foundation for proposed technology upgrades. For a more complete review of infrastructure, turn to Chapter 7. The following points provide a brief outline of things to consider when reviewing infrastructure:

• Decide how existing equipment and infrastructure can be integrated into the project.

• Visit other schools to evaluate successful programs for structural adaptations that could be copied and, in particular, look for unique ideas to solve local problems.

• Ensure that placement of network wiring will accommodate the instructional configuration required by teachers.

• Analyze what space, remodeling, and expertise is required to ready the infrastructure for implementation.

• If needed, arrange for professionals to handle remodeling or other infrastructure necessities.

Community Awareness and Support

In current educational contexts, community support is necessary during the planning stages of the technology initiative. This is because many parents want to be informed observers in their children's education. Neither are community members likely to be idle bystanders when costly reforms are about to change the way significant portions of children's education are delivered. To find out more about community awareness and support, refer to Chapter 5. Several factors are listed below to provide general information to guide your deliberations.

- Evaluate community willingness to fund such technology initiatives in district schools.

- Determine the level of congruence between the school's new technology initiatives and the technology focus of the board of trustees and education.

- Consider how you will be able to show community members that teachers will adopt this technological direction into their curriculum.

- Address parents' and community members' concerns over how technology in the classroom will enhance student learning and achievement.

- Show parents and members of the community how they and their children can benefit from the process of networking technologies in district classrooms.

- Develop guidelines for presenting information to the public. Be sure all news releases are verified with the public relations director before they go public.

Evaluation and Assessment

The work of leaders is not done when computers or other learning technologies are networked in schools and classrooms. In fact, a very important part of the work remains in the form of program evaluation and assessment. To learn more about this process, refer to Chapter 8. The list that follows contains a selection of ideas that are pertinent to evaluation and assessment of the technology initiative.

- Decide who will evaluate the overall project and how the evaluations will be done.
- Set specific dates for the evaluation process.
- Outline how changes or revisions will be handled.
- Review various evaluation and assessment methods and choose the most appropriate methods available for sharing information with the community.

After reviewing the above factors and tailoring feedback to reflect school or district realities, school leaders should be well prepared to develop more-specific plans for the initiative. At this point in the process, administrators should understand the project parameters well enough to form the committees that will make the plan work for students and teachers.

Technology Standards for Administrators

To specifically define project parameters, administrators can use Technology Standards for School Administrators (TSSA) to optimize benefits of school technology use. The notion behind these standards is the assumption that technology reform requires large-scale systemic change. These standards can then be used as technology targets for administrators to aim for. The following material was originally produced as a project of the TSSA Collaborative.[7]

STANDARDS

I. **Leadership and Vision.** Educational leaders inspire a shared vision for comprehensive integration of technology and foster an environment and culture conducive to the realization of that vision.

Educational Leaders:

A. Facilitate the shared development by all stakeholders of a vision for technology use and widely communicate that vision

B. Maintain an inclusive and cohesive process to develop, implement, and monitor a dynamic, long-range, and systemic technology plan to achieve the vision

C. Foster and nurture a culture of responsible risk taking and advocate policies promoting continuous innovation with technology

D. Use data in making leadership decisions

E. Advocate for research-based effective practices in use of technology

F. Advocate on the state and national levels for policies, programs, and funding opportunities that support implementation of the district technology plan

II. **Learning and Teaching.** Educational leaders ensure that curricular design, instructional strategies, and learning environments integrate appropriate technologies to maximize learning and teaching.

Educational Leaders:

A. Identify, use, evaluate, and promote appropriate technologies to enhance and support instruction and standards-based curriculum leading to high levels of student achievement

B. Facilitate and support collaborative technology-enriched learning environments conducive to innovation for improved learning

C. Provide for learner-centered environments that use technology to meet the individual and diverse needs of learners

D. Facilitate the use of technologies to support and enhance instructional methods that develop higher-level thinking, decision-making, and problem-solving skills

E. Provide for and ensure that faculty and staff take advantage of quality professional learning opportunities for improved learning and teaching with technology

III. **Productivity and Professional Practice.** Educational leaders apply technology to enhance their professional practice and to increase their own productivity and that of others.

Educational Leaders:

A. Model the routine, intentional, and effective use of technology

B. Employ technology for communication and collaboration among colleagues, staff, parents, students, and the larger community

C. Create and participate in learning communities that stimulate, nurture, and support faculty and staff in using technology for improved productivity

D. Engage in sustained, job-related professional learning using technology resources

E. Maintain awareness of emerging technologies and their potential uses in education

F. Use technology to advance organizational improvement

IV. **Support, Management, and Operations.** Educational leaders ensure the integration of technology to support productive systems for learning and administration.

Educational Leaders:

A. Develop, implement, and monitor policies and guidelines to ensure compatibility of technologies

B. Implement and use integrated technology-based management and operations systems

C. Allocate financial and human resources to ensure complete and sustained implementation of the technology plan

D. Integrate strategic plans, technology plans, and other improvement plans and policies to align efforts and leverage resources

E. Implement procedures to drive continuous improvement of technology systems and to support technology replacement cycles.

V. **Assessment and Evaluation.** Educational leaders use technology to plan and implement comprehensive systems of effective assessment and evaluation.

Educational Leaders:

A. Use multiple methods to assess and evaluate appropriate uses of technology resources for learning, communication, and productivity

B. Use technology to collect and analyze data, interpret results, and communicate findings to improve instructional practice and student learning

    C. Assess staff knowledge, skills, and performance in using technology and use results to facilitate quality professional development and to inform personnel decisions

    D. Use technology to assess, evaluate, and manage administrative and operational systems

VI. Social, Legal, and Ethical Issues. Educational leaders understand the social, legal, and ethical issues related to technology and model responsible decision making related to these issues.

Educational Leaders:

    A. Ensure equity of access to technology resources that enable and empower all learners and educators

    B. Identify, communicate, model, and enforce social, legal, and ethical practices to promote responsible use of technology

    C. Promote and enforce privacy, security, and online safety related to the use of technology

    D. Promote and enforce environmentally safe and healthy practices in the use of technology

    E. Participate in the development of policies that clearly enforce copyright law and assign ownership of intellectual property developed with district resources

Technology Leadership Tasks

To formulate a technology mission statement, school administrators should keep the following specific technology leadership tasks in mind. The school superintendent, principal, and district program director will take on technology leadership tasks that provide ways and objectives to solidify overriding goals of technology for a school district.

Superintendent: Technology Leadership Tasks

Superintendents who effectively lead integration of technology typically perform the following tasks:

Leadership and Vision

1. Ensure that the vision for use of technology is congruent with the overall district vision

2. Engage representatives from all stakeholder groups in the development, implementation, and ongoing assessment of a district technology plan consistent with the district improvement plan

3. Advocate to the school community, the media, and the community at large for effective technology use in schools for improved student learning and efficiency of operations

Learning and Teaching

4. Provide equitable access for students and staff to technologies that facilitate productivity and enhance learning

5. Communicate expectations consistently for the use of technology to increase student achievement

6. Ensure that budget priorities reflect a focus on technology and its relationships to enhanced learning and teaching

7. Establish a culture that encourages responsible risk taking with technology while requiring accountability for results

8. Maintain an emphasis on technology fluency among staff across the district and provide staff development opportunities to support high expectations

9. Use current information tools and systems for communication, management of schedules and resources, performance assessment, and professional learning

Support, Management, and Operations

10. Provide adequate staffing and other resources to support technology infrastructure and integration across the district

11. Ensure, through collaboration with district and campus leadership, alignment of technology efforts with the overall district improvement efforts in instructional management and district operations

Assessment and Evaluation

12. Engage administrators in using districtwide and disaggregated data to identify improvement targets at the campus and program levels

13. Establish evaluation procedures for administrators that assess demonstrated growth toward achieving technology standards for school administrators

Social, Legal, and Ethical Issues

14. Ensure that every student in the district engages in technology-rich learning experiences.

15. Recommend policies and procedures that protect the security and integrity of the district infrastructure and the data resident on it

16. Develop policies and procedures that protect the rights and confidentiality of students and staff

Principal: Technology Leadership Tasks

Principals who effectively lead integration of technology typically perform the following tasks:

Leadership and Vision

1. Participate in an inclusive district process through which stakeholders formulate a shared vision that clearly defines expectations for technology use

2. Develop a collaborative, technology-rich school improvement plan, grounded in research and aligned with the district strategic plan

3. Promote highly effective practices in technology integration among faculty and other staff members

Learning and Teaching

4. Assist teachers in using technology to access, analyze, and interpret student performance data, and in using results to appropriately design, assess, and modify student instruction.

5. Collaboratively design, implement, support, and participate in professional development for all instructional staff that institutionalizes effective integration of technology for improved student learning

Productivity and Professional Practice

6. Use current technology-based management systems to access and maintain personnel and student records

7. Use a variety of media and formats, including telecommunications and the school Web site, to communicate, interact, and collaborate with peers, experts, and other education stakeholders

Support, Management, and Operations

8. Provide campuswide staff development for sharing work and resources across commonly used formats and platforms

9. Allocate campus discretionary funds and other resources to advance implementation of the technology plan

10. Advocate for adequate, timely, and high-quality technology support services

Assessment and Evaluation

11. Promote and model the use of technology to access, analyze, and interpret campus data to focus efforts for improving student learning and productivity

12. Implement evaluation procedures for teachers that assess individual growth toward established technology standards and guide professional development planning.

13. Include effectiveness of technology use in the learning and teaching process as one criterion in assessing performance of instructional staff.

Social, Legal, and Ethical Issues

14. Secure and allocate technology resources to enable teachers to better meet the needs of all learners on campus

15. Adhere to and enforce among staff and students the district's acceptable-use policy and other policies and procedures related to security, copyright, and technology use

16. Participate in the development of facility plans that support and focus on health and environmentally safe practices related to the use of technology

District Program Director: Technology Leadership Tasks

District program directors who effectively lead integration of technology typically perform the following tasks:

Leadership and Vision

1. Ensure that program technology initiatives are aligned with the district technology vision

2. Represent program interests in the development and systematic review of a comprehensive district technology plan

3. Advocate for program use of promising practices with technology to achieve program goals

Learning and Teaching

4. Participate in developing and providing electronic resources that support improved learning for program participants

5. Provide rich and effective staff development opportunities and ongoing support that promote use of technology to enhance program initiatives and activities

6. Ensure that program curricula and services embrace changes brought about by the proliferation of technology within society

Productivity and Professional Practice

7. Use technology and connectivity to share promising strategies, interesting case studies, and student and faculty learning opportunities that support program improvement

8. Model, for program staff, effective uses of technology for professional productivity, such as in presentations, record keeping, data analysis, research, and communications

9. Use online collaboration to build and participate in collaborative learning communities with directors of similar programs in other districts

Support, Management, and Operations

10. Implement technology initiatives that provide instructional and technical support as defined in the district technology plan

11. Determine financial needs of the program, develop budgets, and set timelines to realize program technology targets

Assessment and Evaluation

12. Continuously monitor and analyze performance data to guide the design and improvement of program initiatives and activities

13. Employ multiple measures and flexible assessment strategies to determine staff technology proficiency within the program and to guide staff development efforts

Social, Legal, and Ethical Issues

14. Involve program participants, clients, and staff members in dealing with issues related to equity of access and equity of technology-rich opportunities

15. Educate program personnel about technology-related health, safety, legal, and ethical issues, and hold them accountable for decisions and behaviors related to those

16. Inform district and campus leadership of program-specific issues related to privacy, confidentiality, and reporting of information that might affect technology system and policy requirements

Formulating a Mission Statement

A project mission statement can be very helpful as a guide to participants in any major project. Paul Houston alluded to the importance of mission statements:

> To get to where we need to go, we will need to have a vision for what we want, a sense of mission that will shape how we carry out the vision and a deep sense of purpose to ensure that it happens.[8]

Remember, it is crucial that the mission of this refocusing of school technology remains consistent with the overall mission of the district or school. (See Box 2.1 for an example.) This consistency helps maintain congruence between all levels of the organization and those working on the project. Also, a mission statement that includes students, learning, and teaching is one that is most likely to direct the project toward successful implementation for students, teachers, and schools. Technology-oriented mission statements should include

- Statements about student learning
- School and district priorities
- General objectives and expectations associated with the shift in technological focus

---

Box 2.1. Vermillion School District 13-1
Vermillion, South Dakota

District Mission Statement

To empower all students to maximize their success in our global society.

Technology Mission Statement

To provide students and staff with the tools and instruction to utilize appropriate technology in a global society.

Technology Objectives

- Students and staff will acquire the capabilities of the Information Age, including recognizing barriers to technology regarding access, handicap, mobility, sex, and religion.

- The district will provide the software and hardware, as well as a knowledgeable staff, to assist students in utilizing technology to accomplish their learning goals.

- Students and staff will maintain an ability level that enables them to adapt their learning with advanced technology.

- Targeted technological training will be provided to the students and staff to enable them to utilize technology as a learning tool in all areas of the curriculum.

SOURCE: Dr. Robert Mayer, Superintendent, Vermillion School District, South Dakota (2002).

Establishing and Maintaining Commitment

Obtaining and maintaining commitment from administrators, teachers, parents, and school board members is important to the success of each phase of the process. Establishing strong backing from each of these groups requires the development of several strategies. Following are a number of approaches for building and maintaining commitment from these groups.

School Administrators

- Encourage school administrators to attend state and national technology conferences. Conferences can bring administrators up-to-date on technological developments and provide useful information to meet district and school needs.

- Allow school administrators to visit schools that have successfully integrated technology into their classrooms. A picture is worth 1,000 words, so get out there and see what is being done.

- Require school administrators to develop management plans for the technology in district schools. School administrators must know that their job is not over when the technology is in place. Their influence and insights will be needed in other areas.

School Board Members

School board members have the ultimate responsibility and authority for almost all decisions and activities that take place in the school district. Therefore support from school board members is critical for the successful implementation of this technology initiative. Some ways to obtain (or maintain) board support and keep board members abreast of new developments in technology are as follows:

- Encourage board members to attend technology presentations at state and national conferences.
- Continually upgrade board members' knowledge by making the latest research available to them.
- Keep the school board informed about district technology needs and initiatives.
- Keep board members up-to-date on the status of technology problems.
- Remember that school board support is important during the entire project but particularly during the planning stages.

The guidelines mentioned above are important because "to compete, public school board members across the country need to spend more time and energy focusing on the big picture in their districts."[9] David Campbell, executive director of the California School Boards Association, believes that,

> all too often, school board members are like firefighters on the ground, battling the flames, when they should be in a helicopter above the fire, able to see how extensive the blaze is, which way the wind is blowing, and where the resources need to be deployed.[10]

Teachers

It is a reality that teaching is a complex occupation. It is also a reality that bringing computers into school learning environments can add to the complexities that teachers must learn to deal with on a daily basis. Inherent in properly functioning classrooms is an energy that is fully understood only through experience. It is within the hustle and bustle of classroom activities that technology initiatives will ultimately succeed or fail. Savvy planners will understand this reality and provide a good deal of attention to teachers and classroom needs. The following ideas can help teachers adapt to the technological changes:

- Encourage interschool visits for teachers to see what classroom technology use looks like and how it is integrated into the curriculum and regular classroom work.

- Distribute up-to-date literature and research findings about technology use in schools' classrooms. This will build confidence in the staff when they know that their administrator is informed regarding the research base on this issue.

- Ensure that the administrative emphasis is on student learning and development and not on the technology. If teachers know that administrators support innovative learning opportunities for students, they may be more likely to use technology in their classrooms.

- Provide in-house workshops for classroom educators. Let teachers know where the expertise is and, more important, that it will be shared.

- Consider targeting teachers at specific grade levels to implement pilot projects with the new technological approach. Allow these teachers to explain to and sell other teachers on the advantages they are experiencing, and to discuss difficulties encountered.

- Build a user-friendly environment for teachers. Provide prompt access to expert guidance when they have questions or problems. Remember, if teachers become stuck, they rarely have time or energy to deal with technical shortcomings because students come first!

- As part of the budgeting agenda, administrators should set aside funding to send teachers to technology workshops or conferences. This is where they can learn from those who are already using learning technologies in their classrooms.

- Remember that teacher input and support for the technology projects is critical for real success.

Parents

Parents constitute a group of educational stakeholders whose voice is more frequently being heard at all levels of public school education. When working with parents, consider the following suggestions:

- Involve parents in the planning process—it can be very beneficial to a project. Make sure they know what is expected of them from the start.

- Arrange for formal and informal meetings between school personnel and parents. These meetings can be used to set positive expectations for the intended technology project.

- Provide the latest information to parents and be willing to discuss information with them.

- When practical, invite a few parents to attend professional development visits to see how students and teachers in other schools are incorporating similar technology initiatives into their curriculum.

- Develop working relationships between home and school to provide an avenue for parental viewpoints and contributions. Parent support can help a project immensely.

PROJECT OUTLINE

The project outline provides structure and direction for the leadership and committee activities required to make this technology project successful. In Forms 2.1, 2.2, and 2.3, it is important to note that staff development and technology evaluation will continue well beyond the initial two-year period. Lengthening the time span for staff development is consistent with the research that shows teachers often require up to five years to become competent at understanding and using classroom technology.

Project Calendar

Administrators and committee members must work closely together to construct a practical calendar for the project. The calendar of events in Form 2.2 marks important reference points for the technology advisory committee to reach in order to keep the project on schedule. Realistic target dates are a key ingredient, and committee members should be included as this is the only way to really ensure a workable schedule of events. In this respect, it is important to remember that committee members are usually chosen because they know how to get tasks done, and they are also the ones who usually have the best idea of how long it will take to get these tasks done.

Developing a Schedule

The project outline differs from the calendar in that it is more specific in nature. The calendar sets general benchmarks to notify participants where they are in the process. The project outline, on the other hand, identifies the specific activities that committee members will do to meet the benchmarks outlined in the calendar. Before planning begins, all participants must understand their roles in the project. Leaders should hold meetings to discuss project guidelines and group responsibilities with the technology advisory committee members. Once a tentative outline is developed, a second meeting should be convened to discuss the project in more detail. Representation at this meeting should include

- Local technology dealers and company representatives
- Community leaders
- District leaders for the teacher association
- District maintenance adviser
- Members of groups interested in or affected by the project

Keep minutes of meetings to direct the efforts of committee members. During preliminary meetings, list the names of individuals or organizations willing to assist with any aspect of the work. Create an implementation document outlining the duty of each group or individual on the technology advisory committee. This document is important because it ties everyone together and ensures successful scheduling of the project.

(Text continues on page 62)

Form 2.1 PROJECT OUTLINE
Phase One: Initial Planning and Commitment

Note: This phase deals with organizing people and creating the plans necessary in moving the technology initiative forward.

Step One: Gaining Support for the Project

Administrative Commitment	Faculty and Staff Commitment	School Board Commitment
Yes ❑ No ❑	Yes ❑ No ❑	Yes ❑ No ❑

If "No," indicate reasons.

Parental Commitment	Community Member Commitment
Yes ❑ No ❑	Yes ❑ No ❑

If "No," indicate reasons.

Additional insights and concerns regarding support:

Step Two: Formulating Core Committees

Note: The number of members on any of the suggested committees will depend on the amount of human resources available.

Technology Advisory Committee

Chairperson:

Administrative Members   Faculty Members

Parent Members   Community Members

Chairperson: **Steering Committee**

Note: These members will come from the technology advisory committee.

Members:

Step Two: Formulating Core Committees (continued)

Subcommittees:

Note: The following list suggests subcommittees that could be established to help with this technology initiative. Some of these can be separate committees, or they can be combined as needed.

Curriculum Committee

Chairperson:

Note: These members will be responsible for developing a working base of information that will assist teachers in implementing the technology in the curriculum.

Members:

Staff Development Committee

Chairperson:

Note: This committee will be responsible for ensuring that all staff members receive appropriate professional training regarding the technology initiative.

Members:

Step Two: Formulating Core Committees (continued)

Budgeting Committee

Chairperson:

Note: This committee will be responsible for dealing with all financial issues associated with the technology project from garnering financial support to pricing out needed equipment.

Members:

Infrastructure Support Committee

Chairperson:

Note: This committee will be responsible for deciding how the technology can best be integrated into the existing school facility.

Members:

Evaluation and Assessment Committee

Chairperson:

Note: This committee will decide on and formulate the approaches needed in evaluating and assessing all stages of the project.

Members:

Step Two: Formulating Core Committees (continued)

Public Relations Committee
Chairperson:
Note: This committee will guide and direct how information will be released to the external community.

Members:

Step Three: Determining Leadership Roles

Note: In this area of the project outline, you want to determine the degree of leadership, input, and involvement you want core members to play.

Superintendent

Leadership:	High ❑	Medium ❑	Low ❑
Input:	High ❑	Medium ❑	Low ❑
Involvement:	High ❑	Medium ❑	Low ❑

Local School Administrators

Leadership:	High ❑	Medium ❑	Low ❑
Input:	High ❑	Medium ❑	Low ❑
Involvement:	High ❑	Medium ❑	Low ❑

Technology Instructors

Leadership:	High ❑	Medium ❑	Low ❑
Input:	High ❑	Medium ❑	Low ❑
Involvement:	High ❑	Medium ❑	Low ❑

Step Three: Determining Leadership Roles (continued)

Classroom Teachers

Leadership:	High ❑	Medium ❑	Low ❑
Input:	High ❑	Medium ❑	Low ❑
Involvement:	High ❑	Medium ❑	Low ❑

Parents

Leadership:	High ❑	Medium ❑	Low ❑
Input:	High ❑	Medium ❑	Low ❑
Involvement:	High ❑	Medium ❑	Low ❑

Community Members

Leadership:	High ❑	Medium ❑	Low ❑
Input:	High ❑	Medium ❑	Low ❑
Involvement:	High ❑	Medium ❑	Low ❑

Step Four: Goal Formation

1. **Write some possible introductory mission statements:** This is to provide general direction for the committees and to align the project with district philosophy statements.

Step Four: Goal Formation (continued)

Step Four: Goal Formation (continued)

2. **State specific objectives:** This will provide a framework for what the main participants and committees should work to achieve.

   Objectives List

   1.
   2.
   3.
   4.
   5.
   6.
   7.
   Other:

3. **Committee recommendations:** This will provide direction for the committees as they work toward goal attainment.

   Recommendations List

Step Five: Establish Communication Networks

Lines of Communication

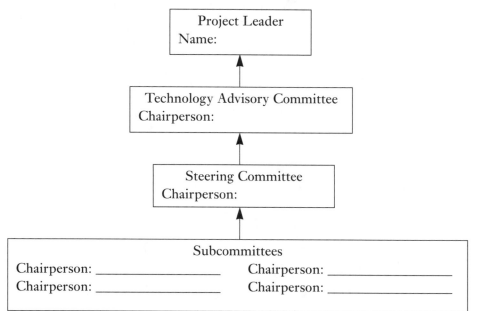

Note: Make sure that you provide a list of all committees and their members to everyone involved in the project. In doing so, stress the importance of using proper channels when discussing project issues or concerns. As part of this, project-related communications should go through committee chairs to disseminate to committee members.

Step Six: Needs Assessment

Note: In this particular category, you want to ask yourself if you have general needs in each of these three areas. The key is that you want to start to consider what already exists in the school and what can be used and what is needed to begin to align your existing technology program with the new technology initiative outlined in this book.

General Assessment

A. Hardware Needs

Yes ❑ No ❑

B. Software Needs

Yes ❑ No ❑

C. Technology
Financial Assessment

Yes ❑ No ❑

Step Six: Needs Assessment (continued)

A. Hardware Inventory

Faculty Computers: [　　　]　　Needed Amount: [　　　]

Student Computers: [　　　]　　Needed Amount: [　　　]

Available Printers: [　　　]　　Needed Amount: [　　　]

Current Computer Hardware Specifications

PC ❏ Macintosh ❏

Processor Type: _____

Memory: _____

Monitor: _____

Video Card: _____

Keyboard Type: _____

Mouse: _____

Expansion Slots: _____

Hard Drive: _____

Floppy Drive: _____

CD-ROM: _____

Sound System: _____

Operating System: _____

Network Card: _____

Warranty: _____

Other Relevant Data:

Step Six: Needs Assessment (continued)

B. Current In-School Software Programs

1.
2.
3.
4.
5.
Other:

C. Technology Financial Assessment

Sources of Funding	Current Amount	Potential Amount
In-School Funding	$	$
District Funding	$	$
Contributions	$	$
Grants	$	$
Donations	$	$
State Initiatives	$	$
Federal Initiatives	$	$
Fund-Raising	$	$
Totals	$	$

Step Seven: Course of Action

1. List specific purposes for the technology change.

2. Project Evaluation: Determine how the computers and programs will be evaluated for use.

3. Preliminary Supplier Evaluation.

    Company: _____

Step Seven: Course of Action (continued)

Expertise:	Excellent ❏	Good ❏	Poor ❏
Price:	Excellent ❏	Good ❏	Poor ❏
Service quality:	Excellent ❏	Good ❏	Poor ❏
After-sale service:	Excellent ❏	Good ❏	Poor ❏
Warranty:	Excellent ❏	Good ❏	Poor ❏

➤ Repeat this process until an appropriate company can be found.

4. Preview software and software support services.

Findings:

Step Seven: Course of Action (continued)

5. Assess general costs for hardware.

Cost per computer:

PC ❏ Macintosh ❏

Processor Type: _____	$_____
Memory: _____	$_____
Monitor: _____	$_____
Video Card: _____	$_____
Keyboard Type: _____	$_____
Mouse: _____	$_____
Expansion Slots: _____	$_____
Hard Drive: _____	$_____
Floppy Drive: _____	$_____
CD-ROM: _____	$_____
Sound System: _____	$_____
Operating System: _____	$_____
Network Card: _____	$_____
Warranty: _____	$_____

Note: You may not have to purchase all new computers for the project. You may be able to upgrade existing computers and then only buy a few new ones. Make sure that everything is compatible in the end.

Total cost per computer:

$_____

Option: Some schools and school districts are opting to lease their computer systems instead of purchasing them outright. Leasing agreements allow schools to acquire equipment without using capital funds, create an integrated computer system, establish flexible financing, and keep computer systems current. Most leasing agreements are based on 48-month terms. It is something that could be discussed and considered based on district needs, finances, and resources.

Step Seven: Course of Action (continued)

6. Evaluate existing network wiring and school physical facilities. Unless you have a qualified technical expert, it would be best if this was evaluated through school district personnel or contracted privately.

List specific needs:

Step Seven: Course of Action (continued)

7. Establish staff development program and prepare anticipated budget. Include such factors as

Training courses: $

Conferences: $

Research resources: $

Leave time: $

Travel allowances: $

Other: $

Projected Totals: $

General Comments:

Step Seven: Course of Action (continued)

8. Review all proposed maintenance agreements, contracts, costs, warrantees, legal documents, and so on. Make sure to get the various committees and school officials to double-check and list any concerns.

Notes:

Form 2.2 PROJECT OUTLINE

Phase Two: Action Planning and Implementation

Step One: Committee Action

Assign specific tasks to committees. Consider factors such as
- ➤ Committee description
- ➤ Who they will work with
- ➤ Timelines for work projects

Committees should now be actively working on their areas of focus and should be providing clear direction to how the computers will be brought into the classrooms.

Step Two: Financial Review

1. Verify funding sources accessed by appropriate committees. You should now be starting to work with actual figures and not projected numbers.

2. Confirm hardware and software costs.

3. Confirm infrastructure and networking costs.

4. Confirm staff development costs.

5. Finalize financial plans with appropriate district and school authorities.

Step Three: Public Relations Program

1. Committee chairperson or administrator should now be able to inform the larger community and public of the technology project.

2. Assign school and technology spokesperson.

3. Ensure that parents and the public are consistently informed of the stages and progress of the technology initiative. This can occur through school newsletters, articles in the local paper, radio, and television.

Step Four: Calendar of Events

1. Finalize dates for completion of purchases.
2. Set dates for introduction of computers into classrooms.
3. Set tentative dates for staff development.
4. Set program evaluation dates.
5. Set dates for public relations information and events.

Calendar of Events Checklist

District Approval	Date:	Done: ❏
School Board Approval	Date:	Done: ❏
Financial Agreements and Contracts Signed	Date:	Done: ❏
Computer Purchase	Date:	Done: ❏
Support Materials Purchase	Date:	Done: ❏
Infrastructure and Networking Project	Date:	Done: ❏
Staff Development Meetings	Date:	Done: ❏
	Date:	Done: ❏
	Date:	Done: ❏
	Date:	Done: ❏
	Date:	Done: ❏
Evaluation Program Schedule	Date:	Done: ❏
	Date:	Done: ❏
	Date:	Done: ❏
	Date:	Done: ❏
Public Relations Announcements and Events	Date:	Done: ❏
	Date:	Done: ❏

Step Five: Hardware and Software Implementation Checklist

1. Sign contracts to purchase hardware, software, and network accessories.   Done: ❏

2. Sign contracts to purchase support materials like tables, chairs, headsets, extension cords, power strips, etc.   Done: ❏

3. Prepare schools and appropriate personnel to facilitate delivery and setup.   Done: ❏

4. Check all products for damage.   Done: ❏

5. Return damaged materials for replacement.   Done: ❏

6. Place equipment in classrooms according to agreed-on plans.   Done: ❏

7. Consult teachers to see if changes are needed regarding placement of computers in their rooms.   Done: ❏

8. Load all software and check for problems.   Done: ❏

9. Run all factory-installed programs and check for problems.   Done: ❏

10. Check network to make sure that connections work as needed.   Done: ❏

11. Make sure support materials are available and equitably distributed (manuals, tutorial programs, textbooks, etc.)   Done: ❏

12. Run final integrity checks on networks, computers, and software before clearing the system for classroom use.   Done: ❏

13. Sign contract for service and maintenance of system.   Done: ❏

14. Develop schedule for regular cleaning and preventive maintenance.   Done: ❏

Form 2.3 PROJECT OUTLINE
Phase Three: Staff Development and Assessment

Note: Staff development is critical for the overall success of this technology initiative. It requires foresight and patience by administrators and teachers, because introducing computers into classrooms can require a good deal of time for some teachers to adjust. As such, all staff will need differing levels of technical support, encouragement, and elbowroom so that they can find the best ways to link the technology with the curriculum and their personal teaching style. It is important that staff development programs are developed according to teacher needs. Often, a homegrown program will work best. Also be aware that phase three will begin as phase two is being finalized.

Instructions for the Staff Development Committee

1. Establish a staff development program that has a commonsense focus and will provide essential help to all staff members.

2. Consider various forms of staff development activities: conferences, inservice days, staff meetings, individual tutoring, and so on.

3. Identify and hire experts to run key staff development exercises, if needed.

4. Purchase needed materials for staff development meetings and activities.

5. Prepare a budget of expected staff development costs.

6. Set dates for staff development activities and meetings.

7. Set guidelines for evaluation and assessment of staff development activities.

8. Establish a communication network so that information and concerns can be shared. This information can be used for future staff development activities.

Instructions for the Evaluation and Assessment Committee

1. Develop and implement the evaluation format.

2. Review evaluation information to determine strengths and weaknesses and areas requiring alterations.

3. Make necessary alterations and continue evaluating the project.

Moreover, precious time, significant sums of district money, and needless duplication of labor can be saved because channels of communication will remain open and responsibilities will be clearly outlined.

Forms 2.1, 2.2, and 2.3 will help school administrators develop the core elements necessary to implement this technology initiative. It is intended to help you focus on the specific needs of your own school and to provide the framework necessary to construct this technology plan based on local contexts. Administrators can use the outline as a model, keeping the plans that are relevant and making changes to suit local needs and conditions when prudent to do so.

ANNUAL PLAN

When the overall three-phased process is put in more specific form and placed on a timeline, it might look something like the model in Form 2.4.

Form 2.4 CALENDAR OUTLINE

ANNUAL PLAN

When this overall, three-phased process is put in more specific form and placed on a timeline, it might look something like the following model.

YEAR ONE: Planning Phase

September	➢ Determine initial commitment to project.
	➢ Form technology advisory committee.
	➢ Form project steering committee.
October	➢ Develop project philosophy and mission statement.
	➢ Create calendars for specific committee work.
	➢ Develop project benchmarks and indicators.
November	➢ Finalize goals and targets for project.
	➢ Carry out needs assessment.
December	➢ Review relevant literature.
January	➢ Analyze needs assessment data.
	➢ Disseminate information from literature review.
	➢ Consider possible options available to planners. (Look at such elements as hardware, software programs, implementation strategies, financing, staff development strategies, student needs.)
February	➢ Determine course of action based on available options and needs assessment data.
	➢ List needed materials and resources.
	➢ Confirm and formalize school board commitment.

YEAR ONE: Phase One–Implementation and Staff Development

	➢ Establish leadership roles for implementation phase.
	➢ Fix calendar for implementation phase.
	➢ Plan public relations program.
March	➢ Meet with committees to discuss implementation strategies.
	➢ Purchase hardware, software, and supplementary materials.
April	➢ Initiate staff development programs.
	➢ Continue public relations program.
May	➢ Network installation begins.
Summer (June to August)	➢ Complete installation and troubleshooting of system.
	➢ Carry out as much teacher inservice as possible before classes begin.
September	➢ Continue with staff development activities.
	➢ Use of new technology in instructional program begins.
	➢ Administrative monitoring of equipment and programs begins.
October and November	➢ Public relations program continues.
	➢ Ongoing help to teachers provided in various forms.
December	➢ Continue administrative monitoring of equipment and programs.

YEAR TWO: Phase Three–Evaluation

January	➤	Begin formal project evaluation, which should include

Reports from administrative monitoring from September to December

Continuing administrative monitoring

Feedback from teachers

Feedback from students

Feedback from in-house technology experts

February	➤	Continue monitoring and gathering information.
March through May	➤	Complete formal evaluations.
	➤	Make revisions according to information gathered during evaluation phase.

Note: Planning, implementation, and evaluation schedules are based on a two-year calendar. Requirements for each month are noted above to simplify and structure the project. As illustrated above, planning and implementation should be completed in year one, with program implementation and evaluation continuing throughout the second year. The staff development phase begins after the planning stage is completed and continues indefinitely. Staff development activities will end when teachers are comfortable and confident in establishing a close relationship between technology and the curriculum in the classroom.

REFLECTIVE ACTIVITIES

1. Describe your personal philosophy regarding leadership in technology.

2. Identify what planning infrastructures exist in your school or school district.

3. Analyze the relationship your school has with the community.

4. Identify the school's and school district's technology mission statement and objectives. Explain how they meet student needs.

5. List which elements of steps one through seven in Form 2.1 are in place at your school or school district.

6. In relation to step three of Form 2.1, identify and list teacher perceptions regarding technology in your school. Identify their levels of technological expertise.

3

Technology and Staff Development

SETTING PRIORITIES

The key to providing staff inservice for technology learning centers is to make staff development a priority from the onset. Being able to integrate multimedia technology as a tool along with the traditional resources is now one of the essential elements of any classroom experience. So instituting the appropriate professional development for faculty, staff, and students is critical to the success of linking technology to the curriculum. It is essential to remember that computer technology is a tool, and, as with any educational tool, teachers need to be trained in its appropriate use.

Staff Development Needs

At least 20% to 25% of all technology money should be allocated for staff development. Many teachers across the nation are inadequately trained in the use of technology resources and particularly in the use of advanced computer-based technologies. What this scenario perpetuates is the belief that computers are just glorified typewriters. Although many teachers see the value of enhancing students' learning through computers and other technologies, just as many teachers are not aware of the resources technology can offer them as professionals in carrying out the implementation of the curriculum in their classrooms. This gap between those who see technology's practical value and those who do not is further increased because many schools do not have an on-site support person officially assigned to coordinate training or facilitate the use of technologies. Figure 3.1 displays how few staff members operate at a more

Figure 3.1 Teacher Skill Level

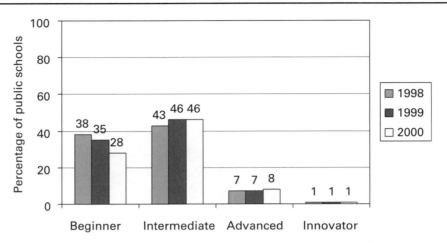

SOURCE: The Editors. (2001). Technology counts 2001: The new divides. *Editorial Projects in Education, 1*(1), p. 53. Retrieved from www.edweek.org/sreports/tc01/charts/tc01chart. cfm?slug=35challenges–c6.h20

advanced skill level with technology. In an advanced global economy, can we afford to work at a beginner level when it comes to technology use? Even in schools where a technology coordinator exists, efforts become consumed with supervising students or selecting and maintaining software and equipment. As a result, staff development falls to the bottom of a technology coordinator's to-do list.

Sharon McCoy Bell, director of educational technology in New Orleans, implied that staff development should be an ongoing program. She said, "Unless you have initial teaching followed by coaching, someone going into the classroom to co-teach, demonstrate, or watch the teacher teach and then offer suggestions, it's not going to work." She also said, "If I had a magic wand, 25% of all technology money would go into teacher training."[1] This is still 5% less than the recommendation given to the president of the United States in 1999.

Another major barrier to staff development appears to be the lack of awareness and understanding by school administrators as to the role of technology in the classroom. Many administrators are unfamiliar with advanced-technology applications and how they can be applied administratively and in the classroom. To alleviate this problem, many states have a degree requirement that all educators seeking an administrative endorsement from any accredited institution of higher learning take coursework in educational technology. Currently, only 26 states require technology training for licensure, as Figure 3.2 indicates. School administrators now certified would be required to take coursework in educational technology for certificate renewal.

Another barrier is state educational agencies that lack resources and funding needed to develop leadership in the area of technology. Both state and national organizations involved in leadership development for

Figure 3.2   State Teacher and Administrator Technology Requirements

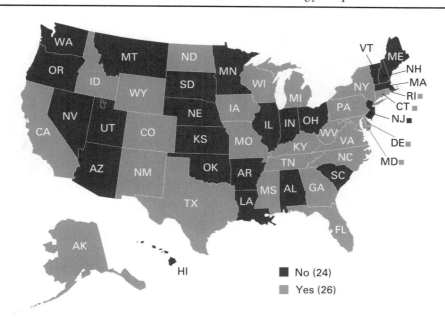

SOURCE: The Editors. (2001). Technology counts 2001: The new divides. *Editorial Projects in Education, 1*(1), p. 52. Retrieved from www.edweek.org/sreports/tc01/charts/tc01chart. cfm?slug=35challenges–c8.h20

administrators need to continue to explore ways to provide training in the area of technology. Many states need to develop strategies to implement a hierarchical staff development model that includes the development of regional resource-training centers. In addition, university and college systems need to work collaboratively with school districts and private businesses to develop a cadre of educational leaders versed in educational technology application.

Appropriate funding of technology staff development programs is another area that remains a barrier. School inservice and staff development programs continue to be underfunded across the country. Lessons from experienced-implementation sites suggest that those who wish to invest in technology should plan to invest substantially in human resources. Currently, most funds for technology are spent on hardware and software. Refer to Figure 3.3 for distribution percentages among staff development, hardware, and software in school technology plans. There appears to be little doubt that inservice training should be ongoing throughout both the planning and implementation process. Staff development depends on teachers being able to integrate technology with the curriculum, and on the kinds and extent of technologies available.

The quality of technology training for new teachers is another problem. Preservice teachers graduating from teacher education programs at both university and college levels appear to be receiving a minimal amount of technology training. There is especially very little training as to

Figure 3.3   School Technology Expenditures

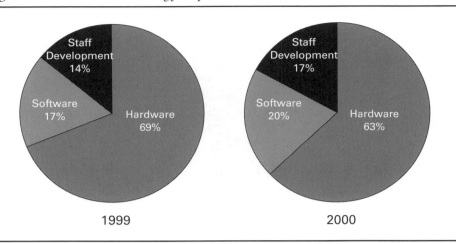
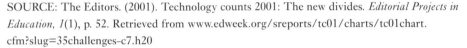

SOURCE: The Editors. (2001). Technology counts 2001: The new divides. *Editorial Projects in Education, 1*(1), p. 52. Retrieved from www.edweek.org/sreports/tc01/charts/tc01chart. cfm?slug=35challenges–c7.h20

how to integrate technology into various subject areas, how to acquire telecommunications information, and how to use technology in the area of assessment. Each state, therefore, needs to fund universities and colleges in a manner that will allow them to effectively use technology in preservice programs. Many states need to revise teacher education program standards to include a requirement that all students enrolled in a K-12 teacher preparation program must have a course in basic technology literacy and software applications as well as instruction in how to integrate and effectively use technology in an instructional setting.

Another barrier to staff development is the current structure of school days. School districts across the country should be provided more flexibility in structuring the school day in order to establish time for ongoing, educational, technology staff development programs. In addition, each state should require districts to plan a minimum of one pupil instructional related day (PIR) of technology inservice each academic year. Renewal certification should include educational technology training. From all this, there is a clear indication that teachers are not feeling prepared when it comes to integrating technology into classroom activities and into the curriculum. Figure 3.4 displays teachers' perceptions regarding technology in the classroom.

In addition, there is no consistent delivery model that currently coordinates educational technology staff development instruction in the various educationally related nonprofit organizations found throughout the United States. The U.S. Department of Education, as well as state educational agencies, needs to explore the possible coordination of efforts and encourage the various organizations to become partners in a national or statewide training model.

Figure 3.4 Teachers' Feelings About Technology Preparation

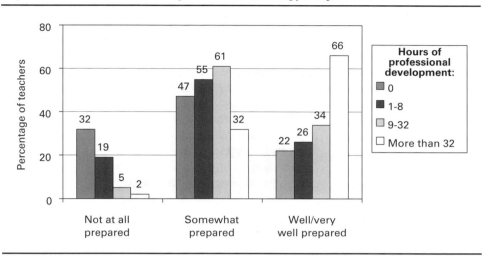

SOURCE: The Editors. (2001). Technology counts 2001: The new divides. *Editorial Projects in Education, 1*(1), p. 55. Retrieved from www.edweek.org/sreports/tc01/charts/tc01chart.cfm?slug=35challenges-c12.h20

What this information is directing administrators to understand is that there are many barriers to teachers successfully implementing technology in regular classroom activities. Figure 3.5 shows that some of those barriers are lack of time, lack of equipment, lack of support, lack of training, and lack of access. Furthermore, the best way for administrators to approach these barriers is to develop a concentrated staff development program around the technology initiative.

One of the keys to successful staff development in technology is simply to have teachers teach other teachers. According to Andrew Latham of the Educational Testing Service, "The bottom line appears to be that computers can indeed enhance student outcomes. Clearly, teacher training needs support across all school environments."[2]

To achieve sustained use of technology, teachers need hands-on learning, time to experiment, easy access to equipment, and ready access to support personnel who can help them understand how to use technology in the classroom. A number of school districts are currently using a number of different approaches for training teachers and implementing technology. These include developing technology-rich model schools, training a cadre of teachers who support and help their colleagues, providing expert resource people, giving every teacher a computer, training administrators alongside teachers, and establishing teacher resource centers.

CADRES OF TECHNOLOGY SPECIALISTS

Numerous state educational agencies provide a cadre of specialists to help train teachers in technology. Some governmental agencies work collaboratively with local schools to develop state technology demonstration sites.

Figure 3.5   School Barriers to Technology Use

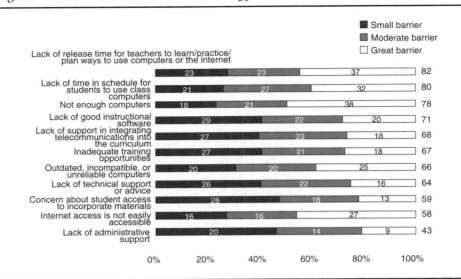

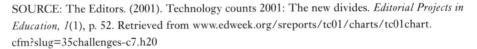

SOURCE: The Editors. (2001). Technology counts 2001: The new divides. *Editorial Projects in Education, 1*(1), p. 52. Retrieved from www.edweek.org/sreports/tc01/charts/tc01chart. cfm?slug=35challenges-c7.h20

These demonstration sites train specialists who then help teachers in local school districts. Some state agencies currently provide contract services to local schools.

Management Planning Matrix

The management planning matrix has been one of the most successful tools used by school leaders in designing effective staff development programs in the country. The Northwest Regional Educational Laboratory in Portland, Oregon, has developed a management planning matrix that can be used to plan, implement, and evaluate an effective staff development program (see Form 3.1 and Form 3.2).[3] The matrix design encourages planners to not only develop technology staff development goals, but also formulate measurable indicators of successful inservice. The matrix also forces planners to detail activities and leadership roles and to set implementation and evaluation dates.

Hardware, Software, and Services

Little in the way of quality staff development can occur without proper equipment, software, and technical-support services. The ideal method is for school districts to use uniformity and high standards when selecting and using equipment, software, and support services for staff development. It is also recommended that teachers and administrators who take inservice programs be able to develop competencies in using a variety of technology applications. Competencies should include using the Internet,

Target Area: _____

1. Goal: _____

Product: _____

End Point: _____

Form 3.1   Management Planning Matrix

6. STATUS TODAY What is the status today?	5. ACTIVITIES What must be done to get from 4 to 3?	4. LEADERSHIP Who is responsible to initiate and follow through with activities?	3. SCHEDULE What is the time frame for accomplishing each activity?	2. INDICATORS If the goal were attained, what would really be happening: What would the target area look like? List 8 to 10 indicators.
A.				A.
B.				B.
C.				C.
D.				D.

SOURCE: Northwest Regional Educational Laboratory (1990). Modified and adapted by Bruce Whitehead.

73

Form 3.2   Sample Management Planning Matrix

Target Area: Language Arts   Product: Writing-to-Read-Software Program

1. Goal: Integrate software program into classroom activities   End Point: Spring 2002

6. STATUS TODAY What is the status today?	5. ACTIVITIES What must be done to get from 4 to 3:	4. LEADERSHIP Who is responsible to initiate and follow through with activities?	3. SCHEDULE What is the time frame for accomplishing each activity?	2. INDICATORS If the goal were attained, what would really be happening: What would the target area look like? List 8 to 10 indicators.
A. No scheduled inservice for writing-to-read software program	Data collection	Principal	Spring	A. Completion of Northwest Evaluation Association student test
	Early-out inservice schedule	Principal	Fall	Writing-to-read software program in place
	Implementation	Consultant & tech director	2nd Thursday each month—9 programs	
B. No special block schedule for mentor-teacher program	Follow-up	Principal	Fall	B. Lesson plans include using the program.
	Align prep periods	Principal	August	
	Assign trainees	Principal	August: music, PE, library, art	
	E-mail communications	Tech director	September to June	E-mail log indicates increase in teacher communication.
C. No conference scheduled	Team selected for conference	Principal	Spring: IBM Conference, Atlanta, GA	C. Team report (positive) Program design Portfolio Parent involvement
	Schedule arranged	Mentor-teacher	January	
	Staff inservice by participants	Tech team	May	
D. No implementation of writing-to-read software program	Program implementation	Mentor-teacher	October	D. Increase in computer use
	Student performance assessment	Mentor-teacher	May	Increase in student achievement
	Parent involvement	Principal	October to June	Increase in quantity of student writing

SOURCE: Northwest Regional Educational Laboratory (1990). Modified and adapted by Bruce Whitehead.

TECHNOLOGY AND STAFF DEVELOPMENT **75**

a scanner, cable, and satellite; designing and developing instructional materials and multimedia presentations using hypermedia, voice recognition, videodisc, CD-ROM, and compressed video.

Regional Resource Centers

An important step in the development of quality preservice and inservice programs will be the development of regional as well as statewide resource centers. Resource centers will not only assist the effort of developing an awareness for the use of technology in our nation's schools but will also be instrumental in providing much-needed staff development in technology. The key, however, is to fund and place technology resource centers strategically throughout all states.

Instructional Design and Computer Skills

To enhance instructional design and computer skills, it is recommended that the specific skills be included in preservice and staff development programs. The following list of instructional design and computer skills was obtained from the Alabama State Technology Plan developed by the Alabama Commission on Higher Education.[4]

Instructional Design Skills

- Identify criteria for achievement and skill objectives
- Delineate relevant expertise and techniques to develop the program
- Diagram content for subject matter
- Use appropriate authoring language to create the program
- Develop internal and external documentation
- Use multimedia tools to generate interactive video materials
- Insert graphics, text, and questions into existing video
- Create a branched lesson using existing video frames under computer control
- Create simulation with combined computer-assisted instruction and video
- Develop appropriate testing programs to accompany instructional programs
- Design an evaluation strategy for validation of products
- Conduct an evaluation of the effectiveness of a product
- Write an evaluation report of findings

Basic Computer Skills

- Navigate desktop environments
- Use common commands, copy, and transfer
- Load and install software
- Use a word processor
- Use database and spreadsheet programs

- Use test generators, grade books, and management systems
- Use graphics programs for educational illustration and animation
- Install cards in ports, connect and disconnect peripheral devices, cables, and modem
- Operate laser optical devices: CD-ROM and videodisc
- Install touch-screen, penlight, and other alternative devices for computer control, alternative computer keyboards, alternative computer displays
- Create a product with desktop publishing
- Create products using draw-and-paint and animated graphics
- Access bulletin board services and online services via modem
- Participate in one-way and two-way interactive satellite classes
- Send and receive electronic mail (e-mail) to a local area network (LAN) address
- Use Internet
- Use LAN for file transfer and e-mail
- Search CD-ROM for specific information
- Compile compressed video sequences and use time-base corrector
- Use optical scanner
- Use LCD projection system
- Prepare a video lesson for use in presentation with QuickTime or Real Player.
- Identify computer software and video programming available and appropriate for K-12 schools

STRATEGIES FOR SUCCESS

A creative and innovative use of physical and human resources for staff development at the local level is going to make the real difference as to whether technology will be successful. In the end, it is the development of a vision, the formation of a sound plan, and implementation of that plan at a local level that will determine the success or failure of any program. You can consider the creative staff development ideas that follow, and that have proven successful with limited resources, as catalysts for your technology and staff development efforts.

Project-Based Approach

A cadre of five to six individuals is selected from the staff periodically to meet with the school administrator or technology director in a project-based meeting. In addition to this cadre, any staff member can participate in the group at any time. The school administrator figuratively lays several thousand dollars on the table and asks the group to come up with a project that uses technology to heighten the teaching and learning process. The money is primarily targeted for inservice or staff development associated with the project. With money up front, the group cannot use dollars as an excuse for not taking a risk and trying something innovative. The only requirement before the allotment of real money is that the group place in writing predetermined indicators of success or measurable assessment indicators.

Flexible Scheduling

The rule of scheduling is to align preparation periods in order that teachers needing assistance with technology can receive help. Art, library, physical education, and music preparation periods can be scheduled in a manner that matches a successful technology teacher with a staff member having difficulty incorporating technology. This provides quality time either in the lounge or in the classroom for specific staff members to get together and share ideas about technology. A bonding often occurs between the mentor-teacher and the staff member needing encouragement. This new-found relationship helps solve technology problems and misunderstandings and opens the way for future inservice opportunities.

Rule of Traveling Pairs

A minimum of two staff members should attend workshops, seminars, and conferences. Teachers feel more comfortable working and training in a cooperative and supportive environment. Having at least two teachers (preferably from the same grade level) obtain the same inservice background is a tremendous way to increase the success of the technology programs. Many programs have failed because only one teacher received the training and did not have the time or energy to carry the program through all of the implementation stages.

Early-Out Time for Students

Numerous schools have found ways to adjust schedules and provide one hour of planning and inservice time for teachers while maintaining state requirements for student contact time. In some schools, teachers have agreed to start earlier and end later each day as well as give up some recess or duty time in order to develop a one-hour block of time per week for inservice and planning. A key is to make sure that at least one early-out per month is devoted to a technology inservice activity. It is also important to make sure that state requirements for student contact time are met.

Presenter Stipends

The school district pays a nominal fee to local teachers to teach inservice programs after school, on weekends, or during summer months. Again, this is a small nominal fee for planning the inservice. The purpose is not to extend salary commitments but to reward local teachers. An emphasis should be placed on having a local teacher, who has credibility with the staff, be the presenter.

Extended Contracts

The school district pays teachers a nominal fee per day to attend inservice on weekends or during the summer.

Adult Education

Adult education funds can be used to provide courses on technology usage. Staff can be reimbursed and take the adult education courses along with parents and community members.

Substitute Rotation

School leaders have developed blocks of time by having a set of substitutes rotate through the schedule. For example, a set of five substitutes could release five teachers in the morning while the same five substitutes could release another set of teachers in the afternoon. Because this procedure diminishes regular teacher and student contact time, it is recommended that this procedure be used sparingly. This process does work well when scheduling a special consultant for a certain period of time.

Free Consulting Services

Innovative school districts have collaborated to obtain the services of free national consultants during a textbook adoption process. Textbook companies are often happy to provide consultants without obligation in hopes that their book series and technology materials will be selected. Naturally, some publishers do provide such services while others do not. It is up to the creative administrator to contact publishing companies for possible free consulting services. A key here is to work with company representatives and collaborate with several adjoining school districts to justify costs for a company to bring consultants into the schools.

Staff Development Cooperatives

More school districts are now realizing the benefits of developing technology cooperatives. This is especially true for small rural school districts. What cannot be achieved singularly can be achieved through the collaboration of resources. School districts have banded together and have hired technical coordinators who can provide the training and staff development needed at a local level. Some school district cooperatives have joined with colleges and universities to provide credit to experienced teachers acting as instructors as well as credit for participants.

Staff Development Consortiums

Throughout the country, consortiums are often developed via collaborative efforts among universities or colleges, school districts, and technology companies. Consortiums not only provide an opportunity to bring in technology specialists from other states but also provide teachers with an opportunity to obtain technology training and university credits inexpensively.

College and University Preservice Programs

Higher education is always looking for ways to extend learning beyond the campus. Recent restructuring efforts have led to major changes in preservice and student teaching programs. Additional core classes now not only address educational technology but also include multicultural studies as well as professional leadership projects. Innovative programs now being used by a number of universities include the use of e-mail to create mentor lines between student teachers, first-year teachers, and university professors. Another involves the use of interactive video between a school district and university.

School, University, and College Partnerships

College and university faculty members are always looking for ways to integrate their students into local schools whether they are small or large. Some schools are using college and university students for faculty inservice on technological innovations and model teaching strategies in classrooms. Local school faculty members learn new ideas, and university students receive grades and credit for their experience. A number of universities and colleges are using school districts as a base for ongoing research studies involving the educational use of technology.

Community Resources

Both small and large school districts across the country have found valuable resource people within their communities. Individual community members who have a great deal of technical experience can provide equipment and knowledge to school districts. Many individuals in the private sector are especially good at providing inservice in the areas of word processing, electronic mail, modems, satellite, cable, and other technical applications. The key is that school leaders seek out and involve community members who can make contributions in the area of technology to the district.

In sum, successful school administrators are focusing on staff development as, probably, the single most important factor in developing an effective technology program in classrooms. Tailoring staff development and inservice programs to teachers and classrooms should become a focal point of any school.

TECHNOLOGY FOR LEARNING AUDIT

As part of their technology initiative, Mid-Continent Research for Education and Learning (McREL) has developed an audit procedure that will help schools to determine how technology is being used in a district, in a school, and by teachers. The audit will help school administrators answer such questions as these:

How are teachers integrating technology in the curriculum?

What professional development resources do teachers need to expand and refine their technology proficiencies?

What are the critical hardware, software, and network issues that keep staff and students from using technology effectively?

How are decisions about technology made?

What resources should be managed at the department, building, and district levels, and how?

Including this audit as part of the staff development plan adds a measurable element to the scheduled activities and provides essential information to help schools to be more efficient in their technology-learning efforts. As part of this approach, the audit includes a Teacher Technology Profile (TTP) survey and an Administrator Technology Profile (ATP) survey. See the forms in Resource A for examples of these surveys. Information obtained from these surveys is then used to create individual teacher profiles and individual administrator profiles. An example of completed individual teacher profiles is also included in Resource A as Form A.1. From this information, administrators get a clear picture of how technologically skilled their teachers are. The profiles help administrators understand the level of expertise among their staff and can be used as the catalyst for future staff development technology initiatives (see Box 3.1). To use the Technology for Learning Audit, contact McREL directly.[5]

FUTURE CHALLENGES

Technology continues to become an increasingly integral part of our schools. Our nation's schools cannot address the problem involving educational equity without first talking about substantial teacher preparation linking technology, pedagogy, and curriculum development. If teachers are to make the most effective use of technology applications available for classrooms, then state leaders will have to focus on providing adequate funding for staff development. Currently, many school districts are investing thousands of dollars for technological equipment and software but very little toward inservice programs. It is now time to establish an equitable balance between technology and staff development.

REFLECTIVE ACTIVITIES

1. Identify your school or district's technology coordinator. List the responsibilities he or she has in relation to staff development.

Box 3.1. Levels of Technology Use

1. **Entry: Teachers who are just starting to use technology for learning**
   - They usually use technology for word processing and data bases.
   - With their students, technology is used predominately as a reward activity or specifically for technology training such as keyboarding.
2. **Adoption: Teachers who have some comfort level with technology and are taking initial steps to use it in their curriculum**
   - They use email and the Internet on a regular basis.
   - Technology is employed in collaborative-learning projects with their students.
   - Technology is used in student-directed learning where the students design the projects and implement them.
3. **Adaptation: Teachers who are shifting toward more student-based project learning and encourage the use of a variety of technology tools**
   - They use a variety of multimedia tools, and they distribute documents electronically.
   - Student activities become more project based, and a wide variety of technology tools is used in those projects.
   - More technology activities involve student-designed projects with the teacher serving as a facilitator.
4. **Appropriation: Teachers who are so comfortable with technology that it is integrated throughout all learning activities**
   - They use technology for multidisciplinary and problem-solving activities.
   - They facilitate the use of multiple technologies, and learner ownership increases as these teachers become facilitators.
5. **Transformation: Teachers who create new ways to use technology tools for real-world applications**
   - They involve students in the development of authentic, technology-rich activities.
   - They guide others in applying information resources.

SOURCE: © 2001 McREL. Reprinted with permission.
May not be reproduced without permission from McREL.

2. Formulate what percentage of your current technology budget is allocated toward staff development. What percentage would you like to get it up to and why?

3. List what you do as an administrator to support technology training in your school. Evaluate some examples of your efforts.

4. Describe some ways that the teachers in your school support each other with integrating technology into the curriculum.

5. If someone in your school is having a problem with or has a question about technology, chart the lines of communication for this. Evaluate how this could be improved.

6. Using the Levels of Technology Use (Box 3.1), rate yourself, individual staff members, and your school on this scale. Explain why you believe this way.

7. Identify what requirements you have at the local and district level for technology training of both administrators and teachers for licensure.

8. Reflecting on McREL's technology audit, consider what you perceive as the benefits of conducting such a survey of your technology staff development efforts.

4

Teaching and Learning With Technology

THE POWER OF TEACHERS

When all is said and done, it will be teachers who determine the success or failure of a technology plan. They are the people who connect technology with curricular practice in a way that will enhance student achievement. It is the interaction between teacher and student that truly accentuates learning in a technological environment. Technology is a proven tool that can help lower dropout rates, enhance student achievement, provide access to information around the world, and raise students' self-esteem. In every class, teachers must contend with a variety of learners, such as the fast-paced learner, the less-motivated learner, students with learning difficulties, and the list could go on. With computers in the classroom, teachers have access to tools that have the potential for providing learning experiences relevant to each of these unique learners.

A normal classroom is a very complex setting to work in and technology, for many teachers, only makes matters more complicated. As such, a lack of understanding as to how technology can be used effectively in the classroom is the greatest barrier to having a successful technology program. A lack of knowledge about technology can lead to what researchers call "soundless barriers." Examples would be educators and parents being out of their comfort zone with technology and thus developing a fear of change. Physical settings in schools have also been cited as barriers to effective implementation of technology. One example is the many older schools that dot the country. These schools often have small classrooms and no false ceilings, which makes it difficult to establish computer learning centers and the necessary wiring infrastructure required to support them. Many of these problems will be addressed as more schools turn to wireless technology.

One of the components that makes this technology plan so unique is its networking capacity. For example, cross-age tutoring is enhanced via the computer networks. Students from one grade level can exchange information with students at another grade level. Via networking computers, special-service students can pull up their homework assignments in the special-service classroom. Teachers, administrators, and parents can communicate with one another via the Internet. Unfortunately, many schools have not taken this direction with their technology plans and are limiting its potential to help with student achievement.

Teachers and school leaders are also finding that out-of-date hardware is slow and cumbersome. Hardware with low memory capability and slow-processing speed can easily frustrate teachers. Educators need fast, memory-intensive machines with software that is applicable to their classroom instruction. Also, a lack of compatibility with hardware can create problems for teachers and students as well. Staff or students may have success using one type of computer and yet be totally frustrated trying to use a different platform. Educators and students need to have compatible equipment throughout the school to enhance their overall use and effectiveness with technology.

Another technological barrier facing schools has been a weak focus on staff development. Teachers, in many cases, have been poorly trained to deal with using technology in their curricular plans because of a lack of appropriate and school-supported training. School leaders are just now realizing that more funding needs to be provided for staff development so that teachers will be better able to understand how they can best incorporate technology into their classroom settings and into the curriculum.

Computer labs, which are the traditional technological infrastructures in schools, have limited the range of influence that computers can have on student achievement. Box 4.1 lists ways that computer labs have been found to be a barrier to effective technology use.

One of the greatest aspects of networked technology in schools is its ability to enhance communication among teachers, parents, administrators, and students via e-mail. Labs are not really conducive to fostering this type of interaction. For individuals to send an e-mail, they must walk down the hall, check to see if the lab is open, check with the lab assistant, and then risk the possibility of interruption while working on a lab computer.

By their basic design, computer labs may not be as efficient as having computers in classrooms. In fact, an overemphasis on computer labs can hinder the development and effectiveness of technology in schools. School leaders are now realizing the value of having networked computers in classrooms. Many principals are taking dramatic steps to increase the involvement of teachers in classroom computer technology. Teachers, for the first time, are beginning to have access to hardware and software

> **Box 4.1. Barriers With Computer Labs**
>
> ➢ Limits access to teachers and students
> ➢ Reduces teacher ownership
> ➢ Limits integrated learning
> ➢ Limits cooperative learning
> ➢ Limits internal and external communication and interaction
> ➢ Available time to complete student assignments is short
> ➢ Lab times may not align with a student's schedule

within their classrooms. Administrators and teachers now believe that computers should be incorporated as a tool for daily learning and not taught in isolation.

The key to success with technology is allowing teachers to develop a sense of ownership of the school's technology. Once teachers develop a sense of ownership, they will be ready to move on to higher levels of technology use. According to Mathew Maurer and George Davidson, "Educators are striving to improve teaching and learning through the power of technology."[1] For example, technology can help some students to be more efficient because they are more inclined to write with a word processor than without one. Students also feel a greater sense of achievement with expanded access to information and a wider selection of data that comes with networked computers.

Only recently have educators across the United States had the hardware, software, support services, and training to integrate technology into their classrooms. The whole process of making technology available in the classroom is an exciting challenge. It is not going to be an easy and simple transition, but initiatives of value are worth the effort.

PROVIDING CONNECTIVITY

Using banks of high-speed, networked computers has the effect of turning a regular classroom into a powerhouse of connectivity and learning. Developing school connectivity should include the implementation of a minimum of at least five networked, high-speed computers with CD-ROM, multimedia presentation capability, and the Internet. The computers should also be networked to a class printer and scanner.

Connectivity refers to the interrelationships, connections, and rapport among the student, the teacher, and the learning process. Technology can be the tool that facilitates and heightens this relationship. When technology is used appropriately and effectively in classrooms, students can more easily make transitions from one concept level to another. They can more actively engage multiple sources of stimuli that allow them to reconstruct, analyze, apply, synthesize, and evaluate solutions to complex problems.

Students can literally plug in locally, nationally, and globally to information sources previously unavailable to them. Using technology in this manner can help to stimulate learning in the classroom. A key, however, is for teachers to make certain that instruction being used in conjunction with technology is based on the core principles and standards of educational technology.

Educational Technology Standards

The following principles of education, developed by a Washington State Technology Task Force Committee, relate to technology.[2]

1. In our rapidly changing world, the economic viability of communities and individuals depends on the ability to access information, build knowledge, and solve problems. Technology plays a key role in this process and students must develop skills in its use.

2. Now and in the future, all learners and educators must have equitable and universal access to information and technology and be skilled in technology applications.

3. Communication linkages among all of the stakeholders in a child's life are critical to the education and well-being of the whole child. Technology is a critical element in establishing these vital linkages.

4. The use of technology is essential to the restructuring of schools through
   - Increased access to information
   - Increased application of appropriate instructional, management, and assessment tools
   - New strategies and tools that involve students in creating and producing meaningful knowledge
   - Greater relevance to the community and workplace.

5. Effective use of technology in schools must be based on coordinated planning and funding efforts at the state, regional, and local levels. To effect change, factors such as training, support, and time must be addressed simultaneously.

These five principles of educational technology are supported by six strategic recommendations included in the1997 *Report to the President:*[3]

1. **Focus on learning with technology, not about technology.** The recommendation was that it is important to distinguish between technology as a subject area and the use of technology to facilitate learning about any subject area. It is important that technology be integrated throughout the K-12 curriculum and not simply be used to impart technology-related knowledge and skills. The report's authors believed that school administrative teams should work toward the use of computing and networking technologies to improve the quality of education in all areas.

2. Emphasize content and pedagogy and not just hardware. Particular attention should be given to the potential role of technology in achieving the goals of current educational reform efforts through the use of new pedagogic methods focusing on the development of higher-order reasoning and problem-solving skills. While obsolete and inaccessible computer systems, suboptimal student-to-computer ratios, and a lack of appropriate building infrastructure and network connectivity will all need to be addressed, it is important that we not allow these problems to divert attention from the ways in which technology should actually be used within an educational context.

3. Give special attention to professional development. The recommendation was that the substantial investment in hardware, infrastructure, software, and content that the report recommended would be largely wasted if K-12 teachers were not provided with preparation and support they need to effectively integrate information technologies into their teaching. The recommendation was that 30% of the educational technology budget should be devoted to professional development. Teachers should be provided with ongoing mentoring and consultative support and with the time required to familiarize themselves with available software and content, to incorporate technology into their lesson plans, and to discuss technology use with other teachers. Finally, both presidential leadership and federal funding should be mobilized to help our nation's schools of education to incorporate technology within their curricula so they are capable of preparing the next generation of American teachers to make effective use of technology.

4. Engage in realistic budgeting. The report recommended that in order for this technology push to be achieved, five percent of all public K-12 educational spending in the United States should be earmarked for technology-related expenditures. At the same time, because amortization of initial acquisition costs will account for only a minority of these recommended expenditures, schools will have to provide for increased technology spending within their ongoing operating budgets rather than relying solely on one-time bond issues and capital campaigns.

5. Ensure equitable, universal access. Access to knowledge-building and communication tools, based on computing and networking technologies, should be made available to all of our nation's students, and special attention should be given to the use of technology by students with special needs. Title I spending for technology-related investments on behalf of economically disadvantaged students should be maintained at no less than its current level, with ongoing adjustments for inflation, expanding U.S. school enrollment, and projected increases in national spending for K-12 educational technology.

6. Initiate a major program of experimental research. The report recommended that a large-scale program of rigorous, systematic research on education in general and educational technology in particular will ultimately prove necessary to ensure both the efficacy and cost-effectiveness of technology use within our nation's schools. To ensure high standards of scientific excellence, intellectual integrity, and independence from political influence, this research program should be planned and overseen by a distinguished independent board of outside experts appointed by the president, and should encompass (a) basic research in various learning-related disciplines and on various educationally relevant technologies; (b) early-stage research aimed at developing new forms of educational software, content, and technology-enabled pedagogy; and (c) rigorous, well-controlled, peer-reviewed, large-scale empirical studies designed to determine which educational approaches are in fact most effective in practice.

As noted in these principles and recommendations for technology, viable technology means obtaining commitments at the local, state, and national levels. It means sharing the vision through a universal and equitable approach to school technology.

So how are these principles being implemented and addressed? The following case reports reflect current technology endeavors being embarked upon by a few states.

Alabama. Students must demonstrate that they are computer literate before high school graduation; local school systems determine competencies and assessment methods. Alabama students who fail a computer skills test must complete a computer applications course that addresses specific skills: computer basics (including issues and ethics of computer use, copyright, appropriate use, and security), word processing, databases, spreadsheets, and telecommunications.

Arkansas. The goals they have set are to have all students demonstrate proficiency in technology standards. The plan includes technology competencies for students and teachers. Teachers can use these competencies in planning technology-rich activities. Technology skills are expected to be incorporated into the state's academic curriculum rather than taught separately.

Florida. This state has established the Sunshine State Standards for Students which includes the use of technology. For example, standards for language arts in high school include the expectation that a student effectively integrate multimedia and technology into presentations. Students in seventh-grade mathematics are expected to use technology to analyze data and create graphs.

Kentucky. This state is taking a long-term approach regarding standards. Technology use is being incorporated into all curriculum guidelines for each subject area and at each grade level. Kentucky uses the National Educational Technology Standards for Students as the basis for these guidelines. These standards have also been incorporated into the state's Core Content and Program for Studies.

Maryland. This state uses the State Content Standards for Learning Outcomes for students in math, science, English language arts, and social studies to which a strong technological component has been added. For example, by the end of eighth grade, Maryland students should be able to prepare writing for publication using electronic resources (e.g., word processing, database, spreadsheet software) and to adopt an appropriate format and principles of design (e.g., headings, margins, spacing, columns, page orientation) that enhance the final product. The standards for science say that students should be able to use computers or graphing calculators to produce visual materials (tables, graphs, and spreadsheets) that will be used for communicating results.

Mississippi. Students in this state must pass a computer skills test or take computer education and keyboarding before they graduate from high school. Students are expected to have a working knowledge of technology-based tools; use technology and information responsibly by understanding their impact on society; select and use appropriate technology-based tools to support learning; use technology to communicate effectively; and use technology to identify, explore, and solve problems and to make quality decisions. See Resources C and D for International Society for Technology in Education (ISTE) standards for teachers and students.

HOW TECHNOLOGY FACILITATES LEARNING

The impact of technology on the classroom environment has been monumental. For example, according to Robert Alfaro of the San Antonio Independent School District,

> In a new program titled the Waterford Early Reading Program, new technology and the old-fashioned buddy system work together to infuse schools with enthusiasm and dynamic teaching practices. The software package allows computers to track each child's progress and give the teacher detailed assessment reports. An independent study found that 90% of the participating children had achieved reading readiness for the first grade.[4]

Schools are finding the buddy system to be an effective way to get students motivated about using technology. For example, Mrs. Stockard's fourth graders are very excited when they visit Mrs. Mires's sixth-grade class. The fourth graders know that they have a sixth-grade buddy there to help them with their social studies reports. The sixth graders sit with the fourth graders and show them how to construct paragraphs and insert pictures into their text documents. When the reports are finished, the sixth-grade buddies show the fourth graders how to send their reports back to their classroom using e-mail and attached documents.

Research studies continue to reveal the positive impact of technology on learning. For example, Cradler compiled research findings summarized in Box 4.2. The effectiveness of technology tends to vary as a function of the curriculum content and instructional strategy delivered by the technology. When content and strategies are determined to meet accepted educational standards, research, as shown in Box 4.2, reveals that technology can enhance student achievement.

Box 4.2. Technology and Student Achievement

- ➢ Increases performance
- ➢ Improves learning attitude and confidence
- ➢ Provides essential instructional opportunities
- ➢ Increases student collaboration
- ➢ Increases mastery of vocational skills
- ➢ Emphasizes problem solving
- ➢ Improves writing skills
- ➢ Provides instant feedback
- ➢ Creates immediate adjustment of task difficulty
- ➢ Provides access for students to advanced or enriched programs

SOURCE: J. Cradler (1995).[5]

Simon Hooper, Chanchai Temiyakarn, and Michael D. Williams, from the University of Minnesota, found similar results in their research on how technology affected student learning.[6] They found that fourth-grade students using cooperative learning in conjunction with technology worked more efficiently, completed lessons more quickly, and demonstrated increased achievement. Overall achievement increased 20% for high-ability students in the study. The researchers also found that high- and average-ability students working in pairs on a computer lesson outperformed students working as individuals.

Other educators are trying to determine how technology affects student learning in classrooms. The Washington State Task Force on Technology suggested that the effective use of technology in the learning process requires that students develop new roles in learning, living, and working.[7] Furthermore, skills linked to technology or "essential learning" should be woven into academic learning requirements in all subjects and areas. They developed the following seven essentials of learning with technology.

1. The student as information navigator. The student recognizes and values the breadth of information sources, browses those sources, differentiates and selectively chooses sources, and retrieves appropriate information and data using all forms of media, technology, and telecommunications.

2. The student as critical thinker and analyzer using technology and telecommunications. The student reviews data from a variety of sources, analyzing, synthesizing, and evaluating data to transform it into useful information and knowledge to solve problems.

3. **The student as creator of knowledge using technology and telecommunications.** The student constructs new meaning and knowledge by combining and synthesizing different types of information through technology, telecommunications, and computer modeling and simulations.

4. **The student as effective communicator through a variety of appropriate technologies and media.** The student creates, produces, and presents ideas.

5. **The student as a discriminating selector of appropriate technology for specific purposes.** Students discriminate among a variety of technologies and media to extend and expand their capabilities.

6. **The student as technician.** Students develop sufficient technical skills to successfully install, set up, and use the technology and telecommunications tools in their life, work situations, and learning environments.

7. **The student as a responsible citizen, worker, learner, community member, and family member in a technological age.** Students understand the ethical, cultural, environmental, and societal implications of technology and telecommunications, and develop a sense of stewardship and individual responsibility regarding their use of technology and telecommunications networks.

Technology and its impact on learning have come a long way. For example, Gary Morrison and Deborah Lowther, of the University of Memphis, stated,

> Since the first microcomputers were used in the classroom, we have witnessed a gradual change from a teacher-centered approach to learner-centered approach. Our methods have changed from emphasizing the acquisition of information to one of constructing meaning. Students are now encouraged to explore, collect data, analyze data, and derive their own conclusions.[8]

HOW TECHNOLOGY FACILITATES TEACHING

Benefits to Educators

Research findings on the benefits of technology for teaching are generally positive due to a shift from teacher-directed strategies to student-directed instructional strategies. According to Cradler, studies show that educator use of technology has many positive effects on student learning and achievement (see Box 4.3).

Classroom Computer Networks

Developing classroom-networked computer technology centers is one of the best ways to integrate technology and enhance teaching. James Kulik, a research scientist at the Center for Research on Learning and

---

Box 4.3. Teacher Instructional Changes With Technology

- ➤ More student-centered teaching
- ➤ Emphasis on individualized instruction
- ➤ Increased time for teacher advisement
- ➤ Increase in interest to explore emerging technology
- ➤ Teacher preference for multiple-technology application
- ➤ Increased teacher productivity
- ➤ Increased planning and collaboration time
- ➤ Increase in revision of curriculum
- ➤ Increase in developing new instructional strategies
- ➤ Greater participation in restructuring efforts
- ➤ Increase in community and agency involvement
- ➤ Increase in teacher and administration communication built into student assessment

SOURCE: J. Cradler (1995).[9]

Teaching at the University of Michigan, has formulated over 100 studies on classroom computer networks.[10] He noted that students who had technology learning centers in their classrooms had a more in-depth exposure to the curriculum and gained the equivalent of about three months of regular classroom-learning progress. Many teachers found that if they used technology to help students and the class solve problems, it actually increased the interaction between teacher and student.

Janet Ward Schofield, senior scientist at the University of Pittsburgh's Learning Research and Development Center, believed that technological changes in schools were largely due to the changes that computers create in teachers. When implemented correctly through proper professional development, teachers often favored classroom computing environments because their students took charge of their own learning, learned to think critically and analytically, worked collaboratively, and created products to demonstrate what they had learned. As a result, classroom computer-learning centers are giving learning and discovery back to the students. Teachers who are effectively integrating technology into the curriculum through these centers are no longer standing in front of the classroom lecturing. They often begin circulating around the room out of necessity and eventually become more facilitators than lecturers.[11]

Classroom Curriculum Connections

As noted in the *Report to the President,* technology in the classroom needs to be driven by the curriculum as opposed to technology driving the curriculum. Technology needs to fit a classroom teacher's style. It also needs to fit the curriculum. Connectivity means that technology is used simply as a tool to collect and organize information and assemble it in a manner that connects meaning and produces learning, understanding, and comprehension. Therefore helping teachers in the classroom accentuate the teachable moment is what technology is all about. For example, successful schools using high-speed, networked, classroom computers, Internet, and a multimedia package help students create presentations that reinforce information retrieval. Sequencing, outlining skills, and information retrieval are normally tedious and boring but, nevertheless, important for students to learn. In essence, the key is to use technological advances to transform normally tedious skills into learning that is fun and productive. Using technology in this manner is what excites teachers and motivates students.

Technology Scope and Sequence

Many school leaders are struggling with trying to develop a technology scope and sequence in their schools rather than allowing teachers to use technology as a tool. Although it is important to develop a scope and sequence for basic technology skills and for keyboarding, school leaders have to be careful not to use technology to determine or direct curricula. There are numerous examples of technology scope and sequences on the Internet. A good example of this is Cupertino Union School District's Web site at www.cupertino.k12.ca.us/Do.www/Scopenseq.html

The Cupertino Union School District, with state and national recognition for the excellence of its schools, serves 15,000 students representing 64 different languages in a 26-square-mile area that includes the City of Cupertino and portions of five other cities in California's Silicon Valley. A copy of Cupertino Union School District's Technology Scope and Sequence can be found in Resource B.[12]

Content Software and Tool Software Selection

Choosing software that matches instructional styles is crucial to enhancing classroom instruction. Gertrude Abramson, Professor at the School of Computer and Information Sciences at Nova Southeastern University, stated that software is a term encompassing all programs and instructional sets stored on floppy disks, CD-ROMs, or the Internet

> that can be used when loaded into the computer. The two major categories are tool software, such as word processing and spreadsheet programs, and content software, which include tutorial programs, drill-and-practice programs, and tools for experimentation, construction, and/or play.[13]

It is also important to limit the amount of software or courseware introduced at any one time to teachers. A key to successful classroom software selection is targeting one curriculum area for technology implementation. Numerous school principals have made the ubiquitous mistake of choosing too much software and overloading the learning curve of their staff. It is best in the beginning to pick a subject area such as language arts and purchase no less than three software packages initially. For example, language arts software might include a word processing program, an e-mail communication package, and a student writing program.

Extensive staff inservice should be provided for each of the software or courseware programs purchased. After six months or as time dictates, another software or courseware package can be introduced. Once school leaders feel that their staff members are comfortable with the new software or courseware programs, they can then move into a different curriculum area.

Classroom and Cooperative Learning

Classroom computer centers help create learning stations that foster cooperative learning. This is an important step because research has found a significant correlation between cooperative learning and student achievement.[14] Arranging technology in classroom learning centers will enhance opportunities for cooperative learning. In addition, the incorporation of programs such as IBM's Teaching and Learning With Computers can provide teachers with innovative strategies on how to use their classroom technology centers as learning stations. With technology centers available, students can use stations at any time during the day allowing maximum use of technology equipment. Teachers are helping students to use classroom technology centers to form learning groups with students from different countries via the Internet. These student groups correspond via e-mail with other international students to study and address problems from a global perspective.

Classroom Technology Strategies

Teachers must think of technology as a regular classroom tool that can be integrated into existing classroom teaching strategies. When technology is used to enhance instruction, it serves to challenge and to involve students rather than to operate as a separate entity to the curriculum. As part of this process, technologists have developed what is referred to as process-learning courseware. Process-learning courseware is based on teaching via the integration of subject areas. This approach uses classroom-networked computers to help enhance cooperative-learning techniques, increase student writing, and enhance the integration of technology into the curriculum. IBM's Teaching and Learning With Computers (TLC) and Apple Classrooms of Tomorrow (ACOT) are examples of strategies and studies used to promote the use of the new process-learning courseware in classrooms. New advances in instructional strategies coupled with unbridled parental support are laying the base for a technology revolution in our elementary schools.[15]

Having Internet, satellite feed, and cable lines in classrooms gives teachers abundant opportunities to integrate subjects. This format encourages teachers to use thematic approaches to incorporate different subject strands into the curricula. For example, fifth-grade teachers implementing a literature unit on the Civil War period can incorporate maps from the National Geographic Society, pictures of slavery from the Smithsonian, and war statistics and agricultural information relating to cotton production from the Library of Congress. The teacher can then create a multimedia presentation that correlates with a children's novel on the Civil War using sound, graphs, maps, and motion pictures. Teachers can model the activity and then have students develop the multimedia presentation through these integrated strategies.

Here is another example of integrating technology in a primary setting. A second-grade teacher first reads a story about a Navajo boy from a textbook. Following the story, the teacher has students watch a Reading Rainbow telecast story on a satellite channel. The segment is a documentary on the Navajo reservation. The teacher then uses the Internet to find maps of the Navajo reservation. The maps are enhanced via a liquid crystal display (LCD) projector. Students then use the maps to mathematically plot distances from the boy's hogan to the nearest town or city. Children also use the electronic maps to better understand distances the Navajo boy had to travel to purchase items in the local market. Children could also be challenged to use a word processing program to write a story about what they have learned about the Navajo boy, the Navajo people, or life on the Navajo reservation.

Learning-Styles Applications

Using technology to maximize learning styles and capabilities via technology in classrooms is paramount to school technology reform. Schools using networked technology in their classrooms provide an environment in which students can access appropriate and challenging information at their developmental levels. Much of a computer's ability to be tailored for individual learning styles has been made possible by the quality of recent educational courseware. Educators are finding out that technology is not just wires and workstations. It is about learning and how students learn. Rita Dunn, learning styles specialist from Johns Hopkins University, stated that "computers are uniquely able to introduce even new and difficult information through a student's preferred learning style."[16]

Student Writing

Many teachers are finding that students using technology in classrooms are currently writing up to three times more than they did previously. It appears to be less physically demanding for most students to write with a keyboard than with a pen or pencil. The result is that students are writing more and enjoying textual expression more. This becomes even more pronounced with the use of voice recognition.

When examining the success of student writing, it is clear that some of the best theory into practice has occurred using technology in the classroom.

This is especially evident when teachers are given appropriate training and support. According to Professor Robert L. Bangert-Drowns of the State University of New York, Albany, 32 studies on word processing and student writing provided evidence that word processing improved the quality of students' writing.[17] Students using technology are more willing to do more editing, and spend more time in reviewing their text and improving it.

Analysis of student writing has shown that word processing does help students become more effective writers. According to Charles Macarthur, a research associate at the University of Maryland, computers can support the cognitive processes involved in planning, writing, and revising text.[18] Equally important is the potential impact of the computer on the social context for writing in the classroom. Anyone who uses word processing to any degree can probably agree with this. Students using word processing can check grammar and spelling and can rewrite their work many times over with greater ease.

Cross-Age Tutoring Via Technology

A major strength of classroom connectivity is the ability of children to cross grade levels. There appears to be a connection between cross-age tutoring and student achievement. In some schools, cross-age tutoring is encouraged at all levels. For example, one half of a seventh-grade class might visit a fifth-grade class as part of a writing project. The other half of that same fifth-grade class would then visit a seventh-grade classroom. This allows for a maximum partnership between seventh- and fifth-grade students. Seventh-grade students use the Internet, scanners, satellite feed, and cable to help stimulate the fifth graders to write a story. Both groups can use the media center in the library to find information resources. Information garnered in the library is then sent back to fifth-grade classrooms so those students can access their work at any time during the day. During the week, fifth graders can send their work via the computer network to seventh-grade partners to preview and edit. This form of partnership and cross-age tutoring has been powerfully successful due to technology. This same format has also been successful with Title I classes as well as with special-services classes. Communication is enhanced because students and teachers can share information and projects in seconds.

Distance Learning

Distance learning in the classroom is having an equalizing effect on education. Distance learning is finding its way into the classroom. Two-way interactive video, satellite, and cable connections are giving students access to courses and instructors that normally would not be available to them. Small and rural schools may not have the resources of larger and more populated districts. It is at times difficult to bring in the depth and breadth of a program or subject area. Distance learning, however, can fill that void. Interactive TV can allow students to listen to and visit with famous professors, artists, and lecturers in both real-time video and audio.

Community Links

Teachers are transforming classrooms through the establishment of educational links between the school and the community. As an example, some classroom teachers are establishing Internet and e-mail links with state museums and libraries. Through these links, students can access hard-to-find books as well as museum artifacts. These connections allow students to explore content areas in greater depth, with more accuracy, and to consult state librarians as well as museum curators. Students are finding that they are not restricted by classroom walls and have the capability to enrich their curricular experience by using a variety of community, state, national, and global information resources.

Classroom teachers are also establishing information links with parents. Classroom computer networks are allowing teachers to access student homework and correspond with parents. Internet e-mail services are providing a direct link between the classroom and home for the first time. Some schools are providing their students with access to laptop computers that can be used at school, on the bus, or at home. Students involved in a number of after-school activities can use a modem to tap electronically into their school at any time and work on their assignments or send messages to the teacher.

Keyboarding Skills in the Classroom

Educators are finding that third grade is generally the best entry level for keyboarding. Younger children are not expected to be able to master the keyboard properly because of the size of their hands and fingers. Teachers have the option of exposing their youngest students to networked typing-tutorial programs or waiting until third grade to emphasize keyboarding skills. Generally, teachers should not be expected to officially stress keyboarding until at least the third grade unless smaller and age-appropriate keyboards are used. Special keyboarding labs, using outdated computers and independent network servers, can be used to implement various typing programs. The role of keyboarding is changing, though, because voice recognition programs are beginning to offer options to many teachers and students.

Keyboarding Software Checklist

Checking software for appropriateness is an important step in developing a successful keyboarding program. Ernest Balajthy noted questions that can be asked to check keyboarding software.[19] He believes that school leaders wanting to purchase keyboarding software should ask the following questions:

Is the keyboarding tutorial organized and age appropriate?

Are effective graphics used for finger positioning?

Are there a variety of video game drill activities?

Are meaningful language arts activities integrated in the software?

Are additional activities suggested in the manual?

Is there an on-disk management system for keeping track of student programs?

School to Work

With the advent of Internet and e-mail access in classrooms, teachers and students are now finding it easier to tap into career and school-to-work programs. School technology especially has become more interesting to businesses with the shift from administrative processes to learning processes in the classroom. As school leaders begin bringing the world into the classroom, businesses will be interested in responding to this shift. Businesses are now looking for ways to cooperate with schools and become community partners because they realize that they need computer literate employees in the future. As a result, they are finding creative ways to assist schools with donations of equipment, training, support, and service.

Large companies are now providing free links to their organizations for schools and libraries. Others are providing technology trainers, workshops, and consulting services. A few business leaders have even begun communicating with students on a personal level. For example, CEOs are using telementoring programs linked to classrooms as a way to advise high school students on career options and the importance of staying in school.

Student Assessment and Technology

Numerous state educational agencies are currently assisting school districts by using technology to assess student performance. School leaders often turn to state agency content specialists to obtain the latest information regarding student assessment. Content area specialists continue to collaborate with the U.S. Department of Education, other state agencies, universities, and research labs in order to provide the most up-to-date information regarding computer adaptive testing of student achievement levels in classrooms. Collaboration among agencies is best evidenced by the development of numerous state technology task forces. These state task forces have done much to help design technological frameworks that will allow teachers to electronically access student achievement on a periodic basis.

Schools are now using networked computers in classrooms to create comprehensive, computer-generated report cards that provide an electronic summary of the student's exact performance in all subject areas. The teacher can now monitor student progress and performance at any time because computers are available within the classroom. Some assessment programs allow teachers to correlate local student data with local, state, or national norms. These computer-assisted data reports become a powerful tool in curriculum development because they give teachers the ability to focus instruction on certain areas. Computer data reports also provide parents with detailed performance reports.

Certain states are now developing technology and curriculum guidelines that relate directly to student performance in the classroom. Although local control is an important issue in most cases, some states are linking funding to student achievement.

Technology Applications

When planning for the future, it is not enough to simply introduce the latest technology into every classroom. It is essential that the technology be closely linked to the needs of students and the school's curricular focus. According to John Conyers, Superintendent in Palatine, Illinois, "Significantly improved test scores, a high level of student excitement, and renewed staff enthusiasm are the results of a successful technology program."[20] Studies have shown that students' roles in the classroom have changed along with the knowledge and skills they need to acquire in school.

Rather than viewing computers as an add-on in the classroom, teachers and parents now view them as the workhorse of the classroom. It is this transformed thinking that is occurring in classrooms across the nation. As a result, technology is now becoming the basis of a multitude of student performance outcomes.

Impacting Disadvantaged Youth

Educators are finding that computer-based lessons are particularly effective for teaching basic skills to disadvantaged students. The National Science Foundation and Eisenhower Program studies have shown that technology helps to eliminate geographic, economic, language, and disability isolation. Technology is especially beneficial to children at risk because it enhances cooperative learning, addresses learning-style differences, and promotes the use of cross-age tutoring. School leaders are promoting the use of technology in schools in order to address the needs of children from low-income families. Classroom technology centers are helpful for special-services teachers who use network technology to obtain information and assignments electronically from student classroom files or portfolios. Networking not only improves communication but also facilitates learning through the use of visual, auditory, and kinesthetic-based courseware.

Meeting State and National Standards

Some innovative schools are using technology to promote state standards as well as promote their students' achievement on national educational goals. For example, schools using classroom technology centers are finding

---

Box 4.4. Student Best Practices

➢ Use a historical focus with an emphasis on the empowerment and the efficacy of students. We shape our future by present actions.

➢ Use a cognitive research base to concentrate on the human center and on whole-person instruction and interaction.

➢ Regard technology and computers as learning tools rather than teaching environments. Emphasize communication rather than rote learning or technical expertise.

➢ Concentrate on education that is idea- and problem-centered and that is equitably applied across disciplines.

➢ Stress collaborative education and communication rather than isolation.

➢ Provide students with survival skills for a changing world.

➢ Nurture the concept of global stewardship and connection.

➢ Emphasize active learning and the development of critical thinking skills using real problems and enabling the creation of products that are meaningful, relevant, and useful to the community.

➢ Use technology as a viable tool to assist the physically, mentally, or emotionally challenged. If software is used correctly, the programs can be more even-handed in response than humans; students can pace instruction appropriately and can help in the design of individualized lessons.

SOURCE: Washington State Task Force on Technology (1994).[21]

---

student achievement scores increasing in the areas of reading comprehension and math concepts. Robert Gilpatrick and Nancy Holty found that classroom technology centers increase student writing, enhance cooperative learning, enhance integrated curriculum development, address student learning style differences, and enhance cross-age tutoring.[22] The researchers found that in the Merton School District in Milwaukee, Wisconsin, the technology program was responsible for a 22 percentile point increase in achievement test scores.

STRATEGIES FOR SUCCESS

Increasing agreement exists among administrators and teachers about the positive influence that classroom technology centers can have on student achievement and learning. Box 4.4 summarizes findings of the Washington Task Force on Technology of what teachers consider "student best practices" in preparing students for the future (see Box 4.4).

FUTURE CHALLENGES

Although the United States has a number of innovative, technologically advanced school districts, it is imperative that all our nation's students and teachers have access to advanced technology applications. A goal of the U.S. Department of Education is to help coordinate services and plans in order to develop statewide technological infrastructures that are accessible by all schools. School leaders need to visit state demonstration sites and begin the process of formulating their own implementation plans for technology.

REFLECTIVE ACTIVITIES

1. List the advantages and disadvantages of the computer labs that you have in your school.

2. Analyze the level of connectivity that your school has in regard to teachers, students, and the curriculum.

3. Research the technology standards that your school and district have for students.

4. Cite some of the positive results that technology use in your school has had on student achievement.

5. Describe the latest software program that you incorporated into your technology efforts and explain why you selected that program.

6. List two recent, successful technology projects that students in your school have completed. Describe the elements of the task that improved student achievement.

7. Research the percentage of writing assignments that students in your school are asked to complete using computer technology. Is this an acceptable statistic?

8. Describe the link that your school has between technology and student assessment figures. Refer to the section on student assessment and technology for examples.

5

Selling Your Technology Plan

PUBLIC RELATIONS

Many schools have public relations (PR) programs to aid in the continued support of their educational programs. At the same time, many of these schools have not incorporated their technology efforts into their PR agenda. An additional element of this technology plan is to include it in an effective PR plan. This chapter focuses on the importance of developing an effective PR program for shifting from computer labs to networked computer systems within each classroom. Much of the material covered in this chapter has been adapted from Boschee, Whitehead, and Boschee's book, *Effective Reading Programs: The Administrator's Role.*[1]

Barriers to Quality School and Community Relations

By not involving the community and gaining support for technology changes, school leaders greatly diminish their chances for financial and educational support from both local and regional communities. Levies and special bond issues for technology are difficult to pass, because the community lacks a basic understanding and awareness as to the importance of technology to teaching and learning. Without financial and moral support from the community, schools often flounder in their attempt to plan and implement an effective technology program such as the one outlined in this book. It is for this reason that quality PR programs are so valuable.

PR skills are a necessary component in promoting successful technology programs. With increased external commitment in school planning and infrastructure, local school administrators need to develop skills on

103

how to effectively communicate with teachers, parents, board members, community leaders, and the general public. More specifically, effective PR efforts should be more than press releases and publicity events. A quality PR program should be based on vision, leadership, consistent school district PR goals, and well-planned strategies.

Michael Simkins, Project Manager for California's 21st Century Education Initiative, stated that "Support for public schools can be built in two ways: through good public relations and through public engagement."[2] Many leaders attempt to garner support through both components, but are neither consistent nor organized in combining the two elements. Interestingly enough, administrators are usually aware of how important PR skills are but rarely use them because they are not knowledgeable about the how-tos of PR in education. They need to know how to sell their successful technology program to teachers, parents, board members, and the general public. In combining these elements, school administrators can enhance public engagement with the technology program. They also need to know how to keep the public informed about new developments in technology, such as student performance assessment software and information retrieval systems. In addition, administrators need to know how to deal with negative issues. They need to be able to take negative situations and turn them into positive ones. Ultimately, administrators need to know how to make sure that everyone understands and supports the technology program.

Making sure everyone understands and supports the technology program means that administrators are going to have to become more effective external communicators. Effective communication and good school-community relations should be based on visionary goals and well-planned strategies. Before this can be accomplished, it is necessary to determine what PR program the district already has in place. One approach is to ask questions about your technology program from a school-community standpoint. From this exercise, you might do the following:

- Determine that there is an excellent technology program, but no one knows about it
- Realize that parents want to work with technology in the school as volunteers, but there is no parent aide program
- Find that only 60% of parents know about the school's technology program
- Notice that some teachers are hesitant to have parents work with technology in classrooms
- Want to pass a mill levy or building reserve for technology but suspect the voters will vote it down
- Discover that an opportunity for a technology media event was missed because the local newspaper or television reporter became lost trying to locate your school
- Find that students are making great strides in using technology effectively, and yet teachers are not being recognized for their efforts

Many administrators find themselves too busy dealing with day-to-day realities to think about PR opportunities. Even though administrators are rightfully concerned with these problems, it is critical that they develop a PR program to ensure the success of this technology initiative and to ensure it stays focused on student achievement.

One of the first steps in developing a PR program pertaining to technology is to ask the following questions:

What is the role of the building administrator in PR, and how does that role apply to technology?

Why do we need to promote pubic relations in the field of technology?

What key components make up the PR process?

What are some specific communication strategies school leaders can use?

Where should we go from here?

Administrative Role in PR

Since administrators are the leaders of the school, they must play a major role in PR. Effective administrators are dynamic and creative in their communications with others. According to Calabrese, effective school administrators and supervisors are committed to excellence.[3] They have demonstrated a high level of involvement in community work, staff development, instructional supervision, and climate improvement. They are personally committed to technology and to communicating with the public.

The association between the effectiveness of a school technology program and the administrators is no surprise. The role of the administrator in technology improvement is best exemplified in a study conducted by Crane, who wrote, "A review of the literature reflects a consensus that the role of the principal has a major impact on a school program and student achievement."[4] School administrators and supervisors are realizing that their roles are broadening. Specifically, they are finding that their expertise should also include a wide range of PR skills.

As a result, the instructional leader of the 1990s is becoming the image maker of the 21st century. Roles of administrators in PR are only limited by the creativity of the administrators. To provide a sense of direction, Box 5.1 lists examples of some of the more common PR roles found among effective principals and supervisors today.

The list of administrative roles in PR is extensive. In fact, the demands on any administrator seem endless, but, according to recent research by Snyder, time spent on parent and community relations is only four hours per week.[5] Since such little time is put toward community relations, effective organization is essential. The key is to enlist the help of essential staff, faculty, and community leaders in the PR process. Everyone benefits when the entire community and staff are fully informed about successful technology programs and activities. In this day and age of change and

> ## Box 5.1. Common Public Relations Roles
>
> ➢ Developing a sense of what the public needs to hear, being able to write journalistically, and knowing how to deal with the press
> ➢ Developing a public relations advisory board to address technology curriculum issues
> ➢ Responding to local and state legislation as it relates to technology
> ➢ Improving administrative and staff relations as well as increasing staff morale
> ➢ Preparing communication vehicles like newsletters and brochures to inform the public about changes in technology curriculum
> ➢ Developing school and business partnerships as they relate to technology

progress, administrators have found that a little PR goes a long way in the successful implementation of technology initiatives, especially when everyone is included.

Promoting Public Relations and Technology

It is a very complex process to implement a new technology initiative in a school. One reason for limited success during the implementation stages may be a lack of societal support. According to Seely, reform movements of the past were often based on educational ideas that did not necessarily have widespread support.[6] This has created a pressure cooker for principals and supervisors alike with pressure coming from a host of external stakeholders.

School leaders are trying to respond to pressure-cooker types of problems in education by working hard to develop better school programs and improve school-community relations. In order to develop more effective PR programs, administrators are going to have to do the following:

- Reassess what principals and supervisors can do to help promote their technology programs
- Create and implement strategic-technology PR plans for their schools
- Establish professional relationships with businesses
- Learn how to handle conflict and criticism involving technology issues
- Build trust
- Establish clear and open communications with parents and community members regarding the technology program
- Respond to reform by creating, adopting, and implementing strong board policies on how technology is to be used in schools

- Establish clear and concise communications on how coordinating technology with the curriculum enhances student achievement

Generally, school reform has been slow and not everyone has been pleased with its progress. The Subcommittee on Technology, Terrorism, and Government Information[7] found America at risk, but said little or nothing about the thousands of successful schools in the United States. As a result, many administrators are developing PR programs as a method of self-protection and self-promotion. The idea is not to avoid bad news but to address the problems as well as talk about the success stories in education. We need to spotlight schools with successful technology programs. Good PR programs will highlight schools with high success rates in student achievement, develop new approaches to technology and instruction, and begin the process of change.

THE PUBLIC RELATIONS PROCESS

Any effective PR program should emphasize planning, research, communication, and evaluation. School and community communication problems and a lack of PR planning have been well documented. Walker indicated that a significant problem in community-school communication existed back in the 1970s.[8] Very little communication in the way of newsletters or pamphlets was coming from the school, as noted by the 61% negative response nationally. These school and community communication problems are still evident today.

Currently, researchers are working to turn the problem around. More and more school leaders now believe that PR programs should emphasize planning, research, communication, and evaluation. These components are not necessary in every project but do reflect the essential components. The following section reveals how effective PR programs have been successfully developed in many schools across the United States.

Public Relations Plan

Psencik indicated that a PR Plan should include a mission statement, internal and external analyses, objectives and strategies, action plans, and research.[9] Psencik's model helps by providing a guideline for administrators wishing to review and update their current PR program. Following is a sample sketch of this planning process.

Mission Statement

A PR advisory board consisting of administrators, teachers, parents, and community members brainstorms to clarify their goals in order to develop their philosophy and their mission statement. The philosophy should reveal a general understanding of the beliefs, concepts, and attitudes of a group for a PR technology program. The mission statement must clearly address the need to increase school-community relations: for instance, "The entire community will be informed about all aspects of the technology program."

Internal and External Analysis

Internal and external analyses involve viewing variables from both school-based (internal) and community-based (external) positions. The PR advisory board discusses both school and community strengths and weaknesses. For example, the PR advisory board might address the basic delineation of educational responsibilities as they relate to technology on the part of students, parents, educators, and the public.

Objectives and Strategies

At this point, the PR advisory board develops objectives and strategies, which should relate to the philosophy and mission statement to improve school-community relations. A possible objective might stress the need to develop a newsletter about the technology program.

Action Plans

Following the development of a philosophically-based mission statement and objectives, an action team composed of both members of the original PR advisory board and of new participants should be selected to address each strategy. This team later reports to the original board regarding the completion and success of specific objectives.

An action committee assigned to develop a strategy for creating a newsletter begins by drawing a set of guidelines for the letter. Topics are then researched and data is collected. Next, calendar deadlines are set, assignments are made, and materials and resources are acquired. After a proof with a layout is made, revisions and adjustments are addressed, and the newsletter goes to print. Following printing, the newsletter is distributed to target groups.

PR plans, such as the one outlined above, allow administrators to anticipate problems. As a result, both administrators and supervisors begin to research and to think through problems in strategic ways.

Research

Research is a major element in the PR process; however, this component is rarely used. To be effective, administrators need to target messages for specific audiences.[10] This means having access to research data without requiring professional researchers. Many effective administrators can find accessible research data right in their own schools. Data simply needs to be collected, organized, and clearly presented.[11]

A partial list of local data sources might include

- Former publications of the school district
- Test scores
- High school and college dropout statistics
- Superintendent and principal reports
- Special education and Title I reports
- Official student records
- Former single-purpose surveys and questionnaires
- Interviews with staff members
- Interviews with parents and students

A partial list of nonschool data resources might include

- State departments of education
- State agencies
- U.S. Department of Education
- Federal agencies
- Community and business leaders
- Area resource councils
- Universities
- Professional organizations like the International Technology Association

Data sources such as those listed above provide administrators with quality information about their technology program. For example, let's say that an administrator reviews a single-purpose survey on school technology and finds

- An analysis of achievement test scores revealing students who are making 2-year gains in 9 months
- Teachers on staff who have been using technology with such strategies as cooperative learning, writing across the curriculum, telecommunications, or Teaching and Learning with Computers (TLC)
- A new computer lab using reading software that allows children to achieve big gains in the first grade
- A staff member whose work has been recognized by a technology association
- Several teachers on staff who have discovered a new software program and wish to share it with the staff
- Students who have indicated a desire to participate in the local technology fair

Special projects, such as technology fairs, can provide a wealth of data about students, curricula, and schools. Materials displayed reveal writing abilities, understanding, and special skills, as well as multimedia presentations developed by teachers and children. Administrators who want to develop projects such as technology nights and technology fairs need to work collaboratively with staff and community members to formulate a management plan for the program implementation. Administrators can be especially helpful because of their knowledge of programming techniques.

Innovative PR projects provide administrators with information about their schools, but also provide a plethora of ideas for newspaper articles, television stories, and newsletters. Nonetheless, administrators and PR advisory groups still have to set priorities as to what should be highlighted in PR projects. As a result, administrators planning a PR project should address the following questions:

Is the technology project exemplary?

How does the project focus on student learning needs?

Is the project unique to the school and community?

What aspects of the project can be easily identified?

Is the project timely?

Are financial resources available for the project?

Is there enough time to complete the project?

Does commitment exist on the part of staff and community to complete the project?

Is the project administratively manageable?

Administrators can use information gained from the above questions to determine the scope of the PR plan and to formulate effective communication strategies.

COMMUNICATION STRATEGIES

The strength of any PR program lies with effective communication strategies. PR strategies are sometimes referred to as PR survival skills. They are crucial in improving school climate as well as in promoting success with the technology program. Effective administrators must relate their communication skills and techniques to the basic tenets of PR: proximity, timeliness, prominent people, dramatic events, and ease of reporting.[12]

Proximity often determines how parents and community members receive PR messages. Articles involving technology and national schools are usually not as popular as stories involving the local school or community. For example, parents and community members are more interested in finding out about a local telecommunications program than about one in a national magazine.

Timeliness can make the difference in successful PR programs. Newspapers, radio, and television do not want yesterday's news. When promoting an event, administrators must always remember a fundamental rule: "Publicize an event before it happens and not after." Information about a new school technology program is more interesting than information about a program developed several years ago.

Prominent people usually attract reporters. If administrators really want to get their stories in the newspaper or on TV, they should invite recognizable personalities to their school. Sports figures, politicians, and authors are good choices. For example, one school invited a famous children's author who used technology to share with students her experiences in writing. The event was a media success, with TV and newspaper coverage. When special people are not available due to distances, satellite downlink operations can also prove useful in providing students with access to special personalities. In all cases of providing special presenters, administrators should contact the media early, because editorial decisions on story selection must be made as soon as possible.

Dramatic events often generate "media play." The more controversial the stories, the greater the chance of having reporters arrive at schools. For example, if a large school purchased a great number of computers, reporters might be more inclined to visit. This is especially true if several community members have been vocal about the amount of money spent on technology. For example, Seven Oaks School in Lacey, Washington, developed a model TLC program. The TLC approach emphasizes the use of computers in the classroom in an integrated unit approach rather than in a traditional lab setting. Early in the development of the TLC program at Seven Oaks School, some individuals expressed skepticism as to the success of the program. With effective planning and a positive communication program on the part of administration and staff, the Seven Oaks School is now a nationally recognized TLC demonstration site and a leader in computerized education.

If the situation is extremely controversial, which is often the case with technology, administrators should try to put a positive edge on the situation. This is particularly important when dealing with the press. The best policy is to say as little as possible, to be honest, and to hope that community members and reporters hear what you say. If in doubt, administrators should write a statement and give it to reporters or media representatives. Written documents minimize the chance of miscommunication.

Ease of reporting can be a factor in the success of a PR program. When media people are under the gun, they become increasingly selective about stories. For example, becoming aware of the time of day in which reporters like to cover a story is important. Newspaper reporters sometimes meet with editors in the morning and thus prefer to cover stories in the afternoon or evening if possible. Television reporters have a real time crunch just before the evening and late news. They often prefer stories earlier in the day that allow more set-up time than in the afternoon or evening. If administrators are out of sync with reporters and their time frames, they are not likely to get their story in the media. In addition, administrators can make reporters' lives a whole lot easier, and increase the chance of coverage, if they submit written information to the media about the event. Typing and double spacing information is very helpful. This allows reporters a chance to check details they might have missed.

When dealing with newspapers, administrators should ask editors to send a photographer, because the general public better remembers pictures and visual images. In addition, the editor is more likely to print the story due to the expense of film shot on the project.

Another important step in the communication process is to identify internal or external target groups. Internal target groups include individuals directly associated with the school, such as administrators, teachers, staff, board members, and students. External groups consist of individuals outside the school, such as parents, business and community leaders, and the general public.

Communication Strategies for Internal Groups

A positive connection appears to exist between high staff morale and the development of successful school technology programs.

Classroom Teachers

An old saying applies: "If classroom teachers are happy, students are happy. If students are happy, parents are happy. If parents are happy, school board members are happy. If school board members are happy, superintendents and principals are happy." The bottom line is that if teachers are happy, everyone is happy. This may sound too simple, but it is true.

Many educators believe that fostering pride in schools and providing teacher recognition helps increase staff morale.[13] If this is true, then administrators wanting to promote technology are going to have to focus on motivational approaches. Administrators wanting to increase staff morale should incorporate the following motivational strategies into the PR plan.

Improving Communication Through Instructional Leadership

As instructional leaders, school administrators should remain knowledgeable about current trends in schools and technology. Administrators need to review professional journals such as *Tech Trends, T.H.E. Journal,* and *Electronic Learning.* As experienced school administrators, the authors have noticed the following integral elements in the communication process.

• Use clinical-supervision approaches for teacher improvement with technology. Many teachers need supervision via guidance, knowledge, and understanding rather than just a formal evaluation.

• Work to keep schools small, enabling administrators to know all the children by name and many of the parents as well. The research base on the relative effects of large and small schools is vast and quite consistent.

The research concludes that an appropriate and effective size is 300-400 students for an elementary school and 400-800 students for a secondary school. In essence, a high school with 400 students or more can offer a curriculum that compares quite favorably in terms of breadth and depth with curriculum offered in much larger settings.

• Offer to teach technology classes. A little time taken by an administrator to work with a student on a multimedia project often pays big dividends in enhancing a positive school climate.

• Work to maintain class size at 12 to 17 students at the K-3 level, and classes of 20 or fewer in Grades 4 to 8, regardless of economics.

• Ensure that appropriate planning time is scheduled for teachers.

• Involve teachers in technology planning. The more ideas presented generally mean more options for administrators if they are willing to take the risk and listen.

• Act as a resource person for materials and equipment used in technology. When a problem with technology materials or resources surfaces, most administrators can get on the phone to other administrators and find what is available—fast.

• Set budget priorities to assist classroom teachers with special technology projects.

Improving Staff Morale

To improve communication and increase staff morale, school administrators can:

• Visit with teachers individually and informally about technology programs and about student needs. Personalizing the process will help teachers feel more inclined to take risks and set higher professional technology goals.

• Acknowledge teachers' roles in developing successful technology programs, either verbally or publicly. A well-written and sincere note of thanks to a staff member for work in technology generates a lot of positive feelings.

• Create special packets to be given to substitutes, informing them about the school's unique technology program. Not only does it assist in their teaching but it is also a great word-of-mouth communication.

• Recognize in weekly or monthly memos the teachers who have had success with the technology program. Good administrators take advantage of every opportunity to highlight the achievements of their school and staff.

• Promote leaves of absence, conferences, summer workshops, and professional seminars. Teachers, administrators, and board members who have an opportunity to attend special programs, immerse themselves in new material, and develop new ideas add a new dimension and depth to the school and enrich the lives of its students.

• Have regular staff e-mails in which selected staff members share new information about technology successes in the school.

• Organize cabinet meetings, before school or after school, to air any concerns that are not negotiable. All grade levels should be represented. Cabinet meetings provide good opportunities to discuss problems. One staff member from each grade level provides representation, but any individual should be able to attend.

• Assist the PTA in providing special luncheons honoring teachers using technology effectively.

• Organize a potluck for Technology Awareness Week. The first 10 minutes could be used for a news report during which staff members can report on positive or interesting ideas in technology.

• Develop an in-school task force committee whose purpose is to generate ideas regarding how to promote technology.

Noncertified Staff Members

Successful administrators quickly learn the importance of noncertified staff. Day-to-day operations in the classroom would not run smoothly without the help of secretaries, clerks, custodians, and other support staff. A positive and enthusiastic secretary often sets the tone for the entire school. A cheerful custodian makes children feel secure and comfortable. There is no doubt that these individuals are a tremendous resource for our schools.

Using Noncertified Staff

School administrators can best use noncertified staff beneficially:

• Ensure that noncertified staff members' efforts do not go unnoticed. For example, children can use technology and writing skills to make cards acknowledging positive contributions of these individuals. For example, students can use technology to make special cards acknowledging the contributions of the custodians to the school.

• Encourage noncertified staff members to share their special skills with students. For example, secretaries can share word-processing skills with children in the classroom.

• Organize a career day. Students could read about various careers of their choice. As part of career awareness, students can visit and work with specific noncertified school staff for a period of time. Journals or reports could be written about their experiences.

• Acknowledge staff members in school publications. Students can write articles about the contributions of noncertified staff members and submit them to the school paper. Student leaders can also provide staff members with special awards during assemblies.

Board Members

Successful schools have positive and progressive board members. Trustees often reflect the political, economic, and social commitment of the community. Without their support, administrators will have a difficult time developing an effective PR program. Board support is vital.

Board Member Communication

Communication with board members can be improved in a number of ways:

• Board members should be encouraged to attend the National School Board's International Technology Conference. This conference provides board members with a positive experience about technology. In some states, board members receive no remuneration for their services and thus feel more appreciated and knowledgeable when able to attend state and national meetings.

• Administrators should make sure that board members are aware of successful school activities using technology effectively. Teachers and staff can make presentations to the school board highlighting their successful programs. School board members should be invited into classrooms to work directly with students on computers. The kids love to show off and board members enjoy interacting with the students.

• Board members should be provided with copies of all PR communications. Copies of all notices, newsletters, and other forms of communication can be given to board members each month as part of an information packet.

Students

Since students will be the most active users of technology in schools, it is essential that they have news and information directed specifically to them. How students feel and act helps set the tone for a school, and so it is essential that they feel good and comfortable about the technology program.

Student Communication

Successful school administrators can improve communication with students:

• Keep an open door and allow students to discuss problems.

• Monitor technology groups to make sure students are being challenged with appropriate technology material.

- Reward students who excel in technology with honor passes. Passes provide freedom of movement for the students within the building. Students love them!

- Allow students to form a technology club.

- Support special minicourses or electives that relate to technology. Minicourses allow students to learn about areas such as PowerPoint. Special funds can be set aside for teachers to set up technology clubs as well as special technology sessions for parents.

- Encourage teachers to display stories produced via multimedia technology. Student work can be displayed in hallways, display cases, or in area businesses.

- Encourage teachers to provide positive reinforcement. Students and parents enjoy having teachers call with positive news. Some administrators use cellular phones to call parents on the spot when a child has finished a book or written a story. Parents and students appreciate this.

Communication Strategies for External Groups

Being aware that parent feelings about technology can make the difference between a positive program and an ineffective one.

Parents and the School

Parents are a critical component of the school technology process. Children learn more and like school better if parents are part of the school process. According to Rasinski and Fredericks, "The research is clear: given proper guidance and support, parents can supplement, in powerful fashion, learning that takes place in the school."[14] As a result of research, educators in technology are speaking out about the need to involve parents in their child's education. With this in mind, administrators need to ask these questions:

What are some ways that school administrators and supervisors can involve parents in technology?

How can administrators increase communication between home and school?

The answers can be found within the following communication strategies:

- The first step is developing a parent aide program. Successful parent partnership programs should have at least one enthusiastic parent and teacher willing to coordinate the program jointly. The parent coordinator organizes and administers the program while the teacher acts as a liaison for the staff. Some parent coordinators schedule a minimum of 100 parent aide volunteers each year.

- An example is the School District #4 Parent Partnership Program in Missoula, Montana. The Parent Partnership Program has been so successful that 1 out of every 10 parents is a parent-aide volunteer. A parent-aide coordinator as well as a teacher coordinator manages the program, making sure that parents are matched properly with teachers and students. These coordinators also work to help teachers feel more comfortable with their parent aides as well as to familiarize parents with the curriculum and technology. Parents with educational technology skills assist students in scanning documents, finding information on the Internet, and developing multimedia projects. "Working as a parent aide can be a transforming experience," says parent aide Joann Higginbotham (personal communication to Bruce Whitehead, April 19, 2001). "Being a parent-aide volunteer at School District 4 changed my life. It provided me with a chance to learn new skills and gave me confidence to apply and get a new job." The Parent Partnership Program has been so successful that it received the Montana State PTA Award.

- Encourage parents working in parent-aide volunteer programs to accept assignments to a grade level not occupied by their children. Some parents working with their children in classrooms can cause problems due to a lack of objectivity. Procedures for a successful program include encouraging parents to choose a level above their children's grade. This procedure enables parents to learn more about the technology process and curriculum and allows parents to become better able to assist their children for the coming year. This process also enables parents to develop a more positive attitude toward school.

- Set up an open house, and use the Schools Wanting to Acknowledge Parents (SWAP) concept. Parents are able to swap places with students for a demonstration of a technology lesson. Administrators need to use care in developing a SWAP program because some parents will feel insecure about being asked questions. Being aware of parent feelings can make the difference between having a positive or an ineffective program.

- Develop a technology advisory board that encourages parents to discuss problems and allows parents to provide input into the technology program. Such meetings are becoming more pronounced due to the advent of site-based management strategies.

Increasing Communication With Parents

Administrators can increase communication with parents:

- Have special PTA or parent nights. Display new technology materials, computer software, videos, and textbooks.

- Encourage teachers to report student progress on a regular basis. Some teachers may make personal calls or write notes. Teachers are using e-mail and sophisticated computer programs linked to phone systems that replicate message boards. Parents simply dial a phone number with a precoded extension and wait for a message describing the day's homework assignment. Students don't always like this innovation.

- Develop a summer technology program. YMCAs and other youth organizations have sponsored summer technology programs in schools across the United States.

- Set up coffee meetings in parents' homes. Many parents enjoy having a school administrator meet with them in small groups in a setting away from the school. Many positive communication ideas are nurtured at these sessions. The coffee klatch is an old idea that is being rediscovered by administrators across the country.

Business and Community Leaders

It is also essential to involve business and community leaders in our PR projects. Business involvement in education is becoming more significant, and a major development has been the growth of school and business partnerships.[15] Business leaders now recognize that they can play a fundamental role in improving education. For instance, corporate executives are assisting school administrators with PR and marketing ideas. Executives are opening businesses to students exploring career options and completing research.

Other community leaders can be helpful as well. Mayors, commissioners, police chiefs, and fire marshals enjoy working with children and are usually willing to come to schools. Many people in the community want to help schools; they just need to be asked.

Communicating With Business and Community Leaders

The following examples are ways business and community leaders can work with schools:

- School administrators can invite community and business leaders as well as their employees to share ideas about technology.
- Community and business leaders and their employees can communicate with the teacher and students via e-mail.
- Business and community leaders can provide field trips for children in order to see firsthand how technology is used in careers today.

The above examples are just a few of the many school and business activities that relate to technology. More and more schools are working with business and community leaders to expand students' horizons in how technology will be used in the future. This mobilization of communitywide relations has provided some dramatic improvements in school PR reform.

School-Community Relations

Problems in schools usually need to be addressed with alacrity. Accessible administrators solve problems whereas inaccessible administrators do not. Building trust is an important factor in school-community relations because it means that administrators consistently make decisions in the best interest of children.[16] Maintaining that trust, however, implies two-way communications and involves parents and community members working with administrators to create successful school technology programs. School-community relations are noted in this section as being directed by either teachers or administrators.

Teacher-Directed Community Relations

Successful teachers who use technology with the curriculum can improve school-community relations by providing special community programs that include multimedia productions by children. Children are encouraged to share special technology projects during these events.

- Providing student publications that are produced via computer or multimedia technology for communities is important.

- Formulating a Bring Your Boss to a Technology Breakfast program encourages businesses and schools to have their administrators participate in an activity where students give multimedia presentations and issues about technology are discussed. Many technology councils and schools have developed this program.

- Help students develop multimedia presentations for homeless centers and nursing homes.

- Provide a no-books day when children must use technology rather than books in all aspects of the curricula.

- In the spring, you could give away T-shirts saying Technology with Books.

- Develop a basket CD and video program. The technology club can arrange for children's CDs and videos to be placed in pediatricians' and dentists' offices.

- Technology Club can provide children's CDs as well as videos to new mothers in hospitals.

Administrator-Directed Community Relations

School administrators can improve school-community relations:

- Encourage staff to submit articles to media about their successful technology programs or activities. Using local TV stations and newspapers to share school technology ideas is common in most states.

- Be visible and available on a daily basis to work with parents or community members regarding technology programs or other activities. Problems in schools usually need to be addressed with alacrity.

- Arrange for a distinguished-visitor tour of the school by community, civic, business, media, and political leaders. Some visitors may want to spend more time observing students working with technology on the computer, whereas others like to visit with students about their written stories.

- Provide a school technology award to an outstanding volunteer helping with technology.

- Work with the PTA or parent groups to develop a reader board or newspaper advertisement listing the names of community members supporting technology. The PTA can sell space on the list to supporters for one dollar per name, to help pay for the program. A newspaper advertisement can be from a half page to a full page in length.

- Plan special banquets for students excelling in the use of school technology. Parents are especially pleased to have their children honored. Some vocational centers cater the whole event, considering it excellent online training for vocational students.

- Designate a community I Love Technology Day.

- Develop weekly calendars and newsletters that are produced via technology and are given to faculty, parents, and key community leaders. This is an old idea that should never be forgotten. Specific dates of technology events and stories about students and faculty make them popular with community members. Placing computer-generated newsletters in public places and grocery stores (with the manager's permission) helps administrators reach community members who do not have children.

- Speak to local community organizations. Various groups need to hear and to understand what is happening in technology at individual schools as well as across the nation. Toastmasters, Kiwanis, Lions, and Rotary are a few examples of organizations that welcome presentations on educational issues.

- Volunteer to work on community projects. Involvement in civic organizations shows interest in the community. For example, a principal may work with a local service club to provide additional technology funding for schools.

- Develop a recorded message service. Parents can call a publicized number for information on special events, school activities, and student and faculty accomplishments. Technology activities can be highlighted in the message.

WHERE SHOULD WE GO FROM HERE?

As school administrators, it is essential to make joint decisions about a student's education. At all times, due consideration must be given to linking educational priorities with successful technology programs. Where we go from here depends largely on where we have been. If a school district stands still because it is shrouded in nostalgia, it is denying the inevitability of change, the future.[17] In this chapter, we discussed the importance of PR in introducing a new technology initiative. We also discussed the role of administrators in the PR process. In our search, we found that school leaders play a key role in promoting technology and that they are becoming PR specialists. School administrators need to get the word out about successful school technology programs. Why? Because parents and community members want to know what is happening in their school technology programs and how they are helping their children to explore diverse learning opportunities.

STRATEGIES FOR SUCCESS

It is critical that technology planners focus on simple ways to improve school-community relations. Some obvious ways that technology planners can improve school-community relations are

- Setting PR awareness as the number one priority
- Formulating a PR advisory committee
- Establishing a PR plan
- Determining internal and external target groups
- Increasing parent participation in schools
- Improving staff morale through effective communication
- Tying your PR campaign to measurable student success outcomes

The PR concepts put forth in this chapter do work. They have proven effective in numerous schools. If technology planners need more information about any of the strategies discussed in this chapter, they should consult a PR professional or media specialist. They should also use information from a number of educational professional organizations. For example, the American Association of School Administrators (AASA), the National Association of Secondary School Principals (NASSP), the National Middle School Association (NMSA), and the National Association of Elementary School Principals (NAESP) all provide excellent materials on how to best inform communities on successful educational practices.

Developing a quality PR program is needed to promote the overall understanding of how technology is being used effectively in schools. An awareness of how technology continues to positively affect curriculum is paramount for the foundation of future funding. Educational reform in the 21st century will not happen without support for technology. It is imperative for all school leaders to begin the process of building a national consensus for technology. Only through awareness is it possible to fully appreciate the tremendous impact that technology has had on teaching and learning.

REFLECTIVE ACTIVITIES

1. List the basic characteristics of your current technology PR plan.

2. Identify how much time you currently spend on PR initiatives in relation to the technology programs you have at your school. If this is a low number, list what you can do practically to increase the number.

3. Assess what ways you currently interact with the external community from a PR standpoint.

4. Write a mission statement for your technology plan.

5. List your school's and community's strengths and weaknesses in relation to technology.

6. Formulate some possible objectives for your PR plan.

7. Identify some viable ways that your school could share information about your technology plan. Now list some creative ways that, at first, appear difficult for your school to implement.

8. Inventory existing research you have about technology that can help in your PR plan.

9. Plan how you think you would go about evaluating your PR activities.

6

Financial Management

CREATIVE FINANCING

The key to successfully financing technology in schools is to first establish technology as a priority in the public relations plan. Through this plan, the external community will be made aware of the school's technology initiative, and it will be a means through which financial support can be accessed. Administrators must make their plans known and actively promote their situation to the external community. If this is done successfully, accessing traditional sources of funding—such as special levies, bond issues, building reserves, and grant support—will yield fruitful results. Further, a strategic financial plan will open up nontraditional sources of external funding such as gifts, donations, fund-raising opportunities, and forging partnerships with local businesses to find innovative ways to fund educational technology.

Successful school administrators have found that it is essential to increase community awareness about local school technology initiatives. Andrew Grove, chairman and CEO of Intel, knows the importance of involving the community when promoting technology plans. Grove stated, "I believe that community support of technology is crucial to our nation's future."[1] Grove was the person most responsible for the amazing growth in the power and innovative potential of microchips. He also noted,

> At a time when computers are most needed, schools have been allowed to deteriorate, and worker-training programs have fallen prey to budget austerity. For all the spending on computers and software ($800 billion in the U.S. during the past five years), the most obvious investment has not been made: ensuring that every school child has a personal computer.[1]

Federal Allocations

Administrators need to realize that Federal funds are available to schools via the U.S. Department of Education, the National Science Foundation, and the National Endowment for the Humanities. The Technology Literacy Challenge Fund has also provided technology funding for every state. Other sources of financial support include Technology Innovation Grants, Star Schools Program, Goals 2000, Title I, Education for the Disadvantaged, Title II, Individuals With Disabilities Education Act Amendments, School to Work Opportunities Act, Telecommunications and Information Infrastructure Assistance Program, Public Telecommunications Facilities Program, Teacher Enhancement, Distance Learning Telemedicine Grant and Loan Program, and Teaching With Technology. It is essential that administrators develop a structured application's plan so that these funds can be accessed. More information on funding sources is available from school district offices where people provide help accessing state and federal agencies that financially support technology.

State Financial Support

Sources of technology funding from states are becoming more creative. States now include one-time legislated allotments, competitive grants, state lotteries, and other forms of gambling. Some states are using revenue from resources such as gas, oil, and coal to support technological initiatives in schools. Other states, like Montana, legislated a Technology Timber Act that allows schools to obtain funding from the logging of trees on state school lands. Still other states are turning to taxation, license plate fees, developer fees, special levies, fines, and forfeitures to fund technology.

States are also developing technology trusts as a way to cope with the pressures of funding school technology. State legislative bodies are allocating large sums of money to school technology, but they are finding it prudent to place funds in designated trusts. State trusts allow initial technology monies to earn high rates of interest until such time as leaders agree about how it should be spent. The following funding strategies are used by a number of states across the country:

- State educational agencies are working with both private and public agencies as well as school districts to seek funding sources for technology. Experts in school technology are serving in advisory capacities to state and federal agencies in all matters pertaining to technological implications and opportunities in education.

- State legislatures are funding respective educational agencies in launching alliances, partnerships, and public awareness initiatives that gain broad-based public and private financial support for technology development.

- States are assisting K-12 school districts in securing affordable access to telecommunications services and equipment. These purchases are made through aggregated purchasing; support for education, community, and business partnerships which maximize resources; establishment of tax incentives for the high-tech industry to assist schools in securing affordable access; and legislative action to ensure K-12 access to channel capacity and production support through existing cable systems.

• State legislatures are ensuring that any financial development, adoption, revision, or restructuring of education reflects current technological requirements for learning.

• State legislatures are enacting legislation to revise current constitutional and statutory language regarding bonds and levies to give school districts increased flexibility to effectively purchase, operate, upgrade, and maintain technology and telecommunications.

• State legislatures are establishing ongoing technology and telecommunications grant programs through state agencies to provide funds to school districts to equitably support student learning.

• State legislatures are increasing technology funding to state educational agencies in the areas of increasing and expanding services in technology networking and working with institutions of higher learning.

• State legislatures are appropriating funds to state educational agencies for the enhancement, extension, and maintenance of a state telecommunications network. This telecommunications network should connect K-12 schools, public libraries, public agencies, vocational and technical colleges, and institutions of higher learning.

• State legislatures are appropriating funds to state educational agencies to develop, implement, and assess technology-based curriculum projects.

SUCCESSFUL GRANT WRITING FOR TECHNOLOGY

Grants are one of the most common ways to fund technology, but they can be difficult to attain without an in-depth knowledge of the processes involved. Preparing a successful technology grant for school districts now requires careful research and planning. School districts and communities are matching their technology grants to philosophy, interests, and regulations.[2] The following practical suggestions are for developing a successful grant-writing plan.

Grant Proposal

A grant proposal is a request from a private or government source to fund a specific project. Preparing a grant application form demands careful research, study, and planning. The quality and integrity of the grant often tests the value of the project for which you are seeking funds.

Matching the needs of a school district to the philosophy, interests, and regulations of the funding source is crucial to the process. A large percentage of technology grant proposals are rejected simply because the proposal did not align with the foundation's or the government agency's philosophy. This can easily be countered by contacting the organization through a letter of inquiry or e-mail to determine if your school's interests identify with the funding agency's requirements. You may also be able to determine whether or not funds are presently available for projects such as yours.

By going through the following activities, administrators can ensure that all the essential elements of any grant proposal are met.

Special Grant-Writing Strategies

Grant writers would do well to make sure they use the following strategies if they want to increase their chances of having a project supported through grants. Effective grant writers should:

- Research the background of the funding agency or foundation.
- Find out what types of projects have been approved in the past by the funding source.
- Obtain a copy of other grants accepted by the funding source, and analyze them for style and content.
- Personalize the proposal to fit the funding source. One proposal should not fit all.
- Note statistics and document special references.
- Include visuals, such as graphs and charts, in the proposal.
- Proofread proposals carefully before submission. At least five people should proofread a proposal.
- Reflect a feeling of confidence and success in writing the proposal.
- Highlight measurable outcomes that will derive from the project.
- Link measurable outcomes to the budget and funding allotment.
- Focus on evaluation and follow-up that will be made at various points during the project.

Grant Configuration

The overall organization and configuration of the grant should:

- Identify and address a special educational problem or need that will be addressed by the grant.
- Focus on district technology goals and mission statement.
- Provide a review of the literature.
- Follow guidelines and requirements established by the funding source.
- Highlight key words and phrases in the proposal that were originally used in literature provided by the funding source.

- Attempt to place the grant in perspective. Why should the funding source approve your request and not another?

Writing the Grant

1. Clarify the problem and establish supporting needs assessment data. Answer the question of how the grant will solve the problem and address the needs of the school district. If possible, the grant should always, indirectly or directly, focus on benefiting students and the community.

2. State clear, measurable indicators of success related to the problem. The objectives and outcomes need to be realistic.

3. Focus on the strength of your leadership in ensuring project completion.

4. Establish commitment from the board, staff, and community for the technology project.

5. Develop your plan of action.

6. Develop the evaluation component.

7. Link successful outcomes to initial budget and grant allocation.

Complete the form in Form 6.1 to help in your preparation of the grant proposal.

FUNDING SOURCES

DISTRICT

- Innovative Teacher grants
- Title I
- Chapter II
- Parent-teacher organizations

COMMUNITY

- Local businesses
- Community organizations
- Service organizations

STATE

- State department of education
- State professional organizations
- Colleges and universities

(Text continues on page 143)

FORM 6.1 GRANT PROPOSAL

1. INITIAL CONTACT

Prepare an e-mail or a letter of inquiry requesting written guidelines from the potential funding source. Initial correspondence should be no longer than three pages in length and should reflect essential elements of the project. From this process, you should be able to determine if your project generally matches the mandates of the funding agency and warrants a complete application on your school's part.

2. COVER LETTER

Write a cover letter that represents the best possible image of the district and school. The cover letter should have the name and purpose of the project, amount requested, length of project, and the name of the project director. Special references should be made to community relations and benefits of the project. The letter should also convey a feeling that the district will remain committed to the project even after the grant timeline expires. The letter should be signed and dated by the board chair.

3. INTRODUCTION

This section should clearly and concisely summarize the overall technology plan. The following elements should be included in an organized manner.

(a) Origins of the Project

(b) Statement of Purpose

(c) Project Philosophy

(d) Relevant School Highlights

School's Opening Date: _____

School Demographics and Community Socioeconomic Status:

_____

_____

_____

Student Population: _____

Faculty and Staff Numbers: _____

School Special Projects:

➢

➢

➢

➢

➢

Current Technology Status: _____

_____

_____

_____

_____

_____

_____

_____

School Technology Awards and Recognition:

➢

➢

➢

➢

➢

Organizational Affiliations:

➢

➢

➢

➢

➢

➢

Articles Published by School Faculty and Administration:

➢

➢

➢

➢

➢

Quotes and Comments of Support From Community Members and Experts:

➢

➢

➢

➢

➢

➢

➢

➢

➢

4. NEEDS ASSESSMENT STATEMENT

This is a statement of why the technology project is necessary and why funding is needed. In order to establish the benefits of receiving the funding, the needs, goals, and problems of the technology project should be stated in measurable terms. Try to avoid the use of jargon, and always focus your discussion on the needs of students, faculty, and parents.

Consider the following questions:

What is the problem being faced by the school in relation to technology and student achievement?

_____

_____

_____

_____

_____

_____

_____

How is this project a response to district technological missions?

_____

_____

_____

_____

_____

_____

_____

How are your needs correlated with needs of other schools in the community? Provide data or information indicating similar needs of other schools in the district.

_____

_____

_____

_____

_____

_____

_____

What statistical or anecdotal evidence do you have in support of your technology efforts? Focus on student achievement and staff development.

_____

_____

_____

_____

_____

_____

_____

What are the experts saying? Cite influential writers and researchers in the field who give support to your technology initiative.

_____

_____

_____

_____

_____

_____

_____

_____

What needs will be met through the funding?

_____

_____

_____

_____

_____

_____

_____

_____

What problems in the technology plan will be solved through receiving the funding?

_____

_____

_____

_____

_____

_____

_____

5. GOALS AND OBJECTIVES

Goals and objectives should describe the desired outcome of your project. Objectives must be quantifiable or measurable. They state how you will know when your goals have been met.

What are the goals of your technology project?

Goals linked to the original problem:
➢
➢
➢
➢
➢

Goals that focus on administrators:
➢
➢
➢
➢
➢

Goals that focus on teachers:
➢
➢
➢
➢
➢

Goals that focus on students:
➢
➢
➢
➢
➢

Goals that focus on parents:
➢
➢
➢
➢
➢

What are the objectives of your technology project? In the objectives, consider target populations and general timelines of completion.

Objectives linked to the original problem:
➢
➢
➢
➢
➢

Objectives that will benefit administrators:
➢
➢
➢
➢
➢

Objectives that will benefit teachers:
➢
➢
➢
➢
➢

Objectives that will benefit students:
➢
➢
➢
➢
➢
➢

Objectives that will benefit parents:
➢
➢
➢
➢
➢
➢

6. FUNCTIONAL COMPONENTS OF THE PLAN

This section describes the processes to be employed to implement the technology plan. It is a description of how project objectives will be accomplished, who is responsible for implementing them, and how they relate to cost.

Administration and Staffing

It is important to identify administrators and staff that will be working with the project. Many funding agencies base their decision on the quality of leadership associated with the grant. General information collected in Formulating Core Committees, completed in Form 2.1, can be extracted to provide this information. Make sure to refer to board trustees, administrators, influential teachers, and community volunteers.

Past Success

List other successes with technology grants or technology projects:

➢

➢

➢

➢

➢

➢

➢

➢

Budget

The budget clearly delineates costs to be met by the primary funding source. It states in dollars and cents what the narrative says in words. It provides the financial backbone of the technology project and delineates what the district expects as expenses. The actual budget helps identify and limit project expenditures, and it reinforces the ideas presented in the initial proposal of the plan. Referral to the appropriate sections of Form 2.1 (see page 41) can provide the figures needed for this section.

Staffing

ANTICIPATED COSTS

Salaries
(e.g., program
director, technical
director) $_____

Wages
(secretarial support,
etc.) $_____

Benefits $_____

Release Time $_____

Other $_____

<u>Totals:</u> $_____

Comments:

Staff Development Costs

<u>Anticipated Costs</u>

Site Visits $_____
Conference Fees $_____
Training Courses $_____
Research Resources $_____
Travel Allowances $_____
Other $_____
<u>Totals:</u> $_____

Comments:

Contracted Services

	Anticipated Costs
Audit	$_____
Consulting	$_____
Printing	$_____
Maintenance	$_____
Totals:	$_____

Comments:

Infrastructure, Technology, and Capital

	Anticipated Costs
Computer Hardware	$_____
Computer Software	$_____
Remodeling	$_____
Maintenance	$_____
Internet Lines	$_____
Office/School Supplies	$_____
Postage/Shipping	$_____
Moving Charges	$_____
Totals:	**$_____**

Comments:

Future and Other Sources of Funding

This component describes a plan for the continuation of the technology project beyond its initial implementation. This aspect of the plan acknowledges other financial resources and reveals the commitment of the school district to the project.

	Anticipated Support
In-School Funding	$_____
District Funding	$_____
Contributions	$_____
Grants	$_____
Donations	$_____
State Initiatives	$_____
Federal Initiatives	$_____
Fundraising	$_____
Totals:	$_____

IMPLEMENTATION PLAN

The implementation plan is an essential component. This plan shows that you are very well prepared and have done everything possible to get the technology plan into action. In preparing this component, consider the following questions:

Why have you selected this technology plan?

_____
_____
_____
_____
_____
_____

Why is this approach better than other approaches for your school?

_____
_____
_____
_____
_____
_____

What benchmarks are needed to guide the successful accomplishment of the project objectives?

_____
_____
_____
_____
_____
_____

How will the media and the external community be involved?

_____
_____
_____
_____
_____
_____
_____

YEAR ONE – *Planning Phase*

September	➤ Determine initial commitment to project.
	➤ Form technology advisory committee.
	➤ Form project steering committee.
October	➤ Develop project philosophy and mission statement.
	➤ Create calendars for specific committee work.
	➤ Develop project benchmarks and indicators.
November	➤ Finalize goals and targets for project.
	➤ Carry out needs assessment.
December	➤ Review relevant literature.
	➤ Analyze needs assessment data.
January	➤ Disseminate information from literature review.
	➤ Consider possible options available to planners. (Look at such things as hardware, software programs, implementation strategies, financing, staff development strategies, student needs.)
February	➤ Determine course of action based on available options and needs assessment data.
	➤ List needed materials and resources.
	➤ Confirm and formalize school board commitment.

YEAR ONE – *Implementation and Staff Development Phases*

	➤ Establish leadership roles for implementation phase.
	➤ Fix calendar for implementation phase.
March	➤ Plan public relations program.
	➤ Meet with committees to discuss implementation strategies.
	➤ Purchase hardware, software, and supplementary materials.

April	➢ Initiate staff development programs.
	➢ Continue public relations program.
May	➢ Network installation begins.
	➢ Complete installation and troubleshooting of system.
Summer (June to August)	➢ Carry out as much teacher inservice as possible before classes begin.

YEAR TWO – Implementation Phase

	➢ Continue with staff development activities.
September	➢ Use of new technology in instructional program begins.
	➢ Administrative monitoring of equipment and programs begins.
	➢ Public relations program continues.
October	➢ Ongoing help to teachers provided in various forms.
November/December	➢ Continue administrative monitoring of equipment and programs.

YEAR TWO – Evaluation Phase

January	Begin formal project evaluation, which should include
	➢ Reports from administrative monitoring from September to December
	➢ Continue administrative monitoring
	➢ Feedback from teachers
	➢ Feedback from students
	➢ Feedback from in-house technology experts
February	➢ Continue monitoring and gathering information.
	➢ Complete formal evaluations.
March to May	➢ Make revisions according to information gathered during evaluation phase.

Evaluation

Who is conducting the evaluation of the technology project?

_____

_____

_____

_____

_____

_____

Data Gathering Methods

Administrators', trustees', teachers', parents', and community members' satisfaction:

_____

_____

_____

_____

_____

_____

_____

Success of program objectives:

_____

_____

_____

_____

_____

_____

Degree to which achieved objectives were correlated to the success of the program:

_____

_____

_____

_____

_____

_____

(In)Effectiveness of the program:

_____

_____

_____

_____

_____

_____

Cost-effectiveness of the program:

_____
_____
_____
_____
_____

How will the data be distributed to those involved?

_____
_____
_____
_____
_____

What processes will occur to ensure that alterations in the program will be implemented?

_____
_____
_____
_____
_____
_____
_____

Attachments

Letter of support from chair of board of trustees
Letters of commitment from cosponsoring agencies
Newspaper articles or media samples
List of awards and recognition for school and staff
Staff resumes: directors and coordinators of technology
IRS letter confirming tax-exempt 501(c)(3) designation

FEDERAL SOURCES

- Block grants
- Discretionary federal funds
  Guide to U.S. Department of Education Programs
  U.S. Printing Office
  web99.ed.gov/GTEP/Program2.nsf

  The Federal Register
  Office of the Federal Register
  National Archives and Records
  Washington, DC 20408

FOUNDATIONS

> The Foundation Center
> 79 Fifth Ave.
> New York, NY 10003
> 1-800-424-9836

The Foundation Center provides informational sources on private philanthropic organizations. Its dialog information services provide an online database on foundation grants: fdncenter.org/

In summary, grants are often a one-time opportunity and can leave a school district open to financial problems in the future. Administrators and community leaders need to use care in using grants as their sole funding source. School leaders are finding that it is best to establish a successful technology program first and then search for grants to help accentuate the program.

Whatever the price tag, successful schools are finding it crucial to make financing technology their number one budget priority. As part of that priority, school leaders are continuing to look for more creative ways to fund technology via grants.

SUCCESS IN FINANCING TECHNOLOGY

Setting Priorities

A traditional approach to planning technology programs involves focusing on cost first and then moving to hardware needs, ease of implementation, courseware, curriculum, and, finally, philosophy of teaching. Perry Brown, director of the office of technology for Anderson Schools in Clinton, Tennessee, believes that the process should be reversed.[3] He believes that when financing technology programs, educators need first to look at the philosophy of education as the foundation of the program, and then the other elements should follow. Once the community and school district establish a consensus on the philosophy of the technology program, they will be better prepared to link it to the school curriculum. The curriculum, in turn, will determine the scope and sequence of courseware and other software used in the classroom. Implementation and hardware follow. Once all these factors are considered, then cost and financing will come into play. Adjustments can then be made to meld the desired program with its cost, at the top of the purchasing pyramid: Figure 6.1 portrays how this would look.

Purchasing Policy

Challenges facing purchasers of expensive hardware and software for schools include compatibility, connectivity, and planned obsolescence, maintenance, lease or purchase alternatives, and support of educational objectives. Susan Cole and Melodie Friedeboch, technology coordinators

Figure 6.1 The Purchasing Pyramid

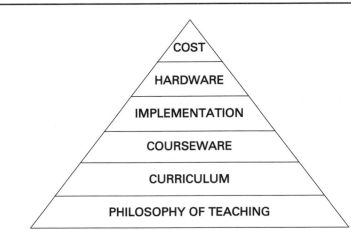

for the Missouri State Education Department, offered a list of key questions that technology coordinators should ask as they consider purchasing both hardware and software.[4]

1. What is the memory capacity of the system to efficiently operate current and projected hardware and software including adaptations?

Substantial access would include memory needed to run standard applications plus additional memory needed to accommodate adaptations.

2. What is the processing capacity of the system to efficiently operate current and projected hardware and software adaptations?

Substantial access would include processing speed needed to run standard applications plus additional memory needed to accommodate adaptations.

3. What is the capacity of the architecture of the system to allow for expansion, such as the addition of specialized cards, memory chips, and port connections?

Substantial access would include the availability of open ports, slots, etc. to meet adaptation needs.

4. What is the capacity of the architecture of the system to allow for ease of physical access to features such as on/off switches, volume, contrast, brightness controls, and disk/CD-ROM drives?

Substantial access would include controls on the front of the system or accessible from the control panel.

5. What is the capacity of the individual user station in a network system to provide adaptations, both built-in and add-on access features?

Substantial access would include network ability to deliver adaptations from the server and independently through the end unit.

6. What is the capacity of the cabling system to transmit a variety of electronic information?

Substantial access would include cabling able to deliver multiple types of electronic information, e.g., adaptations of visual information to auditory and auditory to visual.

School Technology Purchasers

Electronic Learning Magazine conducted a study to determine who buys technology for schools.[5] The survey found that 80% of districts and 96% of schools reported that principals are heavily involved with technology decisions. When it comes to purchasing technology and implementing technology plans, the principal was named as most involved.

E-Rate

The Federal Communications Commission decided to provide virtually every school and public library with a specially discounted "educational rate" (E-rate) on telecommunications services, internal connections, and Internet access. The E-rate discount ranges from 20% to 90% depending on a school's poverty level, which is determined by the federal free and reduced-priced lunch program. Companies providing the discounts are reimbursed through a universal services fund paid by all telecommunications companies. Information about E-rate can be obtained from the U.S. Department of Education online at 165.224.220.66/Technology/eratemenu.html

Funding Staff Development

One way to fund staff development for technology is through Title II money.[6] School leaders are effectively using block grant money to provide the necessary inservice needed to support their technology programs that relate to science and math. Using federal dollars for staff development is one of the best ways to support and reform education and, at the same time, free up money for hardware and software needs.

Fund-Raising Campaign

It is important for school leaders to understand and know the key elements associated with technology fund-raising. Stimson wrote that the strategies will vary from district to district and that his list is, by no means, an exhaustive formula for passing a levy but does describe the essential elements for mounting a successful campaign for locally funding technology:[7]

1. Find a point person. This person's job is to deliver the message about technological change with unflagging enthusiasm.

2. **Devise a sales pitch.** Show voters you have a problem, show them how big it is, and then show that you have a solution.

3 **Talk to any group that will listen.** You have to sell your ideas to the people who matter most—the taxpayers. School leadership should actively solicit opportunities to meet with local businesses, labor, and political leaders, as well as civic organizations.

4. **Involve lots of people.** Every person in your community has a stake in a technology levy. Don't be shy in asking for support to do the legwork essential for any campaign, such as distributing flyers, raising money, demonstrating technology, and making phone calls. Make it an issue with every person in the community. Try to get as many people as possible excited and committed to the technology-funding project.

5. **Court the local media.** To a great degree, they are the people who will report the facts and figures of your technology levy or tax to the general public. Their perception of your campaign will be important for convincing the community that spending the money is worthwhile.

6. **Throw a community party or plan another activity.** Once you're certain the crucial part of your funding message has been delivered and people understand what you plan to do with technology, celebrate with a fun party or other activity. Remember that people are more likely to attend if food is served. This is a great way to reward people for their efforts and support and to help solidify their commitment to the technology project.

7. **Start early.** Don't wait until 90 days before a vote to explain what your measure is supposed to do. It's not unusual to work two years or longer on developing technology plans and plotting a course to win taxpayer support.

Finding Local Funds for Technology

Although a majority of technology funds should come from the general school fund budget, some school administrators are finding supplemental funds from alternative sources. The following ideas on how to find local funds for technology were developed by Kate Collins and presented to the IBM National Schools Executive Conference:[8]

- Hold off buying textbooks
- Purchase used textbooks rather than expensive new ones, and use remainder of money for technology
- Technology jog-a-thon
- Bake sales for technology
- Mall technology fairs
- Hot dog lunches for technology
- Technology Bingo night
- School business partners

STRATEGIES FOR SUCCESS

Technology in education is not an option; it must be budgeted and paid for like any other vital operational need. School administrators are rethinking budgeting processes that restrict teachers in their quest to innovate and create. Teachers are taking responsibility for success in their classrooms and thus providing success stories to foster technology funding. Costs are coming down, and the quality of technology is improving. Educators are in a better position to obtain new innovative technology. With costs of technology coming down, administrators and technology planners need to develop some basic strategies in how to finance technology in their schools. The following ideas reflect a number of financial strategies that have been used successfully by school administrators and technology planners.

Effective Finance Strategies

Technology Line Item. Successful schools formulate a specific line item in their general fund budget for technology. This not only establishes a priority for technology but also provides a known dollar base for a starting point. Administrators can now plan for technology needs knowing that a specified dollar amount will be available.

Five Percent of General Fund Budget. At least three to five percent of the entire general-fund budget should be earmarked for technology. This allotment provides a stable base of guaranteed dollars for technology planning, purchasing, implementation, maintenance, replacement, staff development, and evaluation.

Building-Level Technology Budget. Building-level teachers often want certain pieces of technological equipment for their classrooms that may not be determined by the district as a priority. It is important to have a set sum of money set aside in building-level budgets to maximize purchasing power.

Reallocation of Budget. Schools sometimes find that funds still remain in specific accounts at the end of the budget year. By combining these funds, administrators are often able to apply these reallocated dollars to technology. For example, some educational agencies in northern states encourage school administrators to set aside additional money to pay for heat during the harsh winters. If these states have a mild winter, the school district may have a large amount of money left over at the end of the budget year to reallocate to technology.

Building Bonds and Reserves. Setting building levies and reserves at full bonding limits helps finance technology infrastructure. When constructing new buildings, it is best to set the building bond or a building reserve levy at full bonding limits. This provides school leaders with an opportunity to allocate money for technology infrastructure. A number of school leaders are using this approach to develop connectivity in new buildings, construct phone systems, and develop state-of-the-art technology labs.

Emergency Funding. School leaders experiencing student enrollment increases may be able to use state emergency funds if available. These funds, used in conjunction with the district general fund, can be used to maximize purchasing power for technology. Some states allow schools to apply for additional money if they have high enrollment increases.

Fund-raising. Fund-raising should be an essential element of your technology project. For example, some parent-teacher associations have raised over $20,000 in just 2 weeks each year with their Christmas gift-wrap program. The parents love the program and the school benefits from the money generated.

Corporate Donations. Schools benefit from donations of hardware and services to schools from local corporate businesses. Schools can network older and slower machines into keyboarding labs. Telephone and cable companies are donating free fiber-optic hookups to many schools throughout the country. In some cases, companies are allowing schools to use their lines free of charge.

Low-Interest Loans. Banks and credit unions can provide special services to schools needing assistance with their technology program. For example, innovative school districts are collaborating with local banks and credit unions as school-business partners to provide low-interest, signature, payroll deduction loans for teachers and administrators to purchase their own computers.

Adult Education Funding. Adult Education money in some states can be used to partially fund a technical director's position if the director is an adult education instructor. In addition, adult education classes held in public schools can serve as a source for staff development at a reduced rate or at no cost to the district.

College and University Partnerships. Schools are benefiting from collaboration between their school and a local college or university. For example, some universities will provide Internet access for local area schools.

Technology Consortiums and Cooperatives. Technology consortiums and cooperatives are a cost-effective way to maximize purchasing power, create staff development programs, and provide maintenance service for technology.

The need for schools to establish sound financial plans is a crucial step. Typical school purchasing procedures across the country are primarily based on infrequent and unreliable capital outlay that is out of sync with the needs of education, the growth of new technologies, and the demands of the competitive world. Nonetheless, many school, state, and federal leaders throughout the nation are now making a shift in thinking about how to finance technology. This means that educators need to look not only at the local community for funding but also to state and federal revenue sources. These leaders are realizing that personal computers, courseware, and related networking technologies must be reclassified as ongoing operating expenses like salaries, telephone, electricity, and other necessities.

There should be little doubt that our state and federal educational agencies will have an important say in how technology is funded in the future. It is vitally important, then, that educational leaders continue to work at state and federal levels to build an awareness and an understanding as to the impact of technology on teaching and learning.

FUTURE CHALLENGES

The bottom line to funding is setting priorities and establishing community awareness. Successful technology programs are based on collaborative community efforts and sound funding practices. The future is based on generating partnerships and programs that can become economically self-sustaining. This process includes the matching of curriculum, funding, objectives, and assessment with appropriate media and transmissions systems. Collaboration needs to involve K-12 users as well as experts from higher education, libraries, community centers, businesses, homes, consortiums, and museums. School leaders must seek varied funding sources to extend the learning environment and to enhance participation through interactive technologies and multimedia.

REFLECTIVE ACTIVITIES

1. Describe the current structure in place at your school for the financial management of your technology program.

2. Analyze the current support you have from both the internal and external community for new technology initiatives.

3. Detail the types of financial support you have for technology in your school. Consider district, state, federal, and private support.

4. Highlight the funding strategies that exist in your state for technology.

5. Evaluate the current administrative structures and procedures you have in place for writing technology grants.

6. Envision your new fund-raising program for this technology initiative. Describe its core components, resources, and personnel.

7. Generate a list of creative ways you can locally fund technology in your school.

7

Infrastructure

COORDINATING THE EFFORT

A crucial element of this technology initiative to consider is your school's infrastructure. Infrastructure relates to such things as the wiring of the physical plant, networking systems among schools in a district and within a state, telecommunication systems, and state and federal regulations for technology. This is a very technically complicated area and so it is essential that administrators consider both internal and external issues so that your technology program is well linked with the systems already in place and with future state and federal technology directives. The more that the infrastructure is configured to meet state and federal standards and systems, the more effective the technology plan will be. It is also important to realize that it would be near to impossible for this book to address the specifics of wiring a school and the specifics of establishing individual school technology infrastructures. This chapter provides a framework for discussion and analysis. The specific details should then be considered with a school's or district's technology expert to see how to best implement it based on the local context. So, in dealing with this issue, it is vitally important that we learn from the mistakes, successes, and barriers that others have experienced. The following list reflects barriers or obstacles that have impeded the effective integration of computer technology into American schools and classrooms.

- The inability to properly finance a successful technology infrastructure has been a great handicap to bringing computers into the classroom. Local, state, and national efforts will have to be coordinated to eliminate this barrier.

- For rural schools, the inability to provide line service and Internet service continues to be a major problem, because they are great distances from Internet providers and fiber-optic capability.

- A lack of up-to-date hardware, courseware, support materials, and software quickly frustrates teachers and students. Teachers experience a great deal of anxiety using outdated equipment and materials, which usually means that new software programs lie idle.

- Poor networking capabilities, due to a reliance on stand-alone computers, reduces flexibility in linking technology to the school's curriculum and to the rest of the world.

- The existence of multiple platforms (Apples and PCs) within and among schools makes transferring and coordinating technological efforts complicated.

- There is a problem with a lack of interchangeable parts. For various reasons, many schools have numerous brands of computers and peripherals, and this has made it difficult to upgrade and interchange components. With this as the reality, technology has not been a cost-effective venture.

- Rapidly changing technology has created a backlog of outdated equipment that is not being recirculated.

- Leadership can be a decisive factor in developing a successful technology program. Not having a technology director or coordinator is a major barrier to technology infrastructure development.

- Many schools have suffered because of a lack of maintenance and service capability. Not having access to proper maintenance and service can be a major obstacle to successful implementation.

- The traditional focus for technology in schools has been toward computer labs. Schools using only computer labs are often limiting their teachers' and students' access to technology. Computer labs make it difficult for teachers to easily incorporate technology into daily curricular activities.

- Another barrier to technology has been a lack of staff training and inservice opportunities. Hundreds of computers lie idle in schools because few teachers know how to use them effectively.

NETWORK CLASSROOM TECHNOLOGY CENTERS

One of the most exciting new ways to restructure education and to control technological barriers has been the development of networked classroom technology centers. Classroom technology centers consist of at least five high-speed and memory-intensive networked computers with one printer. Technology centers are located within classrooms and are designed to house a set of computers with multimedia peripherals and Internet access. All computers are networked using high-speed wire or wireless technology and have interchangeable parts.

School leaders are turning to these classroom center formats to make technology more accessible to teachers and students. Building-level file servers make up the core of the networked classroom technology centers. These servers are often connected to a school district's centralized file server via fiber optics or wireless technology. Smaller districts often use just one centralized file server for both building and district technology operations. For information regarding other configurations, educational planners should contact qualified technology consultants or computer outlets.

Software in the classroom technology centers can be used in a multimedia format. Phones, modems, satellite cable, and other multimedia applications accentuate the use of the classroom center. The design also helps to provide an efficient platform for the use of both Internet and intranet capabilities (a detailed description of an intranet is provided toward the end of this chapter). The truly exciting aspect of classroom technology centers is that teachers and students have access to multimedia applications whenever and wherever they want. The applications are right in the classroom. As a result, classroom technology centers are finding increased acceptance among the nation's teachers as a way to enhance student achievement through technology.

Technology Learning Stations

Classroom technology centers allow networked computer clusters to blend into classroom environments as learning stations because they offer subtle changes in how technology works in the classroom. The ability to connect classrooms and communicate technologically in real time helps break down possible teacher and student feelings of isolation and frustration. In addition, self-managing computer centers in classrooms provide students with an opportunity to acquire a deeper understanding of the key concepts in many subject areas. Computer centers also assist in creating an environment that enables students to develop critical work skills, including self-direction, perseverance, and commitment to quality.

The use of computers as learning activity centers has been especially effective at elementary and intermediate levels but is also becoming popular at secondary levels. Teachers at all levels of education are finding that a cluster of computers in the classroom makes technology much more accessible.

Teacher Work Stations

Classroom technology centers are linked to a teacher workstation, which is usually right at the teacher's desk. Teacher station computers are generally faster, have greater memory, and should, ideally, include CD-ROM capability. The teacher station can also serve as the print station as well as provide a platform for phone, satellite, and cable links.

NATIONAL TELECOMMUNICATIONS INFRASTRUCTURE

As research and educational practice continue to show a link between technology and student achievement, national leaders are becoming more interested in funding school technology programs. There appears to be a positive change in Washington, D.C., to a belief that technology can drive educational improvement. Government leaders are now coming to the conclusion that technology does impact learning.

The positive attitude on the part of policymakers in Washington, D.C., has done much to help pump billions of dollars into school technology initiatives. Federal support for technology infrastructure comes from a multitude of departments, foundations, and competitive grants. The focus has been to decentralize the funding of technological infrastructure through the individual states as much as possible. According to Cheryl Lemke, vice president of education technology for the Milken Exchange Program, "The centralized model is not always the best one. Change happens when local school officials, educators, and parents become part of the program."[1]

In addition to state and local support, one of the most successful ways to support technology on a national level is to provide funding for regional educational centers such as the Northwest Regional Educational Laboratory in Portland, Oregon. This special education center provides technology planning, implementation, and evaluation strategies for school leaders, teachers, parents, and community members in six western states.

State Telecommunications Infrastructure

State leaders are becoming more interested in the impact technology is having on teaching and learning in the classroom. Understanding infrastructure design and how it relates to integrating technology in classrooms is becoming the foundation for the change process. Many states are now establishing financial funding that promotes and protects the integrity of technology use in classrooms and across networks. Making sure that schools are able to purchase proper wire, wireless servers, high-speed network servers, and high-speed computers with large amounts of memory continues to be of critical interest to state lawmakers.

Several states are looking at what they can do to speed up the implementation of technology in school classrooms. Most states currently maintain a network of leased lines and microwave links that connect counties and schools. Districts around the country now use existing and evolving telecommunications technologies within their respective areas. Of primary importance are those communications that support Internet provider- (IP) based data and multimedia delivery. Many state and federal agencies, university systems, and private businesses now work collaboratively to deliver stable and sustainable multimedia-based applications. Networking current infrastructure systems within each state has facilitated this effort by establishing models for connectivity, training, and curricula for K-16 education. Requests for large blocks of IP addresses are being made using an IP addressing scheme to support efficient routing and IP-based connectivity to schools and libraries throughout each state.

Multimedia delivery for individual states is often supported through partnerships with other online services, compressed video networks, satellite uplinks available from the university systems, tribal and technical colleges, or private industry—as well as from community access television stations and television cable infrastructures. Many states now have multiple telecommunications corporations, resource centers, and other commercial entities that are coming forward to invest in developing statewide, infrastructural telecommunications systems that can be accessed by schools.

State Telecommunications Networks

Community and school leaders want statewide computer networks that provide dedicated access for voice, video, and data transmissions. Communities and schools are now linked through fiber channels. Linking independent school networks together with state fiber channels remains the primary economic challenge for many states. Telephone companies are now discussing how to offer price breaks on usage fees to allow sustained use of these fiber networks by schools. While compressed video is less expensive than fiber-optic, interactive TV, it suffers from similar scheduling problems. As the use of site networks grows, conflicts in scheduling when all sites are free can be expected to become increasingly problematic. Compressed video sites often have two screens, one that shows the home site, and a central "speaking" or point of origin site. Interactive sites typically have several TVs that allow viewers and speakers to see participants at all or some sites simultaneously or alternately. Frame relay is one method of providing high-bandwidth data communications statewide, such as Internet access.

A few states have been funding their telecommunications programs by requiring companies that are seeking deregulation to contribute to school technology. Companies must provide discounted telecommunications services to schools and contribute an agreed dollar amount per year over a period of 10 years. This money is used to fund and upgrade technology infrastructure.

The use of satellite networks will help to reduce technology barriers and equity issues in schools across the country. The Texas satellite network, known as T-STAR, links districts, regional educational service centers, and the Texas Education Agency together.[2] Each district in Texas has a satellite dish that allows it to participate in the system. As costs come down, more schools in the future will depend on satellite technology to enhance their contact with the external community. There are thousands of school-based satellite dishes throughout the country, and more schools will be turning to satellite to increase desktop Internet access. The problem is the logistics of organizing enough sites to receive the same broadcast and to justify the expense of transmission and use.

South Dakota provides a cost-effective, innovative model for creating infrastructure. Governor William J. Janklow provided fiber-optic cable and training for inmates in the state penitentiary. Schools hired the prison inmates at penitentiary salary to wire every school from kindergarten through higher education in the state of South Dakota to create the Dakota Digital Network, a two-way audio, two-way video telecommunications network.

STATE REGULATIONS AND GUIDELINES

One direction being taken is to tie the funding of technology infrastructure to specific standards and guidelines. The following sections are areas of concern in relation to state and federal regulations and guidelines.

Equity Issues

Technology equity is a major concern for state lawmakers and leaders. States continue to work to eliminate a wide disparity among individual districts as to how they use technology. In order to address equity concerns, some state leaders now allocate federal funds to districts according to the number of low-income children in a district. Free and reduced-cost student lunch counts are used as a measure for identifying the number of low-income families in districts. State officials also use low property values as a way of determining which schools should receive financial support for technology. Another direction is that districts consider the development of technology consortia to help decrease the gap between the haves and the have-nots.

Technology Plans

Before money is approved for technology, many state agencies are requiring schools to develop a comprehensive network technology plan. These state leaders are requiring that districts take certain steps in developing their technology infrastructure before receiving competitive grants in technology.

Evaluation

Program evaluation and a school's ability to assess student performance are now critical elements that must be included in the formation of most states' technology plans if schools are to receive funding.

Staff Development

Teacher training is being recognized as one of the main reasons that schools have difficulty implementing technology. Therefore, state leaders are now requiring that all technology plans include a provision that addresses how staff development will be funded. Some states are requiring teachers to have advanced skills in technology before a school district can receive state technology funds.

Maintenance and Service

Maintaining and servicing networked equipment continues to be a challenge for schools' effective use of technology. More states are now requiring that districts and schools have a technology specialist or coordinator who supports teachers in integrating instruction and technology before that district can receive state funding.

Infrastructure

Integrating technology into classrooms has been a major priority of many states. Numerous state competitive grants are based on how school districts will develop a higher level of connectivity in classrooms.

REGIONAL CENTERS AND TECHNOLOGY HUBS

Regional Technology Service Centers, sometimes called technology hubs, have the capability of serving as informational resource centers, information management systems, professional-development centers, procurement centers, and research and evaluation centers, as well as grant-writing centers. Technology service centers can often make the transfer of student records easier, and they can also enhance the opportunity for state agencies and schools to share reports on student achievement, attendance, enrollment, demographics, and budgets.

Distance Learning Programs

Most learning centers should have the capacity to train teachers in how to integrate technology into their classrooms as well as how to evaluate instructional resources. School leaders now agree that training and content knowledge will become more important as faculty and students have regular access to technology. Regional centers will thus act as staff development centers or learning academies that offer courses for teachers on how to have a closer link between technology and the curriculum. Teachers and other educators will be provided with workshops and conferences at the regional center with the expectation that they will return to their districts and share what they have learned with their peers. The National Science Foundation uses regional technology centers as a base of operations for electronic learning.

Through competitive grants, regional technology centers will have the service of allowing administrators and teachers wishing to become more proficient in this area of technology to check out laptop computers. With some initial training, instructors believe that laptops help get educators connected electronically at home as well as at school. They also feel that the laptops help spur educators on to swapping ideas and designing new curricula.

Regional centers also provide distance inservice learning. Technology hubs have the capability of housing sophisticated distance learning classrooms that can serve all schools within a state. Participants using these interactive classrooms will be able to see, hear, and interact with other educators, classes, and presenters within their state as well as around the world. Centers can thus provide a way for high school dropout students to graduate by allowing them to take courses over the Internet.

College classes can also be offered electronically to students and teachers. A full menu of classes, such as foreign language, art, anatomy, and advanced math, can be offered through an interactive television network based at the regional technology center. Using Internet and telecommunications strategies, technology hubs can go a long way to "filling in the holes of school curriculum" when necessary.

Procurement

Districts can apply for state funds, which may include matching grants, to provide school districts with electronic connections for voice, video, and data transmissions. The service centers can also work with state education departments to buy technology equipment for school districts through special lease-purchase agreements. School districts can also use regional technology centers as sites to try out hardware and software products before deciding what to buy. Using regional technology hubs as procurement centers helps eliminate unnecessary duplication and increases buying power for schools.

Research and Evaluation

Regional technology service centers can also act as a hub for educational research and evaluation of technology programs. Many states have a variety of agencies that can provide research and evaluation services, but currently, there is often no coordinated statewide approach. Regional technology hubs, on the other hand, provide a central processing location for the coordination of research and evaluation activities. This is often what is needed to help generate data that are essential to best restructure education throughout the country.

In addition, technology centers have specialists who assist local school leaders in formulating strategies for the planning, implementation, and evaluation of technology. Data from research projects is used to inform administrators and technology planners of what works and what doesn't work. This provides a mechanism through which research results can now be shared with educators on a faster time frame because of the Internet. According to Donald Leu Jr., professor at Syracuse University:

Increasingly, classroom teachers, not researchers, may define the most effective instructional strategies for literacy and learning. Teachers can evaluate instructional effectiveness and quickly spread the word on the Internet faster than researchers who require substantial time before results are published.[3]

Financial Advice on Technology Implementation

Regional centers also prove to be effective in providing financial advice on the implementation of technology into schools. Staff specialists work with state government and school leaders on the best ways to disperse money for technology. They know and understand the best ways to integrate technology into classrooms and work with schools to ensure that grant dollars are being well used. Centers also have the capability of providing training to administrators and technology planners on how to successfully write and receive competitive technology grants.

Technology Cooperatives

One of the best ways to purchase, service, and upgrade school technological infrastructure is through technology cooperatives. School leaders are now realizing the benefits of technology cooperatives. Cooperatives are making schools more efficient in how to buy, what to buy, and where to buy the latest technology.

National organizational leaders are now assisting school leaders in developing technology cooperatives. Such organizations include the American Association of School Administrators (AASA) (www.aasa.org), the National Association of Elementary School Principals (NAESP) (www.naesp.org), the National Association of Secondary School Principals (NASSP) (www.nassp.org), the National Education Association (NEA) (www.nea.org), and the National School Boards Association (NSBA) (www.nsba.org). These organizations also work with state legislators and members of congress to encourage the development of technology cooperatives.

DISTRICT TECHNOLOGY CONFIGURATIONS

Wide Area Networks

Schools continue to build wire and wireless wide-area networks (WANs) that can be accessed by every teacher and every student in the district. Such networks are also being expanded into the homes of parents and into local businesses. Staff can correspond with each other, parents, community members, and others around the world via e-mail. Innovative schools have WANs that provide every classroom with a direct connection to the World Wide Web.

Local Area Networks

School districts are finding the benefits of developing local area networks (LANs) in each of their school buildings. Individual school buildings are now linking LANs to a WAN. As a result, more buildings within a district are able to have access to the Internet in each classroom. School buildings use their computer labs as a central processing point. They develop a LAN by linking their computer labs to one or more computers in each classroom. Other schools simply network all classrooms within the building to a separate, centrally located server. The separate server is used to provide service to all classrooms.

Juneau, Alaska, porvides a good example of how a geographically large school district established a LAN infrastructure. The Juneau school district serves what is probably, geographically, the largest state capital in our nation—at 3,108 square miles—so technology and networking made the greatest sense of all. This district, Juneau Borough School District, stretches 10 miles down the coastline of southeast Alaska and serves about 5,400 students. It had a staff of about 300 when the snapshot was taken. Networking is keeping the school district connected with its local communities as well as the outside world.

Today, Juneau has a fully operating LAN in each of eight campuses, and a WAN linking the district. The citizens of Juneau approved a second technology bond measure to fund a second phase—access to tools and information, providing more workstations per classroom, software, and training. Building the network was the result of a broad technology plan that included restructuring for educational improvement. Diverse people were involved in the planning process that focused on the essential question: What do we want students to be able to do with technology? The answer: Access information whenever they need it, wherever they are located, at any time, from any source. Planning the infrastructure, then, had to relate to this goal, and equipment decisions focused on "Will this piece of equipment provide the access we intend for our students and teachers?"

Local Intranet

Data intranets are becoming commonplace in schools. Intranets give schools an unprecedented ability to manage their budgets, buy supplies, and analyze student data. For example, districts are using the data intranet to delve into student records, test scores, attendance, and health information, to create student profiles.

Laptop Computing

Laptop computers are becoming essential to school personnel and students. School districts are now giving or renting laptops to their students. Programs include giving computers to fifth or sixth graders and then having them buy the laptop for a nominal fee when they graduate.

Other districts are renting handheld computers to students. Students participating in free and reduced-cost lunch programs are able to receive computers free or at a discount.

A key to the success of handheld and laptop computing is making sure that students and parents receive appropriate inservice. Districts are making sure that at least 20% of the budget relating to handheld computers is used for inservice training. The development of wireless computing will increase the use of handheld computers dramatically.

Laptop computers are providing classroom teachers with an added option in word processing. They do not have the capability of larger computers, but students can still use laptop computers to write, edit, spell check, and store limited text. Schools have especially found them to be great ways to have students enhance their keyboarding skills.

Wires, extension cords, or plug-ins are not needed. Laptop computers often come with a security cabinet on wheels that is also an electrical charger. The unit recharges the computers overnight so they can be ready the next morning to use in any classroom. Many units can last three hours or more on a charge. Models also come with wireless printing and data transfer capability. The machines are far less expensive than a regular computer, are durable, and are extremely lightweight. With the machines being less expensive, administrators sometimes purchase whole classroom sets for their schools.

Interactive Television

Telecommunications networks are continuing to connect schools and classrooms to interactive television systems. Interactive television allows teachers to share resources and ideas in a more personal manner.

Web TV is becoming more prominent in schools. Don E. Descy, associate professor at Minnesota State University at Mankato, stated that

Web TV is a unit that contains proprietary software that allows television viewers to use a Web TV Network to browse the web and send email. It is considered by some to be the greatest consumer product or a poorly conceived bit of consumer technology designed to lure a nonexistent audience.[4]

Wireless-Keypad Response Systems

The Great Lakes School in Holland, Michigan, is having success with remote keypad technology. According to librarian Cindy Dobrez,

Wireless keypad response systems use keypads that are remotely connected to software with radio frequency technology. Using this software, users write a list of questions. Respondents enter their answers to these questions into a keypad which is a small remote-controlled-looking device that registers their answers anonymously. This can be used for pre-testing, in-service, mock elections, and for reviewing sensitive questions.[5]

Automated Networked Libraries

Schools continue to use the Library of Congress as an informational source and to share links regarding advances in library technology. Some states are setting examples of what can be done to improve connectivity among local and state schools and university libraries by developing statewide library telecommunications links. Model school libraries are often the electronic distribution points for multimedia applications.

Advanced libraries across America now use district networks, bar coding programs, and phone, modem and Internet access via fiber, satellite, and cable connections. These automated libraries are making checking out books and keeping inventory much simpler for librarians.

Compatibility of Hardware

Maintenance service contracts and access to interchangeable parts make purchasing compatible equipment an important practice. Compatible equipment also makes administrators, staff members, students, and parents more comfortable in using technology because they are not constantly bouncing from one platform to the next.

Upgrading

With technology changing so rapidly, school leaders are learning how to maximize resources. Educators are now finding that older and outdated machines can be easily relegated to other uses. For example, schools are now using outdated equipment to establish keyboarding and writing labs. In addition, old equipment, courseware, and software are being donated to day care facilities and Head Start programs.

MANAGEMENT, SERVICE, AND MAINTENANCE

Technical Director

One of the most important steps to developing a successful technology program is hiring a technical director or coordinator. Technology is becoming too complex and too expensive to leave to untrained teachers and administrators. Networking computers and multimedia tools today is presenting a series of difficult challenges to schools. School leaders need to know what type of equipment to purchase, where to obtain the best buys, how to train teachers to use it, and when it should be upgraded. It is, therefore, important that administrators have access to personnel who have a technology background and understand how to address these problems.

There continues to be a nationwide shortage of information-technology specialists. Large and better-funded districts are often able to lure the best-trained technologists to their schools first. Small and rural districts are however, finding it essential to share the services of a technical coordinator.

More schools are banding together to create technology cooperatives that have greater buying power and can attract top-notch people.

Optimally, it is best if technical directors have experience in the classroom, but it is not a necessity. Under the proper administrative guidance, technical directors will learn how to best consider technical matters in direct relation to the needs of teachers, students, and the curriculum. For example, Box 7.1 highlights the job description of a typical school technology coordinator.

Teacher Technology Coordinators

One of the most common ways that small and rural schools have addressed the problem of maintaining and servicing their computer infrastructure has been to train their own experts. Training a technology coordinator on-site has had mixed results but continues to be a common practice in many small and rural schools. Librarians and teachers are sometimes asked to become half-time technologists. Half-time technologists need to lead technology planning, purchase and assemble equipment, load software, train teachers, and troubleshoot the system as well as doing their jobs as librarians or teachers.

The part-time technology coordinator often becomes the lightening rod of political struggles over technology funding, training, and service. Although some staff members make it through this gauntlet and become full-time technology coordinators, most do not.

Whether the technology coordinator is a part-time teacher/librarian or an outside expert, Craig Nanson from the Minot School District provides additional practical advice (see Box 7.2) on how technology coordinators should cope with their diverse responsibilities.

Student Technology Assistants

Small and rural schools continue to turn to students for technical support. Schools are having success in organizing their middle and high school students into teams to maintain networks and run the school's Internet services. As part of their student career services, districts are also sending teams of students into the elementary schools to help make wiring connections, load software, train teachers and students, manage Internet accounts, and perform routine maintenance and repair functions. Students obtain course credit, and their skills lead to well-paying summer jobs or permanent employment.

Some school leaders, however, are cautious about relying too heavily on students to help maintain the district's technology program. Their concern is valid in that there may be litigation concerns. Whatever the outcome, educators need to make sure that the students helping to maintain technology programs are being supervised and are working under designated guidelines.

Box 7.1. Job Description for Technology Coordinator

Position Title: Technology Coordinator

Type of Authority: Staff

Reports to: Assistant Superintendent

Supervises: Technology Facilitators and Technicians

Basic Function: To assist the Assistant Superintendent and Superintendent to provide leadership in curriculum, instruction, staff development and technology.

Position Responsibilities:

- Develops a long-range plan for the use of present and emerging technology designed to improve the teaching/learning process.
- Coordinates the use of technology by teachers, administrators, support staff and students to enhance the efficiency and effectiveness of programs and services.
- Reviews, evaluates and informs instructional staff of recently developed commercial software including recommendations to integrate same into the curriculum.
- Coordinates the purchase of technology equipment and materials to insure that needs of the district are being met in the most cost effective manner.
- Coordinates the distribution of technology equipment and materials in manner that effectively implements the long-range technology plan.
- Maintains an inventory of technology equipment and materials.
- Provides training for teachers, administrators and support staff to insure the appropriate application of technology.
- Provides consultation for teachers, administrators and support staff to assist with problems and concerns that arise on a daily basis.
- Consults with curriculum committees to insure that technology applications are effectively integrated into all academic and vocational programs.
- Prepares grant proposals designed to secure additional funding for the school district in the area of technology.
- Submits an annual report regarding the effectiveness of the instructional technology program including recommendations for improvement.
- Supervises and coordinates services available through utilization of the VAX mainframe, LAN networks and WAN networks.
- Provides leadership and coordinates the planning and implementation of telecommunication partnership efforts involving neighboring school districts and other organizations and agencies.

(Box 7.1 continued)

> • Assists in developing the budget for purchase of technology hardware and materials.
> • Performs other duties assigned by the Assistant Superintendent or Superintendent of Schools
>
> ---
>
> SOURCE: Craig Nanson (2002).[6]

Work-Tracking System

To best manage and attend to problems on network servers and hubs, schools are using work-tracking systems. Without leaving their offices, technicians can use these types of management systems to address network problems quickly and efficiently. School technical directors and teachers can now receive technical assistance by contacting a company's troubleshooting division 24 hours daily. Company software can analyze the school's network and individual machines electronically and provide solutions on how to correct problems. Troubleshooting a network electronically has vastly improved how schools maintain and service their equipment even though the parent company may be thousands of miles away.

STRATEGIES FOR SUCCESS

The following strategies are effective for implementing a technological infrastructure in schools.

1. **Rule of Three.** The rule of three is one of the most important tips provided in this book: *"Ask three and then me."* Teachers and staff members are required to ask three other staff members before requesting help from the technical director or coordinator. The purpose of the rule is to reduce the burden on the technology staff so that they are not troubleshooting minor problems such as a computer that is not plugged in, a print cartridge that needs changing, or a loose wire. The rule of three reduces time restraints on the technical staff and allows them to be much more productive and helpful to the staff.

2. **Teacher Application of the Rule of Three.** This same rule, *"Ask three and then me,"* also helps teachers save time in the classroom. Teachers simply require students to ask three other classmates to help solve a computer problem before going to the teacher. Students know which students are more proficient on the computer and will usually go to them first. Students knowledgeable about the computer eventually become great troubleshooters for the class.

3. **Teacher System Operators.** Successful school technology leaders train selected staff members to become system operators. At least two grade level teachers (or two teachers in adjacent grade levels within rural schools)

Box 7.2. Collectively Defined Job Description

PART I: Things you want to DO:
(You need to be the one doing these things)

- Develop technology team (visionaries, people onsite, troubleshooters, people you can delegate pieces to)
- Define a technology plan
- Communicate your priorities to others
- Delegate pieces to your technology team
- Act as liaison for implementing technology plan
- Finding champions ("special friends," visionaries, parents, community)
- Staff development (could also be delegated)
- Presentations to staff, PTA, district council, board, etc. (Can also give input or delegate)
- Community/Parent/Staff/District/Board Liaison
- Attend conferences & workshops
- Research & development (could also be delegated)

PART II: Things you want INPUT on:
(You don't have the ultimate responsibility, but you want to be consulted and involved)

- Define technology plan
- Define technology goals
- Prepare budgets
- Develop Acceptable Use Policies
- Develop Scope and Sequence
- Write grants
- Preview equipment & software (could also be delegated)
- Order, install and maintain equipment & software (could also be delegated)

PART III: Things you want to DELEGATE or COORDINATE:
(You are responsible for these things, but other people can do them. This is why you built a team of supporters & champions!)

- Troubleshoot problems
- Take inventory
- Manage network
- Develop and maintain web site
- Provide parent & community classes
- Run a student group

SOURCE: Craig Nanson (2002).[7]

are provided with inservice to become technology troubleshooters. It is crucial that at least two system operators be trained so that if one becomes tired or changes jobs, the other team member can continue providing technical support to the staff.

- A system operator's role is to mentor other teachers having difficulty in implementing the technology initiative. Teachers like to talk to teachers, especially teachers they know and respect. Teachers trained as troubleshooters are often more credible and more accepted into classrooms than technology directors or coordinators. System operators or teacher troubleshooters help provide on-site technology instruction during recesses and breaks, after school, or on weekends. It is easy for them to develop collegial relationships with other teachers in their grade level or at other primary, intermediate, middle, or high school levels.

- Besides developing a collegial relationship and mentoring other staff members in technology, system operators also help save technical directors and coordinators enormous amounts of time. System operators are trained to look for obvious technology problems. Minor problems can occupy much of a technology coordinator's time. With the help of teacher system operators, technical directors and coordinators can address larger and more pressing issues as well as have more time to plan. System operators are generally not paid but are rewarded with the latest upgrades in equipment or are sent to local, state, and national technology conferences. This gives them a sense of pride and accomplishment in that they are improving themselves as well as helping others in their respective school districts.

4.   Internet, Scanner, and Multimedia Applications. School technology leaders are finding that a triad of Internet, scanner, and multimedia presentation applications provides a strong base for teacher and student use of technology. This combination allows teachers and students to more efficiently gather data from local, state, national, and international sources as well as providing them with a way to present their material in a multimedia format. Teachers at intermediate levels are finding that the combination helps teach students how to sequence and outline material for electronic presentations.

5.   Intranet. The intranet is a communication link similar to the Internet but is developed within the district. Networked computers can access current academic standards and tips on teaching strategies and can recommended technologies. School districts are developing intranets to act as multimedia libraries and repositories. Intranets are now connecting classrooms and media centers as well as offices electronically so that students, staff, and administration can find and locate previously stored information and communicate with each other. Such connections can include everything from telephones and e-mail that allows staff to exchange ideas more conveniently to centralized databases.

Some teachers and students are using intranets to store media presentations and electronic research papers as well as lesson plans. For example, a high-quality student report on pyramids could be linked to a set of lesson plans on the Middle East developed by a teacher within the district. Other teachers could use the district intranet to electronically obtain the Middle East lesson plans as well as the student report on pyramids (for information on any relevant intellectual property laws, contact your district office). If used in this manner, the intranet can become a locally developed, districtwide, electronic resource file for teachers and even for students.

When all is said and done, there are three main components to a school technology infrastructure. The following section is derived from information contained on the Computer Strategies, LLC, Web site that is used with permission.[7]

Three Main Parts

Generally, a network is a communications system used to connect two or more users. A computer network connects users of devices such as computers, printers, or application programs so they can share information. The largest of these networks is, of course, the World Wide Web—the network of networks. In the simplest sense, every computer network consists of three parts:

1. **Clients:** the user workstations and peripherals

2. **Infrastructure:** the wires, fiber optics, or transmission media that the data moves through

3. **Networking electronics:** devices that move, route, and store data for users

A network with 5,000 users might have thousands of components, but each would be one of the types described above. The simplest networks are called *peer-to-peer* networks. In these networks, each client has its own storage area, which might be shared with other clients. There is no central storage in this type of network. Peer-to-peer networks are often used in small classroom computer labs.

The most common are *client-server* networks. These networks have storage devices on the network that may hold data for users to share. The term *file server* is used in reference to these storage devices. A client may use the network to connect to one of these storage devices and get some documents to view or edit.

Computer networks come in all sizes. They are usually referred to by their size and scope. LAN has become almost synonymous with the word network. A LAN is a network in which all clients share a common infrastructure (wires) and are usually in the same building or group of buildings. In contrast, a WAN is one that spans a larger geographic area. For instance, a network that links two or more LANs that are separated by some distance might be called a WAN (see Figure 7.1).

Figure 7.1 LAN and WAN

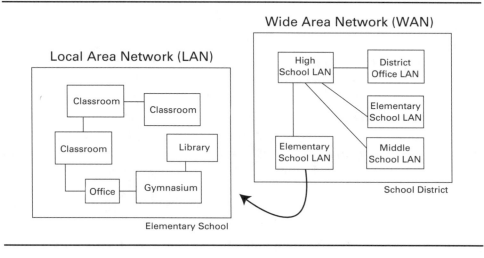

Elementary School

A really big network made up of several diverse LANs and WANs is often called an *internet*. The largest group of interconnected networks in the world is the global network known as the Internet. Increasingly, large groups of networks are interconnected within an organization. As explained above, this type of network has come to be called an *intranet*.

Intranets have become enormously popular because they often rely on the same standard software packages that most of us use for the Internet. For example, using a standard World Wide Web browser, teachers in a large district might navigate their own district's intranet to find class schedule information or a message board for sharing curriculum ideas. Such intranets may look and feel just like the Internet, but access to them is often limited to users within an organization.

Based on this information, a technology coordinator could call up a networking vendor and say, "We are looking to build a district WAN made up of 14 LANs. We estimate about 1,200 clients eventually, and, of course, we want to link our WAN into the Internet." That should get their attention!

Networking Costs

Building and operating a network costs money. Generally, costs are determined by a number of factors; among them are these:

How many users will there be?

Over what distance will the users be spread?

At what speed of communication will the network run?

How complex or simple will the network be?

What type of client services are needed?

How well designed is the network?

It is logical that a network connecting 20 students in a single classroom computer lab will be cheaper than a network that connects 300 teachers across large districts. But some of the other cost factors are not as obvious. For instance, a network in which every user has the same type of computer will be cheaper to build and operate than one in which there are several different types of computers.

The type of services needed is another good example. A network where everyone needs only e-mail will be much cheaper than one where everyone needs live video conferencing. Accordingly, in the planning process, it is really important to separate the need-to-have services from the nice-to-have services. Remember that you will be networked for a long time; there will be plenty of time to add those bells and whistles.

Networking cost analysis should also take into account ongoing support costs. Many network planners use the rule that one full-time support person will be required for every 50 to 75 users. In schools, students and teachers are often involved in the network support. Using certified staff for day-to-day technical support may not be appropriate or practical in many situations. Remember, managing a school network can be a full-time job. What happens when the network goes down and the teacher-network manager is teaching a chemistry class? If the choice is to use student or teacher time, it is important to be realistic about the time demands that will be created by your network-support needs.

Other ongoing costs are related to maintenance and upgrades for the network. In a successful situation, demands for network services will increase steadily, and so will monitoring and maintenance costs. The phenomenal rate of change in the world of technology also requires that school administrators plan for costs due to growth, improvements, and upgrades. With each major change or improvement, there will be costs related to training, both for network users and the network support staff.

Infrastructure Costs

When looking at typical costs for network components, the small percentage spent on infrastructure can be surprising (see Table 7.1).

Table 7.1 Relative Costs for Network Components

Software	53%
Hardware	35%
Networking electronics	7%

SOURCE: Computer Strategies, LLC. (2002). Oakland, California. Used with permission.[8]

Notice, too, that while infrastructure accounts for very little of the overall network cost; it also tends to last longer than the other networking components.

COMPONENT TYPICAL LIFE SPAN

Client stations (PC, Apple): 18-36 months

Network electronics (hubs, routers): 3-5 years

Infrastructure (wires, racks, wiring closets): 10-20 years

Because infrastructure is relatively inexpensive and long-lasting, the obvious conclusion is to build the best infrastructure that is possible. Unfortunately, in practice, many networks are built on poor infrastructure, usually because the network was not planned for growth or costs were cut in the wrong places. For example, when a less-expensive and lower-rated wire is selected, it may not accommodate higher transmission speeds when you want to upgrade. Another common infrastructure mistake is to reduce costs by limiting the number of data ports (or drops) per classroom below the recommended four to six. Most network professionals say that the bulk of the problems a network could encounter come from a poor infrastructure. Think of network infrastructure as you would the foundation of a house. If you were to build a poor foundation under a house, wouldn't that house have problems? It does not matter how well built the house is above ground if the foundation is not solid.

A final note concerns the use of volunteers and students to install network infrastructure. The schools that have done this successfully have used the services of experts to train, oversee, or test the installations. In other words, make expert advice available to get the job done properly.

Building a good, well-planned infrastructure is just one of the many tasks ahead, but it illustrates something that is true of the whole network infrastructure implementation process: planning pays off! A well-planned network will be

More reliable: less downtime

Lower in cost: less expensive to support, expand, and use

More flexible: based on standards, easy to expand, uses parts from many vendors

Simple to support and use

The alternative to good planning is building a network ad hoc. Some people mistakenly assume that eliminating a planning process can save money. They prefer to spend their budgets right away on new hardware and software. The next time there is money in the budget, they run to buy more equipment. This strategy may work for the smallest of systems, but on larger networks, ad hoc networking ends up being expensive, hard to support, and very complex for users.

FUTURE CHALLENGES

Schools and libraries of the future will continue to encourage teachers and students to best use local, state, national, and global informational resources. Schools of the future will not only be considered processors of knowledge; they will also become connectors of knowledge. School leaders will be providing students and teachers with portable technology that will allow them to travel electronically around the world faster than ever before. Wireless portable technology will provide a very high level of connectivity for everyone. New innovations will provide resources, arrangements, and lifelong learning experiences for the full development of all individuals and their communities. New creative designs will provide self-directed, other-directed, individually supported group learning, team building, and societal connections for our world and its people. In sum, educational technology will unfold in a way that nurtures learning and fosters communication among all members of the global community.

REFLECTIVE ACTIVITIES

1.   List the infrastructure barriers that you have experienced in your school as you have tried to implement a technology program.

2.   State your opinions regarding networked classroom technology centers.

3.   Outline the administrative structure for technology that exists in your school, district, and state. Consider wiring and hardware structure.

4.   If you were to work on establishing a regional center and technology hub, describe the resources you have available to accomplish this.

5.   Based on the information about connectivity in this chapter, evaluate where your technology program would rate. Explain your school's perceived need to change this level.

6.   Detail what your school is doing to maximize the interchangeability, adaptation, and use of its technology resources. Identify the infrastructure that exists for the management, maintenance, and service of the computer technology in your school.

8

Program Evaluation

THE FINAL PIECE IN THE PUZZLE

Innovative schools are using technology to make assessment and evaluation an integral part of the instructional design and development process. Built into this technology initiative are procedures for school leaders to monitor and evaluate the direction and implementation of the plan. When appropriate technology is used to facilitate teaching and learning, it becomes an established part of your school. The development of a statewide electronic communication network infrastructure will help assist school leaders in best using and sharing information gained through meaningful program evaluation.

Challenges to Program Evaluation

The single biggest barrier to widespread school technology implementation continues to be basic awareness of the measurable benefits. Unprecedented support for school technology is spurring an investment of billions of dollars, but the lack of research and quality measurement has led to unclear results. The key issue is establishing more effective and accurate ways in which we can measure the real benefits of educational technology and measure the true associated costs in money and time spent learning to use these technologies. Sociological acceptance and adoption of the use of these new communications technologies continues to represent a challenge as well.

Another concern is the lack of leadership in establishing strong evaluation and assessment agendas and programs. There is a special need for leadership and more understanding as to the process of evaluation and how it relates to technology development in schools. Quality leadership is a key component to the success of any educational technology implementation process. One of the most important aspects of that leadership role is that educational planners understand the process of evaluation and how it should be administered.

The rapid changes occurring in computer technology also pose a challenge to establishing effective evaluation programs. Technology capabilities have continued to change faster than educational researchers can keep up. For example, initial evidence on the use of computers in the classroom showed that drill and practice activities were successful in reinforcing skills. Now, with continued advances in software and technology, teachers are using computers in classrooms in entirely different ways. Subsequently, it has been difficult for researchers to complete large-scale, controlled studies that lead to solid conclusions because by the time their research is published, new technologies are providing new opportunities for teachers and students.

A lack of technology standards and guidelines is another barrier to providing quality assessment. Currently, only a few districts in the country have established guidelines for evaluating the effectiveness of technology in their schools (see Table 8.1).[1]

Table 8.1 Regional Data on State Technological Evaluation Requirements

Northeast Region	Connecticut	Maine	Massachusetts	N. Hampshire	New Jersey	New York
State collects technology data	✔	✔	✔	✔	✔	✔
State standards include tech.	✔	✔		✔	✔	✔
Tech. standards are tested						
	Pennsylvania	Rhode Island	Vermont			
State collects technology data			✔			
State standards include tech.	✔	✔	✔			
Tech. standards are tested	✔					
Midwest Region	Illinois	Indiana	Iowa	Kansas	Michigan	Minnesota
State collects technology data	✔	✔	✔	✔		
State standards include tech.	✔	✔			✔	✔
Tech. standards are tested						
	Missouri	Nebraska	N. Dakota	Ohio	S. Dakota	Wisconsin
State collects technology data	✔	✔	✔	✔	✔	✔
State standards include tech.	✔		✔			✔
Tech. standards are tested						
South Region	Alabama	Arkansas	Delaware	Florida	Georgia	Kentucky
State collects technology data	✔	✔	✔	✔	✔	✔
State standards include tech.		✔	✔	✔		
Tech. standards are tested				✔		
	Louisiana	Maryland	Mississippi	North Carolina	Oklahoma	S. Carolina
State collects technology data	✔	✔	✔	✔	✔	✔
State standards include tech.	✔	✔	✔	✔	✔	✔
Tech. standards are tested				✔		
	Tennessee	Texas	Virginia	W. Virginia		
State collects technology data	✔	✔	✔	✔		
State standards include tech.	✔	✔	✔	✔		
Tech. standards are tested			✔			
West Region	Alaska	Arizona	California	Colorado	Hawaii	Idaho
State collects technology data		✔	✔		✔	✔
State standards include tech.	✔	✔			✔	
Tech. standards are tested						
	Montana	Nevada	New Mexico	Oregon	Utah	Washington
State collects technology data	✔	✔	✔	✔		✔
State standards include tech.	✔	✔	✔	✔	✔	
Tech. standards are tested						
	Wyoming					
State collects technology data	✔					
State standards include tech.	✔					
Tech. standards are tested						

Strong evidence of technology's effectiveness will surely further and strengthen public and political support. Richard Mayer, Professor of Psychology at the University of California, Santa Barbara, stated,

> Our research provides encouraging evidence that appropriate experience with educational technology can promote important cognitive changes in children, including improvements in content knowledge about computing, strategies for comprehending written instruction, strategies for devising problem-solving plans and even in basic academic skills."[2]

As the demand for innovative technology designs in the classroom increases, the need for evaluation also increases. Administrators, teachers, and parents want to know and understand the impact that technology has made on district goals relating to student learning, staff development, and curricular content.

Focusing on Student Performance

Thomas Guskey believes that technology and assessment should be important factors in assessing student performance. He stated that "if a performance-based assessment program is to evoke more stimulating, intellectually challenging tasks for students, extensive professional development opportunities for teachers will need to accompany the assessment program."[3] It is essential that the direction for the technology initiative remain focused on student performance. The key behind this program is to create a more symbiotic relationship between technology and the curriculum. In doing so, correlations between student performance and the use of technology in the classrooms will become more evident. Thus appropriate mechanisms and administrative structures will need to be made so that student performance can be measured and assessed in relevant ways. The key here is that we want teachers, students, administrators, and the external community to see that technology is having a positive effect on student achievement and that students are performing better because of the technological changes enacted within your school.

Data Collection

Data collection is a key to finding out how technology is being used to impact teaching and learning. A number of national marketing companies are collecting data on technology use. These commercial marketing firms collect information on school technology and sell that information to technology manufacturers. They conduct mail and telephone surveys of schools throughout the nation, determining what type of high-tech equipment is being used and how it is being used. Results are supplemented by information from departments of education and other surveys. State and school leaders, upon request, may obtain this information after a certain amount of time.

State and school leaders do have to be careful in placing too much emphasis on data collected by marketing companies. One of the weaknesses of this data is that it is usually based on small-sample populations. This can generate misleading statistics that favor the direction of the company sponsoring the survey. Another problem is that district administrators do not always take surveys seriously or rush through them without real consideration. As a result, some states are collecting their own data because they feel that schools take government surveys more seriously and the results will be more accurate. In addition, these surveys have an educational and student achievement focus on technology and are less likely to have a hidden technological agenda like that found in market research. This data is also public property and can be shared more easily among districts and states for comparison studies.

There continues to be a move nationally to gather technology data for research. Federal and state officials are, at times, having schools submit a list of inventory of technology as a requirement for grant applications. According to Don Feuerstein of the U.S. Department of Education, "Data collected from these applications can be used to generate a national database."[4] Information obtained from these databases helps in the study of course content, software development, Internet use, academic standards, and curricula. The benefit to administrators is that they can use the information to help in the evaluation of their technology plan. A partial list of technology databases include information on:

- Access time to national and international networks
- Student time spent on computers
- Teacher time spent on computers
- Number of computers in classrooms
- Number of technology and computer labs
- Student and teacher time using satellite and cable informational resources

These are all areas that can be tapped for information that school leaders can use to revise and update their technology programs.[5]

Leadership

Quality leadership is a key component in the success of any educational evaluation process. One of the most important aspects of that leadership role is for educational planners to understand the process of evaluation and how it should be administered. Educational planners can contribute to the process by understanding the evaluation process and how it relates to program development. Understanding the evaluation process means leaders will have to convey knowledge of technology as well as instructional strategies. They will also have to convey their expectations of how technology can be used throughout the curriculum.

Technology Plan Assessment

An assessment of the technology plan should reveal the quality of change that occurred during the actual implementation process. Assessment indicators need to reveal the quality of change rather than just a snapshot of current conditions. The evaluation process should help determine if the school's vision of technology truly reflects a focus on student learning. School leaders must examine and review the technology plan to make sure that it encourages teachers to use current research and academic development practices in their classrooms. The following questions can provide direction during a review of a technology plan:

Does the technology plan address the meaningful involvement of community members, parents, and other stakeholders who have shown an interest in developing and promoting informational technology?

Should the technology plan be changed to increase community involvement?

Does the technology plan facilitate instruction?

Do action steps in the plan reflect the alignment of up-to-date technological practices with student-learning patterns?

How effective is the technology plan in accounting for student performance?

Are objectives for student performance responsive to the learning needs of students?

Are student achievement goals being met?

In sum, an evaluation of the technology plan should reveal a dynamic perspective of growth in the area of technology use.

Staff Development and Evaluation

Often a strong association exists between effective leadership and the evaluation of staff development programs. Effective staff development programs can be evaluated and analyzed by using indicators of success developed early in the project. Objectives of the professional development program should be consistent with the school's vision and designed to advance the school's goals for student learning in technology.[6] Indicators of staff development success can be measured through the staff's ability to

- Understand the school vision and goals as shown by surveys and documents prepared by staff
- Participate in technology workshops and conferences
- Operate a computer system, connect peripherals, and use software effectively to complete tasks, locate information, and manage data
- Demonstrate ability for data collection and multimedia presentations

- Demonstrate an ability to use telecommunications, online networks, and CD-ROMs to foster learning
- Identify sources of technology support and service
- Model the use of technology as a teaching tool and as a support to instruction
- Explain equity and legal issues involving the use of technology
- Evaluate and assess student performance

ASSESSING TEACHING AND LEARNING

Integration of Curriculum

Determining how technology enhances the integration of curriculum as well as curriculum content is a way to measure the effectiveness of technology. Development of an integrated curriculum is based on expectations for student learning achievement. The formulation of learning objectives is an important component in assessing student growth via the use of technology. The design of the curriculum should provide students with the essential knowledge and skills in information technology that can be applied across the curriculum. Students can use their school's technology network to access the library or the Internet as a way of finding information that relates to different curricular areas.

Classroom Technology Environment

The importance of organizational climate for school success is well known. The classroom must be designed technologically to foster active involvement of students in the learning process. Lessons should be based on high expectations and an application of higher-order thinking skills whenever applicable. The pace of learning should take into account learning styles of children and stages of growth and development. Application of instruction should be based on individual needs of the students and allow them to explore and investigate new forms of informational technology.

The amount of student writing, as well as the completion rate of projects, can be used to measure positive changes. One 10-year study revealed that students using technology were writing more and finishing units of study more quickly. Students using informational technology were becoming independent learners and self-starters, working cooperatively, expressing positive attitudes toward the future, sharing their expertise spontaneously, and representing information in a variety of forms.[7]

Other studies suggest that student attendance rates have gone up in classrooms using technology. Students participating in interactive technology seem to want to come to school. Attendance rates can easily be cross-correlated with classrooms using interactive technology to give administrators a feel as to whether technology may be having an effect on attendance.

Another indicator of technology success in the classroom is teacher and parent support. Teacher and parent support of technology can be monitored via questionnaires or opinionnaire surveys as well as by the collection of positive correspondence. In addition, minutes from board of trustee meetings can provide documentation of positive feelings toward technology and thus reflect possible organizational climate changes.

Student Outcomes

Documenting the effectiveness of improvements made in electronic applications is a way of assessing the impact of technology in schools. Student learning outcomes can include measures of how well students learn, think, reason, and solve complex problems through the use of computers in the classroom. Program attendance, graduation rates, standardized testing, teacher-made pre- and post-tests, observation, portfolios, grades, and the degree of student participation can provide indications of program success.

Teacher and student use of technology can be documented easily by logging the number of times an individual uses the Internet and e-mail. A log of all Internet queries and messages sent and received can be noted on the computer log. This data can be graphed and shared with the community to show how technology is being used in classrooms.

Equity Issues

Monitoring equity issues as they relate to technology planning and implementation is a key to reforming education. Andrew Lantham of the Educational Testing Service stated that "technology can help reduce performance gaps among subgroups of students. Technology has the potential to decrease opportunity gaps by granting students from different backgrounds equal access to a wealth of information on the Internet."[8] On the other hand, an equity problem can arise due to a lack of technology. Schools in urban areas often have an advantage over rural schools in accessing technology. Thousands of rural schools across the country do not have access to fiber optics and thus find it difficult to access the Internet. Hopefully, more research and an improvement on bandwidth restrictions should resolve this problem. Improved satellite technology and reduced costs for satellite transmission should help as well.

Measuring Connectivity

Measuring student access and maintaining equity is of paramount importance to school leaders. Many states are concerned that school computers are not being used and that technology is not cost-effective. According to Jackie Shrago, the project director of ConnecTEN (the name of the organization, ConnecTEN, is an initiative that is part of Tennessee's 21st Century Classrooms project), "If access is only a couple of minutes per week per child, it's not any different than a single textbook in a classroom."[9] School leaders are now becoming more interested in how computers are being used rather than just in noting the number of computers in schools. Researchers are finding that teacher and student use of computers can be measured by a connectivity rate.

A school's connectivity rate is formulated by calculating the number of minutes students use the school's computers divided by the number of computers in the school. This can be tracked daily and averaged at the end of the month. A school's connectivity rate can be one of the major factors when allocating technology funding or competitive grants. For example, Tennessee uses the connectivity rate to maximize computer use in schools.

Accreditation Standards

States are attempting to link technology funding with standards for student performance. To avoid developing paste-in technology approaches, schools are realigning their curricula and technology around student performance standards. Program evaluation for schools using technology is becoming centered on meeting student performance benchmarks. In an attempt to avoid prepackaged technology approaches, schools are realigning their curricula and technology around student performance standards. Program evaluation for schools using technology is becoming centered on meeting student performance benchmarks.

Student Performance Assessment

Technology grant applications in some states are now requiring schools to include student performance objectives and assessments in proposals. As a result, school leaders are continuing to search for the best ways to incorporate assessment packages in grant applications.

Integrated Learning System Assessments

A popular way to develop a database of student achievement is through the use of integrated learning systems. Integrated learning systems (ILS) are computer based and allow students to proceed at their individual challenge level.[10] These software systems also have a teacher management component that provides diagnosis, adjustment, and evaluation features. The courseware packages often have a student performance assessment component built into the program. Information collected from these databases can then be used as part of a larger program evaluation process.

Program Guidelines

Technology is ever changing, and so the best of technology plans must change as well. Due to the scope of most technology plans, it is critical that the evaluation process be viewed as ongoing. Statewide educational agencies should review and evaluate technology in their states at a minimum of every three years. Such evaluations should be coordinated with appropriate resource centers, schools, and other agencies. This type of review process helps to identify standards and interconnection issues that should be evaluated and addressed. It will also identify the success stories and research that is needed to validate the cost and implementation of technology.

Guidelines for program evaluation are listed below:

- Indicators of success for the technology program should be developed at the onset of the project.
- Indicators of success should relate to the original vision of the project as well as to the mission statement.
- An evaluation component for staff development should be a major component of the technology plan.
- A feedback process for information should be incorporated in the evaluation plan.
- Clear indicators of success expressed in terms of student outcomes should drive improvement efforts.
- Assessment should derive from multiple sources of data, both quantitative and qualitative.

EVALUATION CHECKLIST

Evaluation checklists are helpful to educational planners trying to gauge the success of their classroom technology program. The checklist below is easy to administer and provides a quick assessment of program components.

Does the program provide evidence of administrative and school board support?

Does the plan incorporate a technology mission statement?

Does the plan establish a technology task force or advisory committee?

Does the technology plan facilitate community school-business partnerships?

Does the technology program provide for a public relations plan?

Does the technology program allow for research development?

Does the technology plan use student learner outcomes as a measure?

Does the plan have an evaluation tool that provides for the collection of qualitative data?

Evaluation tools such as the checklist do not have to be complicated. These instruments help determine if key components are present in the classroom computer program.

STRATEGIES FOR SUCCESS

Successful school administrators use the following strategies in developing assessment and evaluation programs relating to school technology.

Setting Goals and Indicators. The evaluation and assessment process must be linked to the original mission statement and objectives of the district. Indicators of successful technology integration for the purposes of evaluation should be established during the early planning stages of the program.

Identifying Target Populations. Successful evaluation and assessment procedures should focus on targeting specific external and internal population groups. Parents and community-related organizations and businesses represent external groups. Trustees, administrators, teachers, and students represent internal target groups. Data collection needs to specifically focus on these target areas and how they relate to technology integration.

Evaluation Centers. The National Study of School Evaluation located in Schaumburg, Illinois, provides a wealth of information on technology evaluation and assessment. *Technology: Indicators of Quality Information Technology Systems in K-12 Schools* by Fitzpatrick and Pershing is considered one of the nation's best publications on assessment and evaluation.[11]

Regional Technology Training Centers. The Northwest Regional Educational Laboratory (retrieved May 15, 2002, from www.nwrel.org/) and other regional technology centers across the United States provide a plethora of information on best practices involving assessment and evaluation. They also provide conferences and workshops on evaluation strategies.

Regardless of the process used to evaluate a program, planners need to be willing to use data and to make changes and adjustments where necessary. They must understand that curriculum improvement and instructional improvement are interconnected and that a change in one area will probably elicit a change in another area. Problems and concerns can cloud issues at hand, making evaluation an important tool. With higher quality and more detailed information at our disposal, school leaders will be able to focus more on how technology can help teachers with student achievement in the future.

FUTURE CHALLENGES

Once people know, firsthand, and are able to measure the benefits of advanced technology applications, public support for funding will become viable. Indicators of success used to measure the impact of technology in schools are noted in Chapter 1. It is hoped that future research will be based on these indicators to give educational planners a more complete picture as to the impact of technology on teaching and learning in our nation's classrooms. A key to the success of any technology program in the future is the ability of school leaders to develop awareness and understanding through the implementation of an effective evaluation program. Throughout the entire evaluation process, the focus for administrators should be on combining appropriate technology with measurable results indicating positive correlations between teaching and learning.

REFLECTIVE ACTIVITIES

1. List the current practices and procedures your school has for evaluating technology. Consider elements such as administrative structures, staff, and lines of communication.

2. Describe the current methods that your school uses for collecting data about technology and student achievement. List the internal and external sources.

3. Evaluate your current technology assessment procedures and then consider alternative approaches for your school.

4. Determine the degree to which your school's technology program is linked to student achievement.

Resource A

Individual Teacher and Administrator Technology Profiles

FORM A.1. TEACHER TECHNOLOGY PROFILE

1. **I have been employed as an educator for the following number of years:** *(circle one)*

   1-5   6-10   11-20   21+

2. **I have actively used technology in my classroom for the following number of years:** *(circle one)*

   1-5   6-10   11-20   21+

3. **I have used technology at home or school for the following number of years:** *(circle one)*

   1-5   6-10   11-20   21+

4. **Per average week, I use the following software for _____ hours:**
   (circle one for each item)

(a)	Word processing	0	1-5	6-15	16+
(b)	Spreadsheet	0	1-5	6-15	16+
(c)	Multimedia	0	1-5	6-15	16+
(d)	Database	0	1-5	6-15	16+
(e)	Internet	0	1-5	6-15	16+
(f)	Simulations	0	1-5	6-15	16+
(g)	Reference software	0	1-5	6-15	16+
(h)	Drill and practice	0	1-5	6-15	16+
(i)	Games	0	1-5	6-15	16+
(j)	Drawing	0	1-5	6-15	16+
(k)	Desktop publishing	0	1-5	6-15	16+
(l)	Photo editing	0	1-5	6-15	16+
(m)	E-mail	0	1-5	6-15	16+

5. **My comfort level with each of the following technology activities is:**
    (circle one)

    (a) Communicating with other teachers in the district using the GroupWise E-mail system
    Not comfortable 1   2   3   4   5   Very comfortable

    (b) Communicating with other professionals outside of the district via Internet/E-mail
    Not comfortable 1   2   3   4   5   Very comfortable

    (c) Sharing technology projects with other teachers (such as lesson plans, multimedia presentations and web-based activities)
    Not comfortable 1   2   3   4   5   Very comfortable

    (d) Creating multimedia presentations for my classes
    Not comfortable 1   2   3   4   5   Very comfortable

    (e) Publishing materials on the Internet that I have created
    Not comfortable 1   2   3   4   5   Very comfortable

    (f) Using scanners and digital cameras to create materials for my classes
    Not comfortable 1   2   3   4   5   Very comfortable

    (g) Participating in listservs, news groups, and user groups on the Internet
    Not comfortable 1   2   3   4   5   Very comfortable

    (h) Conducting online searches
    Not comfortable 1   2   3   4   5   Very comfortable

    (i) Using SASI/xp for student information
    Not comfortable 1   2   3   4   5   Very comfortable

    (j) Having students use technology to create projects
    Not comfortable 1   2   3   4   5   Very comfortable

6. **The presence of technology in the classroom and at home has helped me make the following changes:** *(circle one in each category)*

    (a) Students spend more time working in groups
    Minimum or no change   Noticeable change   Significant change

    (b) I use technology to prepare materials (hand-outs and tests) for my students
    Minimum or no change   Noticeable change   Significant change

    (c) I spend more time coaching/advising students
    Minimum or no change   Noticeable change   Significant change

    (d) I use technology to help integrate standards into my curriculum
    Minimum or no change   Noticeable change   Significant change

    (e) I work more with other teachers in the development of lesson plans
    Minimum or no change   Noticeable change   Significant change

    (f) I let students decide how to use technologies in their projects
    Minimum or no change   Noticeable change   Significant change

    (g) I let students decide which technologies to use in their projects
    Minimum or no change   Noticeable change   Significant change

    (h) I use technology to keep students informed of their progress in the class
    Minimum or no change   Noticeable change   Significant change

(i) I evaluate electronic versions of student work
Minimum or no change   Noticeable change   Significant change

(j) I involve students in the development of learning activities using technology
Minimum or no change   Noticeable change   Significant change

(k) I integrate a greater variety of subjects/content into each of my lessons
Minimum or no change   Noticeable change   Significant change

(l) I use more class time for students to work on projects
Minimum or no change   Noticeable change   Significant change

7. **When I use technology in the classroom it is . . .** *(circle one)*

Organized   Chaotic but rewarding   Chaotic and frustrating

8. **I would classify myself as the following type of technology user:** *(Check the one level that best describes your use of technology in your teaching)*

Entry: Teachers who are just starting to use technology for learning

---

Adoption: Teachers who have some comfort level with technology and are taking initial steps to use it in their curriculum

---

Adaptation: Teachers who are shifting toward more student-based project learning and encourage the use of a variety of technology tools

---

Appropriation: Teachers who are so comfortable with technology that it is integrated throughout all learning activities

---

Transformation: Teachers who create new ways to use technology tools for real-world applications

---

9. **I would like to increase my use of technology in the following ways that I can't right now:** *(Check all that apply)*

_____ Create documents with word processing or data bases
_____ Increase communication with colleagues throughout the country
_____ Use e-mail to communicate with other teachers and staff members within the school
_____ Conduct research via the Internet
_____ Create multimedia presentations for the class
_____ Design collaborative projects for my students
_____ Improve classroom record keeping
_____ Design more curriculum that integrates technology
_____ Individualize instruction for students
_____ Let the students use a variety of technology resources to design their own projects
_____ Create more units that integrate multiple content areas

_____ Provide more authentic, real-world activities
_____ Communicate with parents
_____ Change the learning environment
_____ Conduct on-line interviews with content-area experts

10. **How accessible is the computer lab for your classes?** *(circle the most appropriate response)*

Never   Once a week   2-3 times a week   4 times a week   Always

11. **Please respond to the following statements about technology plans.**

(a) I am aware of the content of the building technology plans
Yes   No

(b) I am aware of the content of the district technology plan
Yes   No

(c) I know we have technology plans, but I don't ever refer to them
Yes   No

(d) They help define how I use technology in my classroom
Yes   No

(e) They provide guidelines for the purchase of hardware and software
Yes   No

(f) They establish standards for the use of technology in the classroom
Yes   No

(g) They helped establish the integration of technology in curriculum planning
Yes   No

(h) Because of the way they are designed, it is difficult to implement parts of the plans
Yes   No

(i) I am expected to teach established student technology skills and standards that have been mandated by the district or school
Yes   No

12. **When I need technology help, I go to:**

(a) A building tech person
not at all   sometimes   most of the time

(b) Other teachers in my content area or grade level
not at all   sometimes   most of the time

(c) A media specialist
not at all   sometimes   most of the time

(d) Administration (principal, assistant principal)
not at all   sometimes   most of the time

(e) District technology person
not at all   sometimes   most of the time

(f) Student technology support team
not at all   sometimes   most of the time

(g) Students in my class
not at all   sometimes   most of the time

13. **When I want to obtain a piece of equipment or software that is not currently available, I use the following procedure:** *(Check the one procedure that you use most often)*

    _____ I ask my administrator and if the money is available, it is purchased

    _____ I have to put it in the budget for the following year and wait until then to get it

    _____ I purchase it myself and the school reimburses me

    _____ I can request it through several channels including the district, the PTO, or businesses

    _____ I request it through my administrator and she/he will look for resources to purchase it

    _____ Other:

14. **Do the administrators in your building:** *(Check one)*

    _____ Encourage the use of technology

    _____ Remain neutral about the use of technology

    _____ Show frustration about the use of technology

    _____ Seem uncertain about technology

15. **I have learned to use technology through the following methods:** *(circle one for each method)*

    (a) Self-taught by experimenting with the equipment or software
    Not a useful method for me   Supplemental method   Predominant method
    (b) Through district in-service programs
    Not a useful method for me   Supplemental method   Predominant method
    (c) By reading manuals
    Not a useful method for me   Supplemental method   Predominant method
    (d) By attending vendors' workshops
    Not a useful method for me   Supplemental method   Predominant method
    (e) By attending conferences
    Not a useful method for me   Supplemental method   Predominant method
    (f) In higher education course
    Not a useful method for me   Supplemental method   Predominant method
    (g) With assistance from peers/acquaintances
    Not a useful method for me   Supplemental method   Predominant method
    (h) Through visits to other schools
    Not a useful method for me   Supplemental method   Predominant method

16. **In the past I have had professional development in technology via:** *(check the appropriate choice)*

    _____ Graduate credit

    _____ Content-area conferences that included technology

    _____ Technology conferences

    _____ District inservices

    _____ Vendor workshops

17. I would like to have more training in: (*Check* all *appropriate responses*)

_____ Basic computer skills (e.g., accessing programs, printing documents)

_____ How to use E-mail (e.g., writing, sending, receiving, storing messages, adding attachments)

_____ How to use the Internet (e.g., searches, downloading data, creating and managing Favorites)

_____ Specific software programs (e.g., *Kid Pix, Inspiration,* etc.)

_____ Software evaluation (e.g., picking the best program for my classroom needs)

_____ Technology planning (e.g., how to develop and implement a plan)

_____ Technology leadership (e.g., becoming comfortable with decisions related to technology use)

_____ Integrating technology into the curriculum (e.g., when and how to use technology)

_____ Using technology to teach to various learning styles (e.g., visual, auditory, kinesthetic)

_____ Using technology productivity tools (e.g., SASI/xp, grade books, word processing)

_____ Classroom technology management (e.g., managing technology resources in the classroom)

_____ Using technology for assessment (e.g., ABACUS, STAR)

18. In my classroom, I have the following technology hardware:

(a) type of computers: (*circle the number of machines in your classroom in each category*)

Windows laptops	1	2-5	6-12	13+
Windows desktops without CD-ROM	1	2-5	6-12	13+
Windows desktops with CD-ROM	1	2-5	6-12	13+
Windows AV (with video in/ out capability)	1	2-5	6-12	13+
Macintosh laptops	1	2-5	6-12	13+
Macintosh desktops without CD-ROM	1	2-5	6-12	13+
Macintosh desktops with CD-ROM	1	2-5	6-12	13+
Macintosh AV (with video in/ out capability)	1	2-5	6-12	13+
(b) No. of scanners	1	2-5	6-12	13+
(c) No. of printers	1	2-5	6-12	13+
(d) No. of portable keyboards (like Alpha Smart)	1	2-5	6-12	13+
(e) No. of programmable calculators	1	2-5	6-12	13+
(f) No. of computers connected to school network	1	2-5	6-12	13+
(g) No. of computers with access to Internet	1	2-5	6-12	13+
(h) No. of digital still-shot cameras	1	2-5	6-12	13+
(i) No. of video cameras	1	2-5	6-12	13+

19. **Do you use the video distribution system in your building?**

    Yes   *No*

20. **I am most comfortable using:** *(select one answer)*

    _____ Macintosh computers
    _____ Windows (PC) computers
    _____ Equally comfortable with both
    _____ I don't feel comfortable with either one

21. **Per grading period, I make assignments in which I expect my students to use technology in the classroom or at home:** *(circle the average number of assignments per grading period)*

(a)	Word processing	0	1	2	3	4+
(b)	Spreadsheet	0	1	2	3	4+
(c)	Multimedia	0	1	2	3	4+
(d)	Database	0	1	2	3	4+
(e)	Internet	0	1	2	3	4+
(f)	Simulations	0	1	2	3	4+
(g)	Reference software	0	1	2	3	4+
(h)	Drill and practice	0	1	2	3	4+
(i)	Games	0	1	2	3	4+
(j)	Drawing	0	1	2	3	4+
(k)	Desktop publishing	0	1	2	3	4+
(l)	Photo editing	0	1	2	3	4+
(m)	E-mail	0	1	2	3	4+

22. **Per grading period, I use technology for the following activities:**

    (a) My students keep a journal with word processing
        Never   Seldom   Occasionally   Often
    (b) My students share projects with students in other locations via Internet
        Never   Seldom   Occasionally   Often
    (c) My students design their own projects that incorporate technology
        Never   Seldom   Occasionally   Often
    (d) My students use Internet for research
        Never   Seldom   Occasionally   Often
    (e) I set up files of bookmarks for my students to use in research and projects
        Never   Seldom   Occasionally   Often
    (f) My students and I use Internet to create and publish student work
        Never   Seldom   Occasionally   Often
    (g) I create visual presentations to use for classroom discussions
        Never   Seldom   Occasionally   Often
    (h) My students create visual presentations to use for class discussions
        Never   Seldom   Occasionally   Often
    (i) I use technology to present problem solving situations
        Never   Seldom   Occasionally   Often

(j) My students create and contribute to electronic portfolios
Never   Seldom   Occasionally   Often

(k) My students create multimedia projects in which they use tools such as scanners and digital cameras
Never   Seldom   Occasionally   Often

(l) I use technology to keep my students informed of their progress in class
Never   Seldom   Occasionally   Often

23. **My comfort/confidence level in using technology for each of the following student activities is:** *(rate your comfort level from 1 to 5)*

(a) My students keep a journal with word processing
Uncomfortable   1   2   3   4   5   Very comfortable

(b) My students share projects with students in other locations via Internet
Uncomfortable   1   2   3   4   5   Very comfortable

(c) My students design their own projects that incorporate technology
Uncomfortable   1   2   3   4   5   Very comfortable

(d) My students use Internet for research
Uncomfortable   1   2   3   4   5   Very comfortable

(e) I set up files of internet Favorites for my students to use in research and projects
Uncomfortable   1   2   3   4   5   Very comfortable

(f) My students and I use Internet to create and publish student work
Uncomfortable   1   2   3   4   5   Very comfortable

(g) I create visual presentations to use for class discussions
Uncomfortable   1   2   3   4   5   Very comfortable

(h) My students create visual presentations to use for class discussions
Uncomfortable   1   2   3   4   5   Very comfortable

(i) I use technology to present problem solving situations
Uncomfortable   1   2   3   4   5   Very comfortable

(j) My students create and contribute to electronic portfolios
Uncomfortable   1   2   3   4   5   Very comfortable

(k) My students create multimedia projects in which they use electronic tools such as scanners and digital cameras
Uncomfortable   1   2   3   4   5   Very comfortable

(l) I use technology to inform students of their progress in class
Uncomfortable   1   2   3   4   5   Very comfortable

24. **Per grading term, a typical student uses the following software ____ times in the computer lab during my class:**

(a)	Word processing	0	1	2	3	4+
(b)	Spreadsheet	0	1	2	3	4+
(c)	Multimedia	0	1	2	3	4+
(d)	Database	0	1	2	3	4+
(e)	Internet	0	1	2	3	4+
(f)	Simulations	0	1	2	3	4+
(g)	Reference software	0	1	2	3	4+
(h)	Drill and practice	0	1	2	3	4+

(i)	Games	0	1	2	3	4+
(j)	Drawing	0	1	2	3	4+
(k)	Desktop publishing	0	1	2	3	4+
(l)	Photo editing	0	1	2	3	4+
(m)	E-mail	0	1	2	3	4+

25. **Per average week, my students and I devote _____ hours of class time to:**

(a)	Working in cooperative groups	0	1	2	3	4+
(b)	Independent work time	0	1	2	3	4+
(c)	Organized whole class discussion	0	1	2	3	4+
(d)	Teacher delivered material	0	1	2	3	4+
(e)	Presentations by students to the class	0	1	2	3	4+

26. **I use the following methods to introduce new material in my class:**

   (a) Class lecture
   Never   Sometimes   Frequently
   (b) Class lecture with visuals
   Never   Sometimes   Frequently
   (c) Class discussion around a focus question
   Never   Sometimes   Frequently
   (d) Hands-on activity
   Never   Sometimes   Frequently
   (e) Reading assignment
   Never   Sometimes   Frequently

27. **Per average week, my students and I devote class time to:**

   (a) Developing problem-solving strategies for problems with multiple problems
   Never   Sometimes   Frequently
   (b) Developing effective research techniques that utilize a variety of resources
   Never   Sometimes   Frequently
   (c) Analyzing and synthesizing information
   Never   Sometimes   Frequently
   (d) Conducting inquiry-based research
   Never   Sometimes   Frequently
   (e) Activities with authentic, real-life connections
   Never   Sometimes   Frequently
   (f) Activities that involve manipulatives
   Never   Sometimes   Frequently
   (g) Reflecting on their own learning
   Never   Sometimes   Frequently

28. **The addition of technology in my classroom has changed the learning environment in the following ways:**

   (a) Students complete work quickly so they can use the computers as a reward
   Minimum or no change   Noticeable change   Significant change

(b) Students are physically more active
Minimum or no change   Noticeable change   Significant change

(c) My teaching style has changed
Minimum or no change   Noticeable change   Significant change

(d) The arrangement of the room has been altered to accommodate technology
Minimum or no change   Noticeable change   Significant change

(e) Students are proactive about their own learning
Minimum or no change   Noticeable change   Significant change

(f) Students work together in collaborative groups
Minimum or no change   Noticeable change   Significant change

(g) Student projects involve visuals
Minimum or no change   Noticeable change   Significant change

(h) Students willingly engage in problem solving activities
Minimum or no change   Noticeable change   Significant change

(i) Students use a variety of resources for their projects
Minimum or no change   Noticeable change   Significant change

(j) Student work is creative
Minimum or no change   Noticeable change   Significant change

(k) Student work is rigorous
Minimum or no change   Noticeable change   Significant change

(l) Student work is shared with a variety of audiences
Minimum or no change   Noticeable change   Significant change

29. **Technology has been helpful in meeting district and state student standards:**

    Yes   No

30. **My students and I completed the following lesson in which the technology worked well:** *(Briefly describe the lesson)*

    _____
    _____
    _____
    _____
    _____
    _____

31. **In my classroom, I get frustrated with technology when:**

    _____
    _____
    _____
    _____
    _____
    _____

32. **I find the following strategies motivate my students to work and to learn:** *(check all that apply)*

    _____ Lecture   _____ Student observations
    _____ Group discussion   _____ Manipulatives

_____ Listening to recorded information _____ Dance and movement
_____ Making own recording   _____ Computer-generated
                                                  art & music
_____ Lecture with audio-visual aids   _____ Computer simulations
_____ Showing videos   _____ Multimedia projects
_____ Computer/Internet video clips   _____ Desktop publishing

33. Please share any other comments about technology in education.

_____
_____
_____
_____
_____
_____
_____

Thank you for your thoughtful participation in this process.

Form A. 2   Individual Teacher Profiles

Teacher Name	Grade and Subjects	Proficiency Level Self Rating	Proficiency Level Admin./Peer Rating	Proficiency Level McREL Rating	Pertinent Comments	Training Needs Expressed
Teacher 1	Media and Technology	Adoption	Adaptation	Adaptation	• Software purchases are at a standstill until platform change is completed. • Math Blaster freezes some computers and Manuel is too busy to find the source of the conflicts.	• Windows vs. Mac networks • MS certification course • Wireless lab management • Opportunities to attend specialized workshops for education tech specialists
Teacher 2	Pre-K	Adoption	Entry	Adoption	• Does not use tech in classroom: kids are too young.	• Data management; grade book; exposure to programs appropriate for preschoolers
Teacher 3	2nd	Adoption	Entry	Entry and Adoption	• New to district—has other priorities beyond tech right now. • Is organizing own records on PC.	• One-on-one training in one content area, using resources that are currently available • Troubleshooting printers and scanners
Teacher 4	3rd	Adoption	Adoption	Adaptation and Appropriation	• Extensive user: publishes newsletter, uses scanner. • Needs access to tech: additional equipment and lab time.	• Advanced word processing; assessment and grading programs
Teacher 5	1st	Entry	Entry	Entry	• Needs help with computer and TV interface. • Likes Sam's tech lessons, as they are "job embedded."	• One-on-one training is most helpful. • Scanners and digital cameras • What are other 1st-grade teachers doing?
Teacher 6	Music	Entry	Entry	Entry	• Lacks a computer in his class. • Has no music software for kids.	• Will take Midi keyboard class. • Opportunity to collaborate with other district music teachers
Teacher 7	2nd	Adoption	Adaptation	Adaptation	• Needs more access to computer lab and staff time to collaborate on lesson plans with tech, etc.	• One-computer classroom, opportunities to brainstorm with peers throughout the district
Teacher 8	K	Adoption	Entry	Entry and Adoption	• Uses tech a lot for record keeping—for kids, just wants to expose them to tech at the K level.	• Information on good software for primary levels • Summer tech classes fit her schedule better.

FORM A.3. ADMINISTRATOR
TECHNOLOGY PROFILE

1. **I have been actively employed as an educator for the following number of years:** *(circle one)*

   1-5   6-10   11-20   21+

2. **I have actively used technology the following number of years in my job:** *(circle one)*

   1-5   6-10   11-20   21+

3. **I have personally used technology the following number of years:** *(circle one)*

   1-5   6-10   11-20   21+

4. **Per average week, I personally use the following software _____ hours:**

(a) Word processing	0	1-5	6-15	16+
(b) E-mail	0	1-5	6-15	16+
(c) Desktop publishing	0	1-5	6-15	16+
(d) Spreadsheet	0	1-5	6-15	16+
(e) Multimedia	0	1-5	6-15	16+
(f) Database	0	1-5	6-15	16+
(g) Internet browsers	0	1-5	6-15	16+
(h) Games	0	1-5	6-15	16+
(i) Student information/management system	0	1-5	6-15	16+

5. **Please respond to the following comments:**

   (a) Technology provides me with better data for decision making
   Yes   No

   (b) Technology has increased the amount and types of information people expect from me
   Yes   No

   (c) Technology has enabled me to do my job more efficiently
   Yes   No

   (d) Technology has made my job more complicated
   Yes   No

   (e) Technology has increased communication with parents
   Yes   No

   (f) Technology has improved communication with students
   Yes   No

   (g) Technology has improved communication with faculty and staff
   Yes   No

6. **I would like to improve my ability to do the following with technology:** *(check all that apply)*

    _____ Use e-mail to improve communication with faculty and parents
    _____ Conduct more research via the Internet
    _____ Create more documents with word processing and/or databases
    _____ Improve the reporting processes
    _____ Provide better data for decision-making
    _____ Provide more information about students
    _____ Increase communication with colleagues throughout the country
    _____ Provide staff development opportunities via Internet
    _____ Improve presentations through the use of multimedia
    _____ Change the learning environment throughout the building

7. **Please react to the following statement: I wish technology would go away? Why or why not?**

8. **I would classify myself as this type of technology user:** *(check one category)*

Entry: Educators who are just starting to use technology for learning

Adoption: Educators who have some comfort level with technology and are taking initial steps to use it in their curriculum

Adaptation: Educators who are shifting toward more student-based project learning and encourage the use of a variety of technology tools

Appropriation: Educators who are so comfortable with technology that it is integrated throughout all learning activities

Transformation: Educators who create new ways to use technology tools for real-world applications

9. **Please complete the following phrase: "My personal vision concerning the use of technology in education is . . ."**

10. **I would best describe my participation in the development of the district's technology plan as:**

    Not involved   Plan was written before I assumed this position
    Somewhat involved Very involved

11. **I would best describe my participation in the development of the school's technology plan as:** *(circle all that apply)*

    Organized the committee   Participated in the committee
    Chaired the committee   Committee worked independently
                                from me

12. **The following people were encouraged to contribute to the planning process:** *(circle all that apply)*

    Teachers   Students
    Tech staff   District administration
    Community   School staff & administration
    Parents   Business representatives

13. **How does the technology plan relate to the district's strategic and curriculum implementation plan?** *(circle the <u>one</u> best answer)*

    There is no technology plan
    There is no strategic/curriculum plan
    We have both documents but they are not interrelated
    The curriculum plan drives the technology plan
    The technology plan drives the curriculum plan
    The two plans work as one

14. **How long has it been since the building technology plan was revised?**

    It is being revised now   Four years
    One year   Five years
    Two years   More than five years
    Three years   I don't know

15. **Briefly describe the process for implementing the building technology plan.**

16. **How successfully is the building technology plan being implemented?** *(select one)*

    _____ Progress has stalled
    _____ Progress is slow but proceeding
    _____ Implementation is meeting the plan's time lines
    _____ Implementation has been successful and has moved beyond
            the plan's goals

17. **If parts of the plan are not working, why do you think they aren't working?**

18. **What is the community's attitude toward the use of technology in the school?**

    Non-supportive   Somewhat supportive
    Neutral   Very supportive

19. **Generally, what is the faculty's attitude toward the use of technology in the school?** *(select one)*

    Non-supportive   Somewhat supportive
    Neutral   Very supportive

20. **To what degree is the district supportive of technology efforts?** *(select one)*

    Non-supportive   Enhances our building efforts
    Somewhat supportive   Actively engages us in district effort
    Encourages our building efforts

21. **I have learned to use technology through the following methods:** *(circle one for each item)*

    (a) Self-taught by experimenting with equipment or software
    Not a useful method for me   Supplemental method   Predominant method
    (b) Through district in-service
    Not a useful method for me   Supplemental method   Predominant method
    (c) By reading manuals
    Not a useful method for me   Supplemental method   Predominant method
    (d) By attending vendors' workshops
    Not a useful method for me   Supplemental method   Predominant method
    (e) By attending conferences
    Not a useful method for me   Supplemental method   Predominant method
    (f) In higher education courses
    Not a useful method for me   Supplemental method   Predominant method
    (g) With assistance from peers or acquaintances
    Not a useful method for me   Supplemental method   Predominant method

22. **What incentives are you using to encourage faculty to participate in technology professional development?** *(check all that apply)*

    _____ Tuition reimbursement
    _____ Release time
    _____ Conference/seminars/workshops—expenses reimbursed
    _____ Other: _____

23. **Is technology use part of the teacher evaluation process?**

    Yes   No

24. **Which professional development opportunities are your faculty using?** *(check all that apply)*

    _____ On-site courses and training _____ Conferences
    _____ On-site visits to other schools _____ Peer training and mentoring
    _____ On-site vendor presentations _____ Graduate courses
    _____ Online courses   _____ Summer workshops

25. **Do the computers in your building meet the needs of faculty and students?** *(check _all_ that apply)*

    _____ We don't have enough machines to meet all requests

    _____ Equipment is too old to accommodate new programs and projects

    _____ Appropriate equipment is usually available for programs and projects

    _____ We have enough machines but need additional educational software

    _____ Teachers and students are not using currently available equipment to its full potential

    _____ We have the equipment and software, but it is not easily available where and when the teachers and their students need it

26. **The following has occurred as a result of technology being available at my school:** *(check _all_ that apply)*

    _____ Increased collaborative learning

    _____ More individualized curriculum to meet student needs

    _____ Increased class activities that are appropriate for multiple learning styles

    _____ Increased use of multiple resources in the instructional process

    _____ Increased student motivation

    _____ Reduced tardiness and absences

    _____ Increased creativity in student projects

    _____ Increased collaboration among teachers and staff

27. **How important is it to use technology:**

    (a) Throughout the curriculum

    Not very important   Important   Necessary

    (b) To individualize instruction for students

    Not very important   Important   Necessary

    (c) To communicate with parents

    Not very important   Important   Necessary

    (d) To change the learning environment

    Not very important   Important   Necessary

    (e) To meet standards

    Not very important   Important   Necessary

    (f) For staff professional development

    Not very important   Important   Necessary

28. **Describe the characteristics that achieved successful technology integration:**

29. **My school has a policy for software licensing:**

    Yes   *No*   *Vague*

30. **How is software managed?** *(select all that apply)*

    _____ Software licenses are managed by one person in the building
    _____ Teachers can only use school-purchased software
    _____ Teachers can provide their own software
    _____ Students may bring software and install on school machines
    _____ I don't know

31. **I use management software (including SASI/xp) to perform the following tasks:** *(select all that apply)*

    _____ General spreadsheets   _____ Report standardized test
                                                       scores and performance

    _____ Financial programs   _____ Registration
    _____ Schedule management   _____ Attendance records
    _____ Grade books   _____ Eligibility records
    _____ Report cards and transcripts _____ IEP software *(Excent)*
    _____ Student performance records _____ Student tracking and
                                                       demographics

    _____ Other: _____

32. **I use the following set of priorities for purchasing technology when requests exceed budgets:** *(number these according to their priority with the item having the highest priority labeled no. 1)*

    _____ The technology has a direct impact on student learning
    _____ The technology enables the teacher to work more effectively
    _____ The technology can be used as part of the standards imple-
            mentation plan
    _____ The technology is recommended by the district
    _____ The technology has been requested by a teacher whose work
            sets an example for others to follow
    _____ The district requires the use of this technology with our students
    _____ Technology purchase requests are honored until the budget is
            exhausted

33. **I help a teacher who wants to acquire more technology for class projects by:** *(select all that apply)*

    _____ Filing their request if the money is available
    _____ Asking him/her to put it in the budget for next year
    _____ Asking him/her to purchase it and be reimbursed by the school
    _____ Encourage him/her to find other channels for funding such as
            (select all that apply)
    _____ The district office
    _____ The PTO
    _____ Sponsoring businesses

_____ Other: _____
_____ Helping him/her find resources to purchase it

34. **I help a teacher who is resisting the use of technology by:**

35. **The following people have key responsibilities for technology in my building:** _(List by name and title)_

   1. _____
   2. _____

36. **The implementation of technology has changed the way I work in the following ways:**

37. **The following are examples of technology issues that continue to be a challenge in my building:**

38. **The following are examples of effective technology implementation in my building:**

Thank you for your thoughtful participation in this process.

Resource B

Cupertino Union School District: Technology Scope and Sequence

Cupertino Union School District's technology effort provides a framework to help teachers weave the district-adopted curriculum, student-centered learning practices, and technology into rich learning experiences for children (see Figure B.1).

Research, data organizing and analyzing, and publishing were selected because they build on three broad areas of educational processes which already exist in the classroom. Most curricular and content areas contain

Figure B.1   Learning Tasks Which Can Be Supported by Technology

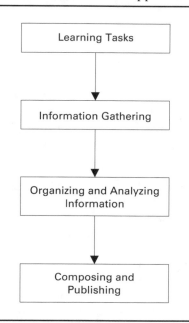

SOURCE: www.cupertino.k12.ca.us/Do.www/Scopenseq.html

Table B.1 Technology Scope and Sequence

Technology Scope and Sequence Research			
Level	**Technology Skill**	**Possible Applications**	**Examples**
One: Exploring • Students assisted by teacher • Students investigate electronic media sources to find information for task • Students read/retrieve data from databases & spreadsheets • Students create simple bibliography and citations • Students use simulation software to broaden learning experiences	• Search/navigate CD-ROM resources • Use WWW search engines • Perform single topic searches • Open and read online databases • Use software templates for bibliographies/citations • Run simulations	• CD encyclopedias, atlases • Instructional TV • Laserdiscs • Simulations: BodyWorks, Great Ocean Rescue, Oregon Trail	• Outlining • Note taking • Mind mapping • Information compilation in organized manner • Bibliography
Two: Composing • Students assisted by peers/teachers • Students use electronic media features to efficiently select pertinent information • Students download files from the Web which make information locally accessible • Students cite information in appropriate manner • Students narrow search parameters by using more than one word • Students communicate with experts via online discussion groups	• Use notepad or note-taking feature of CD • Edit/save skills, cut, copy, paste skills • Download text, graphics, video, sound • Save/Organize data in folders on hard drive • Create formats for bibliographies/citations • Perform Boolean searches (and/or/not) • Use e-mail & online chat rooms/forums/bulletin boards	• Netscape: Yahoo, WebCrawler, Excite • Word processor • Databases/Spreadsheets • TOM or TOM Jr. • Online card catalogs, periodicals, indexes	• Footnotes and other citations • Initiate and participate in online chats
Three: Refining • Students independently select and use software and devices • Students compile information for complex research project/problem • Students use multiple sources including CD-ROMs, ITV, Internet & WWW • Students compare, analyze, synthesize information from downloaded files	• Use technology/software to organize and interpret collected information • Create mind maps, outlines, databases, graphs/charts/tables, …	• What On Earth, X-Press • Inspiration • MS/Claris Works • MS Word	• Compare and contrast collected information

aspects of these three functions. Students gather, organize, and analyze information, then demonstrate their understanding through the process of composition and publishing. The Technology Scope and Sequence[1] overview (see Table B.1) provides direction on how technology can play a role in each of these areas. It is intended to assist teachers in integrating technology into the curriculum. It is designed to be used as a roadmap to help students progress along a continuum of technology skills.

Technology Scope and Sequence further divide the subjects into 4 key sections: research, data organizing and analyzing, desktop publishing, and multi/hypermedia. Figure B.2 illustrates how these basic learning tasks can be supported by technology.

Each section of the Scope and Sequence contains recommended activities, technology-specific skills, possible applications and devices, and curriculum-related examples. It is a continuum that allows students to progress through three different levels of proficiency. In terms of

Table B.1 Continued

Technology Scope and Sequence Data Organizing and Analyzing			
Level	**Technology Skills**	**Possible Applications**	**Examples**
One: Exploring Database • Students investigate existing database in whole group setting • Students create whole group database and input data • Students learn database terminology Spreadsheet • Students create whole group spreadsheet and inputs information • Students produce whole group graph/chart • Students learn spreadsheet terminology	• Sort (filter), find, match to meet one condition • Create fields, format fields, enter data • Know terms – field, records, views (data, list, design, report) • Enter label and value • Use "make chart" feature • Know terms – columns, rows, cells	• The Graph Club • Cruncher • Microsoft/ClarisWorks	• Student information • Favorites • Animals • Reading log • Class surveys
Two: Composing Database • Students assisted by peers/teachers to create database • Students manipulate, present, and analyze data to convey information Spreadsheet • Students assisted by peers/teachers to create spreadsheet • Creates graph/chart • Students use simple formulas • Students use editing features	• Create fields, format field, enter data • Sort (filter) to meet more than one condition • Print using report feature • Enter label and value • Use make and define chart features • Know that formulas begin with "=" (multiply, subtract) • Use paste function (sum, average) • Edit – fill right & down	• FileMaker Pro	• Presidents • States • Explorers • Missions • Literature • Budget
Three: Refining Database • Students independently create effective databases • Students use more sophisticated filters and formatting Spreadsheet • Students independently create effective spreadsheets & graphs/charts • Students manipulate values to explore cause and effect relationships • Students use more sophisticated formulas and formatting • Students use more sophisticated chart features	• Creates appropriate fields and design layout • Create filters using multiple operators (equals, contains, less than) • Format fields (text, number, date, time) • Design appropriate labels and values • Input different values • Use paste function (percent, square root, absolute value) • Format cells (text, number, date, time) • Use draw features to enhance graph/chart	• Excel	• Use database information for reports and projects • Polyhedraville • Recipes

application, this continuum acknowledges two implementation issues: (a) teacher background and comfort with technology and (b) student access to technology. It is independent of grade level and recognizes that teacher experience and students with greater access to technology may lead to more rapid progress through the levels. The first column consists of three levels of activities corresponding to the terms *exploring, composing,* and *refining*. The second column touches on the attendant technology skills students need at each level. The third column suggests possible applications or devices that would help them to perform at that level, and the last column outlines a few examples of how students can exhibit their proficiency at that level. This Technology Scope and Sequence table can help

Table B.1 Continued

Technology Scope and Sequence Desktop Publishing			
Level	**Technology Skills**	**Possible Applications/Devices**	**Examples**
One: Exploring • Students assisted by teacher • Students explore basic word processing functions to produce sentences • Students investigate basic drawing tools • Students investigate basic paint tools	Basic word processing functions • Insert, delete, highlight ... Basic drawing tools • Line, shapes, eraser Basic paint tools • Brush, spray can, patterns ...	• Hypercard • Hyperstudio • Easybook • Storybook Weaver • KidPix • KidWorks 2 • Microsoft/Claris Works	• Letters • Story/Narrative • Picture and/or text • Picture with label
Two: Composing • Students assisted by peers/teacher formats and edits text • Students import, alter, and customize basic graphics/clipart • Students use 2 programs to produce a final product	Formatting Skills • Font, style, justify, tabs, page breaks, margins, page setup Editing Skills • Cut, copy, paste, spell check Graphic Skills • Importing, sizing ... • Uses scrapbook	• Writing Center • Student Writing Center • Works • CD-ROM resources • Use Clipart programs • Printshop, Bannermania	• Newsletter • Report • Letters • Posters, signs, cards, banners • Books • Brochures
Three: Refining • Students independently select and use software and devices • Students import graphics using peripherals • Students add visual elements to the text • Students use sophisticated word processing features • Students use 3 or more programs to produce a final product	Import graphics skills • Digitized images, scanning, quicktake/cam ... • Visual elements • Columns, graphs, tables, borders, shading ... • Word Processing features • Header/footer, footnote, thesaurus	• Works • PageMaker • Student Writing Center • Word • Electronic Resources – CDs, encyclopedia, online • Digitized images • Scanner • Quicktake/cam	• Newspaper • Yearbook • Complex Report • Advertisements • Magazines

teachers incorporate technology into the curriculum as they provide students with rich learning experiences. It addresses only technology skills as they apply to the curriculum. We assume that the writing process, problem solving, and other sound teaching practices are in place and that technology is used to support district curriculum.

Table B.1   Continued

Technology Scope and Sequence Multi/Hypermedia			
Level	**Technology Skills**	**Possible Applications/Devices**	**Examples**
One: Exploring • Students assisted by teacher • Students use tools to create buttons, text, draw pictures, & import clipart • Students use stand-alone devices to support presentation • Students create a simple presentation including text and pictures	• Use text, buttons, & painting tools • Imports/paste clipart • Use video, laserdiscs, CD-ROM	• Hyperstudio • Hypercard • Mediatext • Digital Chisel • KidPix/Slideshow • Word processing • VCR • CD-ROM • Laserdiscs	• Slideshow • Short stack • Using remote control to access a visual aid • Biography • Creative stories
Two: Composing • Students assisted by peers/teacher • Students use tools to import graphics from devices • Students create presentations which include attractive layout, easy navigation, and meaningful content	• Use scanner, CD-ROMs, internet, digital cameras, video cameras as a graphic source • Create animation • Convert video to QuickTime	• Scanner • Quicktake/cam • Laserdiscs • CD-ROMs, audio & photo • Netscape/AOL • Video camera • Apple Video Player	• Reports • Electronic newspaper • Tutorial • Video book report
Three: Refining • Students independently select and use software and devices • Students use tools to integrate sound, video, CDs and access the Internet • Students create clear presentation which require research, formatting, & skillful delivery	• Create internet links • Import sound files • Edit video and sound • Work in a scripting language	• Simpletext • Avid VideoShop • HTML, PageMill • HyperLogo, HyperTalk	• Commercial • Webpage

Figure B.1   Curriculum Subjects Integrated With Technology

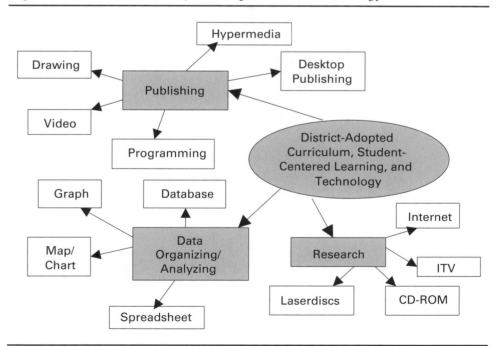

SOURCE: www.cupertino.k12.ca.us/Do.www/Scopenseq.html

Resource C

ISTE National Educational Technology Standards (NETS) and Performance Indicators: Educational Technology Foundations for All Teachers

International Society for Technology in Education (ISTE)
Performance Profiles for Teachers

I. TECHNOLOGY OPERATIONS AND CONCEPTS

Teachers demonstrate a sound understanding of technology operations and concepts. Teachers:

A. Demonstrate introductory knowledge, skills, and understanding of concepts related to technology (as described in the ISTE National Education Technology Standards for Students).
B. Demonstrate continual growth in technology knowledge and skills to stay abreast of current and emerging technologies.

II. PLANNING AND DESIGNING LEARNING ENVIRONMENTS AND EXPERIENCES

Teachers plan and design effective learning environments and experiences supported by technology. Teachers:

A. Design developmentally appropriate learning opportunities that apply technology-enhanced instructional strategies to support the diverse needs of learners
B. Apply current research on teaching and learning with technology when planning learning environments and experiences
C. Identify and locate technology resources and evaluate them for accuracy and suitability
D. Plan for the management of technology resources within the context of learning activities

E. Plan strategies to manage student learning in a technology-enhanced environment

III. TEACHING, LEARNING, AND THE CURRICULUM

Teachers implement curriculum plans that include methods and strategies for applying technology to maximize student learning. Teachers:

A. Facilitate technology-enhanced experiences that address content standards and student technology standards
B. Use technology to support learner-centered strategies that address the diverse needs of students
C. Apply technology to develop students' higher order skills and creativity
D. Manage student learning activities in a technology-enhanced environment

IV. ASSESSMENT AND EVALUATION

Teachers apply technology to facilitate a variety of effective assessment and evaluation strategies. Teachers:

A. Apply technology in assessing student learning of subject matter using a variety of assessment techniques
B. Use technology resources to collect and analyze data, interpret results, and communicate findings to improve instructional practice and maximize student learning.
C. Apply multiple methods of evaluation to determine students' appropriate use of technology resources for learning, communication, and productivity

V. PRODUCTIVITY AND PROFESSIONAL PRACTICE

Teachers use technology to enhance their productivity and professional practice. Teachers:

A. Use technology resources to engage in ongoing professional development and lifelong learning
B. Continually evaluate and reflect on professional practice to make informed decisions regarding the use of technology in support of student learning
C. Apply technology to increase productivity
D. Use technology to communicate and collaborate with peers, parents, and the larger community in order to nurture student learning

VI. SOCIAL, ETHICAL, LEGAL, AND HUMAN ISSUES

Teachers understand the social, ethical, legal, and human issues surrounding the use of technology in PK-12 schools and apply those principles in practice. Teachers:

A. Model and teach legal and ethical practice related to technology use
B. Apply technology resources to enable and empower learners with diverse backgrounds, characteristics, and abilities

C. Identify and use technology resources that affirm diversity

D. Promote safe and healthy use of technology resources

E. Facilitate equitable access to technology resources for all students

---

SOURCE: © 2001 Technology Standards for School Administrators (TSSA) Collaborative. Reprinted with permission.

Resource D

ISTE National Educational Technology Standards (NETS) and Performance Indicators: Educational Technology Foundation Standards for All Students

The International Society for Technology in Education (ISTE) technology foundation standards for students are divided into six broad categories. Standards within each category are to be introduced, reinforced, and mastered by students. These categories provide a framework for linking performance indicators within the Profiles for Technology Literate Students to the standards. Teachers can use these standards and profiles as guidelines for planning technology-based activities in which students achieve success in learning, communication, and life skills.

TECHNOLOGY FOUNDATION STANDARDS FOR STUDENTS

1. Basic operations and concepts
   - Students demonstrate a sound understanding of the nature and operation of technology systems.
   - Students are proficient in the use of technology.

2. Social, ethical, and human issues
   - Students understand the ethical, cultural, and societal issues related to technology.
   - Students practice responsible use of technology systems, information, and software.
   - Students develop positive attitudes toward technology uses that support lifelong learning, collaboration, personal pursuits, and productivity.

3. Technology productivity tools
   - Students use technology tools to enhance learning, increase productivity, and promote creativity.

215

- Students use productivity tools to collaborate in constructing technology-enhanced models, prepare publications, and produce other creative works.

4. Technology communications tools
   - Students use telecommunications to collaborate, publish, and interact with peers, experts, and other audiences.
   - Students use a variety of media and formats to communicate information and ideas effectively to multiple audiences.

5. Technology research tools
   - Students use technology to locate, evaluate, and collect information from a variety of sources.
   - Students use technology tools to process data and report results.
   - Students evaluate and select new information resources and technological innovations based on the appropriateness for specific tasks.

6. Technology problem-solving and decision-making tools
   - Students use technology resources for solving problems and making informed decisions.
   - Students employ technology in the development of strategies for solving problems in the real world.

Resource E

Glossary

automated digital library.   A digital library where all tasks are carried out automatically; computer programs perform the intellectually demanding tasks that are traditionally carried out by skilled professionals.

bus.   A transmission path on which signals are dropped off or picked up at every device attached to the line. Only devices addressed by the signals pay attention to them; the others disregard the signals.

CD–ROM.   An acronym for compact disk–read only memory; a read-only optical-storage technology that uses compact disks.

centralized file server.   A computer or device on a network that manages network resources. For example, a *file server* is a computer and storage device dedicated to storing files. Any user on the network can store files on the server. A *print server* is a computer that manages one or more printers, and a *network server* is a computer that manages network traffic. A *database server* is a computer system that processes database queries. Servers are often dedicated, meaning that they perform no other tasks beside their server tasks. On multiprocessing operating systems, however, a single computer can execute several programs at once. A server, in this case, could refer to the program that is managing resources rather than the entire computer.

computer-aided design (CAD).   Computer software used by engineers in the design of a product.

computer-controlled flexible manufacturing system.   Any production process in which computers are used to help control production.

courseware applications.   Software developed for computer-assisted instruction or computer-based training applications.

data intranets.   Hardwired network systems that serve a local group, for example, a local area network (LAN).

electronic scanning device.   A piece of equipment that varies the sector covered by a transmitting or receiving antenna by electrical means without moving the antenna. Used in scanning a surface to reproduce or transmit a picture or text.

fiber-optic cables. A high-speed physical medium that can be used for transmitting data. Constructed from thin fibers of glass, fiber-optic cable guides the light of transmitting lasers without significant loss, despite twists and turns along the way.

frame relay. A portion of data transmitted by a modem for purposes of checking for errors in other transmitted data. Employs a protocol for sending small packets of data over a network. Frame relay uses packets of variable length, unlike cell relay, and requires less-stringent error detection than other forms of packet switching, because it is designed to take advantage of the more reliable circuits that have become available in recent years. Frame relay is often used for wide area networks, where it can transmit data at high speed more efficiently than point-to-point services. Frame relay is used with digital lines.

hypertext presentation. A method of preparing and publishing text, ideally suited to the computer, in which readers can choose their own paths through the material. Hypertext applications are particularly useful for massive amounts of text, such as encyclopedias.

interactive video. A computer-assisted instruction technology that uses a computer to provide access to up to 2 hours of video information stored on a videodisk.

laptop or notebook. A small, portable computer that is light and small enough to hold on your lap. Small laptop computers which weigh less than 6 pounds and can fit in a briefcase are called notebook computers.

local area network (LAN). A computer network that spans a relatively small area. Most LANs are confined to a single building or group of buildings.

memory expansion. Adding additional memory to a personal computer by means of expansion cards.

mill. A monetary unit equaling .001 of a dollar. A tax rate of 500 mills equals 50 cents.

millage. In some states, this is stated in amount of taxation in dollars and cents per $1,000 valuation.

optical disk drives. A large-capacity data storage medium for computers, on which information is stored at extremely high density in the form of tiny Bits.

peripherals. Devices, such as a printer, scanner, bar coder, or disk drive, among others, that are connected to and controlled by a computer but external to the computer's central processing unit (CPU).

school hotline. A toll-free number available 24 hours per day, 365 days per year to give students, parents, and community members the opportunity to report and receive important notices about daily school activities.

video cards. A video capture card—an adapter that plugs into the computer's expansion bus and enables you to control a video camera or videocassette recorder and manipulates its output. Video capture cards usually compress the video input to a manageable size and are useful for developing multimedia presentations.

voice recognition and translation programs.   Computer recognition of human speech and transformation of the recognized words into computer-readable, digitized text or instructions.

wide area network (WAN).   A computer network that uses high-speed, long-distance communications networks or satellites to connect computers over distances greater than those traversed by LANs.

SOURCES

Flanigan, J. L., Richardson, M. D., & Stollar, D. H. (1995). *Managing School Indebtedness* (2nd ed.). Lancaster, PA: Technomic Publishing.

Pfaffenberger, B. (1995). Que's *Computer & Internet Dictionary* (6th ed.). Indianapolis, IN: Que® Corporation.

Rebore, W. T., & Rebore, R. W. (1993). *Financial and Business Administration.* Needham Heights, MA: Allyn & Bacon.

Webopedia. Online Dictionary for Computer and Internet Terms. (n.d.). Retrieved February 26, 2002, from wysiwyg:2/http://webopedia.com

Welcome to the Computer User High-Tech Dictionary! (n.d.). Retrieved February 26, 2002, from www.computeruser.com/resources/dictionary/startmain.html

Notes

PREFACE

1. U.S. Department of Education. (1996). *Getting America's students ready for the 21st century: Meeting the technology literacy challenge.* Retrieved May 21, 2002, from /www.ed.gov/Technology/Plan/NatTechPlan/title.html

2. Ibid.

3. The Editors. (2001). Technology counts: The new divides. Looking beneath the numbers to reveal the inequities. *Education Week on the Web, 20*(35). Retrieved May 21, 2002, from www.edweek.org/sreports/tc01/tc2001_default.html

4. Layton, T. (2000, September). Digital learning: Why tomorrow's schools must learn to let go of the past. *Electronic School.Com.* Retrieved May 16, 2002, from www.electronic-school.com/2000/09/0900f1.html

CHAPTER 1

1. Layton, T. (2000, September). Digital learning. Why tomorrow's schools must learn to let go of the past. *Electronic School.Com.* Retrieved May 16, 2002, from www.electronic-school.com/2000/09/0900f1.html

2. Panel on Educational Technology. (1997, March). *Report to the president on the use of technology to strengthen K-12 education in the United States* (p. 31). Washington, DC: President's Committee of Advisors on Science and Technology.

3. American Association of School Administrators. (2000, September 11). Only 10% of teachers have more than 5 class computers. *Leadership News.* Retrieved May 16, 2002, from www.aasa.org/publications/ln/09_00/00_09_11 teachtech.htm

4. The Editors. (2001, May 10). Technology Counts 2001: The new divides. Education Week 1(1). Retrieved May 21, 2002, from www.edweek.org/sreports/ tc01/states/tc01state_compare.html

5. Ibid.

6. Ibid.

7. Ibid.

8. Panel on Educational Technology. (1997, March). *Report to the president on the use of technology to strengthen K-12 education in the United States* (pp. 1-20).

Washington, DC: President's Committee of Advisors on Science and Technology.

9. Data from the Ohio SchoolNet Commission Survey Results (1999) used with permission. KPMG Economic Consulting Service, 2001 M Street NW, Washington, DC 20036.

10. Shields, M. K., & Behrman, R. E. (2000, Fall/Winter). Children and computer technology: Analysis and recommendations. *The Future of Children: Children and Computer Technology, 10*(2), 4-30.

11. Panel on Educational Technology. (1997, March). *Report to the president on the use of technology to strengthen K-12 education in the United States* (p. 20). Washington, DC: President's Committee of Advisors on Science and Technology.

12. Trotter, A. (1997). Taking technology's measure. *Education Week on the Web, 17*(11), 6-11.

13. Dunn, R. (1995). Analysis of learning research. *Educational Research Newsletter, 8*(5), 6.

14. Wishengrad, R. (1999). Are paper textbooks ready to fold? *Educational Digest, 64*(6), 57-61.

15. Trotter, A. (1997). Taking technology's measure. *Education Week, 17*(11), 6-11.

16. Field, J. (2001). The learning age—is it just for youngsters, or can adults join in too? *Adults Learning, 12*(7). Also: John, G. (2000). The learning age. *Educational Change, 11*(10).

17. Lowe, M. J., & Vespestad, K. (1999). Using technology as a tool to enhance learning. *NASSP Bulletin, 83*(607), 30-35.

18. Zehr, M. A. (1997). Partnering with the public. *Education Week, 17*(11), 36-39.

19. Data from the Ohio SchoolNet Commission Survey Results (1999) used with permission. KPMG Economic Consulting Service, 2001 M Street NW, Washington, DC 20036.

20. Tapscott, D. (1998). The net generation and the school. *The Milken Exchange on Education and Technology.* Retrieved May 17, 2002, from www.mff.org/edtech/article.taf?_function=detail&Content_uid1=109

21. LeBaron, J. F., & Collier, C. (2001). *Technology in its place* (p. 87). San Francisco: Jossey-Bass.

22. Becker, H. J. (2000, Fall/Winter). Who's wired and who's not: Children's access to and use of computer technology. *The Future of Children: Children and Computer Technology, 10*(2), 66. The article includes the following statistics:

- Only 22% of children in families with annual incomes under $20,000 had a home computer in 1998 compared with 91% of children in families with incomes over $75,000.
- Fewer than 3% of low-income children reported using computers in libraries or community centers in 1998.
- Schools serving predominantly low-income children generally have computers connected to the Internet, but they tend to have older, less functional computers; to have fewer computers in each classroom; and to offer fewer experiences using computers to create presentations and analyze information—compared with schools serving higher-income children.

CHAPTER 2

1. Morefield, J. (1994). Recreating schools for all children. *Principal, 73*(3), 42-45.

2. Kimpton, J., & Considine, J. (1999). The tough sledding of district-level engagement. *School Administrator, 8*(56), 6.

3. Ibid., 7-8.

4. Ibid., 10.

5. Shannon, T. (1996). Plans for technology in Education: An ITTE technology leadership network special report. *The National School Board's Association,* p. 43.

6. Jones, R. (2001, September). How parents can support learning. *American School Board Journal, 188*(9). Retrieved May 22, 2002, from www.asbj.com/2001/09/0901coverstory.html

7. © 2001 Technology Standards for School Administrators (TSSA) Collaborative. Reprinted with permission. Retrieved May 17, 2002, from TSSA Web site: cnets.iste.org/tssa/framework.html

8. Houston, P. D. (1999). To lead my trek, I pick Scotty. *School Administrator, 8*(56), 55.

9. Bushweller, K. (1999, December). Seeing the big picture. *Education Vital Signs*, A 12.

10. Ibid.

CHAPTER 3

1. Bell, S. M. (1994). Teach your teachers well. *Electronic Learning, 13*(7), 34.

2. Latham, A. S. (1999). Computers and achievement. *Educational Leadership, 56*(5), 87-88.

3. Northwest Regional Educational Laboratory. (1990). *Management Matrix.* Portland, OR: Author.

4. McFadden, A. C., & Johnson, E. (1993). Training teachers to use technology: The Alabama plan. *Techtrends, 38*(6), 27-28.

5. Mid-Continent Research for Education and Learning (McREL); 2550 South Parker Road, Suite 500; Aurora, CO 80014. Retrieved May 21, 2002, from www.mcrel.org

CHAPTER 4

1. Maurer, M. M., & Davidson, G. (1999). Technology, children, and the power of the heart. *Phi Delta Kappan, 80*(6), 458-459.

2. Washington State Task Force. (1994). *High standards: Essential learnings for Washington students* (*Report by the Washington Commission of Student Learning*, p. 1). Olympia, WA: Office of the Superintendent of Public Instruction.

3.   Panel on Educational Technology. (1997). *Report to the president on the use of technology to strengthen K-12 education in the United States* (p. 35). Washington, DC: President's Committee of Advisors on Science and Technology.

4.   Alfaro, R. (1999). The technology-reading connection. *Educational Leadership, 56*(6), 48-50.

5.   Cradler, J. (1995). *Summary of current research and evaluation findings on technology in education.* Retrieved May 17, 2002, from www.wested.org/techpolicy/refind.html

6.   Hooper, S., Temiyakarn, C., & Williams, M. D. (1994). Cooperative learning increases achievement with computers. *Educational Research Newsletter, 7*(1), 4.

7.   Washington State Task Force. (1994). *High standards: Essential learnings for Washington students (Report by the Washington Commission of Student Learning).* Olympia, WA: Office of the Superintendent of Public Instruction.

8.   Morrison, G. R., & Lowther, D. L. (1998). Introduction: Learning with computers in the K-12 environment. *Tech Trends, 43*(2), 33-38.

9.   Cradler, J. (1995). *Summary of current research and evaluation findings on technology in education.* Retrieved May 17, 2002, from www.wested.org/techpolicy/refind.html

10.   Kulik, J. (1994). An ecological approach for information technology intervention, evaluation, and software adoption policies. In E. L. Baker & H. F. O'Neil Jr. (Eds.), *Technology assessment in education and training* (Chapter 2), Hillsdale, NJ: Lawrence Earlbaum.

11.   Schofield, J. W. (1998). You don't have to be a teacher to teach this unit: Teaching, technology, and control in the classroom. In H. Bromley & M. W. Apple (Eds.), *Education, technology, power: Educational computing as a social practice* (Chapter 6). Albany: State University of New York Press.

12.   Nichols, C. (1999). Cupertino Union School District's technology scope and sequence. Retrieved May 17, 2002, from www.cupertino.k12.ca.us/Do.www/Scopenseq.html

13.   Abramson, G. (1998). How to evaluate educational software. *Principal, 78*(1), 60-61.

14.   Hooper, S., Temiyakarn, C., & Williams, M. D. (1994). Cooperative learning increases achievement with computers. *Educational Research Newsletter, 7*(1), 4.

15.   Dwyer, D. (1994). Apple classrooms of tomorrow: What we have learned. *Educational Leadership, 51*(7), 4-10.

16.   Dunn, R. (1995). Analysis of learning research. *Educational Research Newsletter, 8*(5), 6.

17.   Bangert-Drowns, R. L. (1993). Word processing in writing instruction. *Educational Research Newsletter, 6*(4), 4.

18.   Macarthur, C. (1988). The impact of computers on the writing process. *Exceptional Children, 54*(6), 27-34.

19.   Balajthy, E. (1987). Keyboarding and the language arts. *The Reading Teacher, 41*(1), 86-87.

20.   Conyers, J., Kappel, T., & Rooney, J. (1999). How technology can transform a school. *Educational Leadership, 56*(5), 82-85.

21. Washington State Task Force. (1994). *High standards: Essential learnings for Washington students* (*Report by the Washington Commission of Student Learning*, p. 1). Olympia, WA: Office of the Superintendent of Public Instruction.

22. Gilpatrick, R., & Holty, N. (1990, Winter). Teaching and learning with computers. *T.H.E. Journal*, pp. 28-31.

CHAPTER 5

1. Boschee, F., Whitehead, B. M., & Boschee, M. A. (1993). *Effective reading programs: The administrator's role*. Lancaster, PA: Technomic Publishing.

2. Simkins, M. (1999). Building public support: Help from the Web. *Principal, 78*(3), 51.

3. Calabrese, R. L. (1991). Effective assistant principals: What do they do? *NASSP Bulletin, 75*(533), 51-57.

4. Crane, G. M. (1989). *Leadership characteristics of elementary school principals related to technology achievement* (p. 38). Unpublished doctoral dissertation, University of Montana.

5. Snyder, T. D. (1990). Trends in education: Elementary schools can expect continued expansion and challenges in the 1990s. *Principal, 70*(1), 6-10.

6. Seeley, D. S. (1990). A new paradigm for parent involvement. *Education Digest, 55*(6), 37-40.

7. U.S. Senate, Committee on the Judiciary. (1997, November 5). *The nation at risk: Report of the president's commission on critical infrastructure protection* (S. HRG. 105-447). Washington, DC: Government Printing Office.

8. Walker, J. E. (1983). Polls of public attitudes toward education: How much help to principals? *NASSP Bulletin, 67*(459), 28-35.

9. Psencik, K. (1991). Site planning in a strategic context in Temple, Texas. *Educational Leadership, 48*(7), 29-31.

10. Armistead, L. (1989). A four-step process for school relations. *NASSP Bulletin, 73*(513), 6, 8, 10-13.

11. Tankard, G. G., Jr. (1974). *Curriculum improvement: An administrator's guide* (pp. 95-120). New York: Parker Publishing.

12. Conners, A. J. (1988). Let's hear about the good stuff! *Clearing House, 61*(9), 399-402.

13. Wherry, J. H. (1986). A public relations secret: Enlist entire staff for PR effectiveness. *NASSP Bulletin, 70*(494), 3-4, 6-8, 10-13.

14. Rasinski, T., & Fredricks, A. (1989). Working with parents: Can parents make a difference? *The Technology Teacher, 43*(1), 84.

15. Seeley, D. S. (1990). Carrying school reform into the 1990s. *Education Digest, 55*(9), 3-6.

16. Fuller, S., & Martin, G. (1991). Nine ways to build better relations with your board. *Executive Educator, 13*(1), 2-23, 28.

17. James, J. (1996). *Thinking in the future tense*. New York: Simon & Schuster.

CHAPTER 6

1. Isaacson, W. (1998). Driven by the passions of Intel's Andrew Grove. *Time, 150*(27), 49.

2. Furtwengler, C. B. (1998). Heads up! The EMOs are coming. *Educational Leadership, 56*(2), 44-47.

3. Brown, P. (1995, February). Total integration of courseware throughout the elementary curriculum. Paper presented at the National IBM School Executive Conference, Chicago, Illinois.

4. Cole, S., & Freideboch, M. (1996). *Basic questions to ask when purchasing technology.* Excerpted from a technical assistance packet developed by the Missouri Assistive Technology Project and the Missouri Technology Center for Special Education. This packet is available through the Missouri Technology Center for Special Education; University of Missouri, Kansas City; School of Education, Room 24; 5100 Rockhill Road; Kansas City, MO 64110-2499; 800/872-7066; 816/235-5270 (fax); TechCtr@smtpgate.umkc.edu (e-mail). Retrieved May 21, 2002, from www.resna.org/tap/aet_bpqu.htm

5. Mageau, T. (1993). Who buys technology? *Electronic Learning, 13*(2), 4.

6. Poris, J., & Gruder, I. (1993). Chapter II funds to be combined with Eisenhower money. *Electronic Learning, 13*(3), 6.

7. Stimson, J. (1993). Local communities will vote to raise taxes for technology in schools: If you sell it the right way? *Electronic Learning, 13*(3), 22-28.

8. Collins, K. (1995, May). The global classroom. Paper presented at IBM National Schools Executive Conference, Atlanta, Georgia.

CHAPTER 7

1. White, K. (1997). A matter of policy. *Education Week's Technology Counts, 17*(11), 40-42.

2. Woodard, L. (1997). State by state profiles. *Education Week's Technology Counts, 17*(11), 88.

3. Leu, D. J., Jr. (1999). The Miss Rumphius effect: Envisionments for literacy and learning that transform the Internet. *The Reading Teacher, 52*(6), 636-637.

4. Descy, D. E. (1998). All aboard the Internet. *Tech Trend, 43*(3), 3.

5. Dobrez, C. (1999). Keypad technology in action. *Media & Methods, 35*(3), 28.

6. Nanson, C. (2002). District technology coordinator for Minot, ND, public schools. Retrieved May 15, 2002, from www.minot.com/~nansen/tech/job_desc.html

7. Ibid.

8. Computer Strategies, LLC. (2002). Oakland, CA. Retrieved from www.compstrategies.com/projects/workshops/forum/am3.html on May 21, 2002. Used with permission.

CHAPTER 8

1. The Editors. (2001, May 10). Technology Counts 2001: The new divides. *Education Week 1*(1). Retrieved May 21, 2002, from www.edweek.org/sreports/tc01/states/tc01state_compare.html

2. Mayer, R., Schustack, M. W., & Blanton W. E. (1999). What do children learn from using computers in an informal collaborative setting? *Educational Leadership, 39*(2), 28.

3. Guskey, T. (1994). What you assess may not be what you get. *Educational Leadership, 51*(6), 52.

4. D. Feuerstein cited in Trotter, A. (1997). Taking technology's measure. *Education Week's Technology Counts, 17*(11), 6-11.

5. The U.S. Department of Education keeps relevant statistics. Retrieved from www.ed.gov/topics/topics.jsp?&top=Research+%26+Stats on May 15, 2002. The National Center for Educational Statistics also has a good Web site: retrieved from nces.ed.gov/ on May 15, 2002. The National Education Association Web site is helpful: retrieved from www.nea.org/publiced/edstats/ on May 15, 2002. And if you type "education statistics" in a search engine, it will find a whole range of Web sites on the topic.

6. Fitzpatrick, K., & Pershing, J. A. (1996). *Indicators of quality information technology systems in K-12 schools* (*National Study of School Evaluation*). Schaumburg, IL: National Study of School Evaluation.

7. Carr, S. (1997). Putting it all together. *Education Week's Technology Counts, 17*(11), 16-18.

8. Lantham, A. S. (1999). Computers and achievement. *Educational Leadership, 56*(5), 87-88.

9. Woodard, L. (1997). State by state profiles. *Education Week's Technology Counts, 17*(11), 88.

10. Among the sites where information about ILS can be found are these (retrieved May 15, 2002): www.rm.com/Primary/Products/Story.asp?cref= PS948, www.ncrel.org/sdrs/areas/issues/methods/technlgy/te8lk2.htm,atschool. eduweb.co.uk/mbaker/material/ils.html, and if you type "integrated learning systems" in a search engine, you will find Web sites related to this topic.

11. Fitzpatrick, K., & Pershing, J. A. (1996). *Indicators of quality information technology systems in K-12 schools*. Schaumburg, IL: National Study of School Evaluation.

RESOURCE A

1. Mid-Continent Research for Education and Learning (McREL); 2550 South Parker Road, Suite 500; Aurora, CO 80014. Retrieved May 21, 2002, from www.mcrel.org

RESOURCE B

1. Nichols, C. (1999). Cupertino's Union School District's Technology Scope and Sequence. Retrieved May 21, 2002, from www.cupertino.k12.ca.us/Do.www/ Scopenseq.html

Name Index

AASA, 121

Bangert-Drowns, R. L., 96
Baucus, M., xviii
Becker, H. J., 18
Bell, S. M., 68
Boschee, F., xix, 103
Boschee, M. A., 103
Brown, P., 143

Cole, S., 143
Considine, J., 23
Conyers, J., 99
Cradler, J., 89, 92
Cupertino Union School District, 93

Davidson, G., 85
Dennison, G., xviii
Descy, D. E., 161
Dobrez, C., 161

Ferrandino, V., xviii
Feuerstein, D., 176
Freidebock, M., 143

Gilpatrick, R., 100
Graves, G., xviii
Guskey, T., 175

Holty, N., 100
Hooper, S., 90

Jacobson, M., xviii
Janklow, W. J., xiii, 156
Jensen, D. F. N., xix
Jones, Rebecca, 25

Keenan, N., xviii
Kimpton, J., 23

KPMG Economic Consulting Service, 9
Kulik, J., 91

Lantham, A., 179
Lowe, M., 13
Lowther, D., 91

Macarthur, C., 96
Mauer, M., 85
Mayer, R., 37
Mayer, R., 175
McREL, 79, 81, 196
Mean, B., 13
Morefield, J., 21
Morrison, G., 91

NAESP, 121
Nanson, C., 165, 166
NASSP, 121
NMSA, 121
NWREL, 72

President's, Panel, 3

Schofield, J. W., 92
Shannon, T., 24
Shrago, J., 179
Simkins, M., 104
SWAP, 117

Temiyakarn, C., 90
TSAA, 29

Whitehead, B. M., xvi, xix, 103
Williams, M. D., 90
Wishengrad, R., 13

Subject Index

Achievement and technology, 10
  benefits of technology, 10
    community relations, 12
    cooperative learning, 11
    cross-age tutoring, 11
    curriculum integration, 11
    global learners, 12
    higher quality, 10
    learning style strategies, 11
    parent communication, 11
    student writing, 10
    teacher communication, 11
Administrator profile, technology, 197
Audit procedures for technology, 79

Baby boomers, 18
Barriers, staff development, 68
  technology use, 72
Buddy system, 89

Coffee klatch, 118
Community awareness, 2, 12, 13,
    15, 97, 123
  development of, 13
  public involvement, 14
  relations, 119
  technology support, 14
Computer labs, xv, 3, 12, 84, 152
  barriers, 85
Computer life span, 171
Computer skills, 75
  basic, 75
  instructional, 75
  successful strategies, 76
Configurations, district technology, 159
  automated libraries, 162
  hardware, compatibility of, 162
  laptops, 160
  local area network (LAN), 160, 168, 169
  upgrading, 162
  wide area network (WAN), 9, 11, 159,
    168, 169
  wireless systems, 161
Cooperative
  learning, 11, 84, 90, 94

Cross-age tutoring, 11, 84,
  90, 94, 96

Dakota digital network, 156
Disparities, rich and poor, 18
Distance learning, 96, 157

Economic vitality, 17
E-rate, 145
Evaluation of technology program, 173
  checklist, 181
  evaluation requirements, state, 174
  staff development, 177
  student performance, 175
  successful strategies, 182
  teaching and learning, assessment
    of, 178-181

Facilitating learning, 89
  student achievement, 6, 13, 89, 90
Facilitating teaching, 91
  instructional changes, 92
Financial management, 123
  federal allocations, 124
  state support, 124
Finance strategies, effective, 147
Fund raising, 145-146, 148
  technology trusts, 124

Grant writing, 125-143
  configuration, 126-127
  proposal, 125
  writing strategies, 126

Hubs and routers life span, 171

Information Age, 13
Infrastructure costs, 170
  life span, 171
Internet, 169
Intranet, description
  of, 160, 167, 169

Job description, technology
  coordinator, 164

Keyboarding, 97

Leadership, 21
  Annenberg Institute, 23
  community support, 28
  financial management process, 27-28
  maintaining commitment, 37
    administrators, 37
    parents, 39, 117
    school board members, 38
    teachers, 38
  planning, 26
  program evaluation, 29
  staff development, 27
  technology project outline, 40-65
    calendar, importance of, 40
    schedule, development of, 40
Learning Age, 13
Levels of awareness:
  NCATE, 16
  state and national, 16
Levels of technology use, 81
Libraries, automated, 162

Maintenance, 162
  student assistants, 163
  teacher coordinator, 163
  technical director, 162
Mission statement, 36-37

Net generation, 18
Network, main parts, 168
  clients, 168
  electronics, 168
  infrastructure, 168
    satellite networks, 155
    state networks, 155
New teachers, training, 69

Partnerships, 14, 79, 118, 148
  parent partnership program, 117
  school and business, 14
Planning matrix, 72
  forms, 73-74
Positive effects on children, 9
Potential of educational technology
  Blackstone Junior High School, 6
  Carrollton City School District, 6
  Carter Lawrence School, 6
  Christopher Columbus, 7
  Clearview Elementary School, 7
  East Bakersfield High School, 8
  Hellgate Elementary School, 8
  Northbrook Middle School, 8
  Ralph Bunche School, 8
  Taylor Elementary School, 8
Professional development
  incentives and requirements, 7
Public involvement, 14, 23, 24, 29, 79, 104
Public relations, 103

administrative role, 105
advisory board, 107
communication strategies, 110-119
plan and process, 107-110
  external groups, 116
  internal groups, 112
successful strategies, 121
Pyramid, the purchasing, 144

Regulations and guidelines, state, 156
Remote keypad technology, 161
Resource centers, 75
Rule of three, 165

School infrastructure, 151
  classroom centers, 152
  telecommunications, 154
Schools for Thought, 7
Staff development, 67
  coaching, 68
  money and training, 68-69, 84, 145
  needs, 67
  skill level, teachers, 68
Stakeholders' role, 24
  important factors, 25
    student needs, 25
    leadership and planning, 26
    teaching and learning, 25
Standards for administrators, 30-36
Strategies in technology, 1
  changing contexts, 1
    flexibility, 2
    learning style, 2
    relationships, 2
    technology, 2
    time, 2
  technology goals, successful, 17

Teacher profile, technology, 185
Teachers and technology, 83
  connectivity, 85
  technology standards, 86
Technology, barriers, 71, 83, 84, 85, 103,
  151, 152, 173
Technology endeavors, states, 88-89
Technology expenditures, school, 70
Technology, financial advice, 159
Technology goals, school, 15
  equipment, guidelines, 15
  school administrators, 15
  student assessment, 15
Technology hubs, see regional centers, 157
Technology preparation, 71
Technology realities, 3
  lack of technological progress, 4
  past educational strategies, 3
  percentages, 3
  public schools, hardware in, 5
  students per computer, 4
  teacher tech training, 6

Technology requirements, 69
Technology scope and sequence, 205
Technology standards (ISTE)
    principals, 33-35
    students, 215
    teachers, 211
Technology, strategic plan 15, 24
    leadership, 32-36

project-based approach, 76-77
teaching and learning, 25,
    26, 30-31
support, 31
training, 69, 70
use, 81

Work tracking system, 165

**CORWIN
PRESS**

The Corwin Press logo—a raven striding across an open book—represents the happy union of courage and learning. We are a professional-level publisher of books and journals for K-12 educators, and we are committed to creating and providing resources that embody these qualities. Corwin's motto is "Success for All Learners."